Ulster Sports
1995

Jerome Quinn

First published 1995 by Jequibooks
46 Royal Lodge Road,
Belfast
BT8 4UL

ISBN 0 95245952 5 2

Previous Books by the author:
Celebrating Ulster Football : Path of Champions (1993)
Ulster Gaelic Games Annual (1994)

This book is dedicated to Justine

Photographs on cover

Front, top left: Malone's Denis McBride touches down behind the Welsh posts to give Ireland the perfect start in their Rugby World Cup tie.

Top right: Britain's costliest player Stan Collymore (8.5 million) tussles with Linfield's John Easton during Liverpool's visit to Belfast in August. 25,000 people saw Ian Rush score the only goal.

Bottom left: Wayne McCullough, WBC champion.

Bottom right: Peter Canavan in action for Tyrone in the Ulster SFC.

Back, from the top: Tony Scullion (Derry) raises the National League cup; Philip Walton, Ireland's only Ryder Cup representative, in action at Belvoir Park where he won the Smurfit Irish PGA Championship; Anthony Tohill in the red and white of Derry City; Dungannon captain Jeremy Hastings with the First Trust Senior Cup.

Printed by Universities Press

Contents

Acknowledgements

Sponsors: Guinness Northern Ireland had confidence in this project from day one, and I, in turn, was confident that their backing would enhance the publication, primarily because of their commitment to a wide variety of Ulster sports, from sponsoring Wayne McCullough's return to Belfast, to local darts, hockey, football, gaelic games, and school sports. Special thanks go to Carmel, Paul, Jean Francois Jamet, and Brian Duffy. I am also grateful to a number of other sponsors for supporting this book - Ulster Bank, Bank of Ireland, First Trust, Smurfit International, Willie John Dolan, Powerscreen, Harry Corry, Wilkinson Sword, Connors Fuels, the Northern Ireland Sports Council, and Sure. I have placed their advertisements strategically, in order to highlight their direct and important backing of local sport.

Contributors: My sincere thanks go to Don Allen, Chairman of the Sports Council, for his foreword, and to Jim Boyce, Mark Robson, Tony McGee, Dermot James, and Edward Smith, for their expert contributions. The list of 'helpers' is much longer - Seamus McAleenan, Paul Welch, Owen McConnon, Tony Dunne, Peter Campbell, Michael Keenan, Michael Daly, Peter Watson, Seamus Mullan, Frank Rodgers, Gerry McClorey, Pat Nugent, John Graham, John Smedley, Glenavon FC, John Flack, Adam Coates, Ritchie Kelly, Carl Anderson, Dick Hinds, Paul McGrory, and many more. Thanks also to Tyrone Times sports editor Kevin Hughes - the newspaper is simply one of the best in the province.

Interviewees: I have to say that all those interviewed were generous in their time and co-operation, including Felix Healy, Trevor Anderson, Roy Walker, Fergal Logan, Paddy O'Rourke, Brian McLaughlin, Davy Tweed, and Hugh Russell, to name but a few.

Photographs: Once again, Tyrone Times snapper Oliver McVeigh has proved that he is always in the right place, at the right time. His pictures tell stories, before words are added. I am also delighted to include some of Hugh Russell's outstanding boxing profiles, and other photographs from the Irish News. All the many sources of photographs are listed at the back of the book.

December Publications: 292 Antrim Road, Belfast (747426) : Thanks to Paul Campbell and his team, especially Colin Thompson and Jake Campbell, for delivering a publication of quality.

I've left the best to last! Paddy O'Hara was once again a friend to treasure and a solid shoulder to lean on, while Justine, Matthew, Kathryn, and Mark were my inspiration.

Jerome Quinn
October 1995

From
BRIAN DUFFY
Managing Director
Guinness Northern Ireland

I am delighted to have the opportunity on behalf of Guinness Northern Ireland to introduce and recommend to you Jerome Quinn's excellent book, *Ulster Sports*.

Guinness Northern Ireland's first venture into sponsorship involvement with a book was with Jerome's *Ulster Football and Hurling: The Path of Champions*, which proved to be, as predicted, a must for every Ulster Sports fan's shelf. It therefore seemed a natural progression for both Jerome and ourselves to extend our involvement to this latest work *Ulster Sports*, which succeeds in bringing both insight and pleasure to the reader across the wide range of sports in Ulster.

The Ulster sports scene has a rich variety and wide participancy and Guinness Northern Ireland have for over thirty-five years enjoyed an unrivalled position as a leader in sports' sponsorship throughout the Province. I am delighted that so many of the sports that we support through sponsorship, feature in this book.

Jerome has fully reflected the richness and diversity of our sports scene and I know that you will derive a great deal of knowledge, insight and enjoyment from reading *Ulster Sports*.

Brian Duffy

Hands across the divide. Antrim GAA and the Irish Football Association each receive a £300,000 windfall. Back, L-R: David Bowen IFA, Don Allen, N.Ireland Sports Council Chairman, Jack Boothman, GAA President, Oliver Kelly, Antrim Chairman. Tony McCusker, Chief Executive of Making Belfast Work, is in the front row.

Antrim Hurler Terence McNaughton and Crusaders goalkeeper Kevin McKeown join John Davidson, Chairman of the N.Ireland Federation of Clubs, to promote 'Clubs Together Day' in June, and to "celebrate the end of the troubles and the beginning of a return to reality", in their own words. Eight clubs twinned with counterparts across the community for a sports social evening.

'The Peace Dividend For Sport'

by Don Allen
Chairman, Northern Ireland Sports Council

In 1995, GAA President Jack Boothman stood side-by-side with Irish Football
Association Secretary David Bowen in Belfast; Willie Anderson took Catholic
and Protestant boys from Dungannon on a rugby trip to Dublin, and members
of the Sandy Row Glasgow Rangers Supporters Club visited Donegal Celtic.
During 25 years of troubles, these refreshing facts may have seemed improbable,
but peace-time has allowed for a massive wind of change in sporting circles in
Northern Ireland.

Consider also that Womens Home International Bowls and the Smurfit
Irish PGA Championship both returned to the province for the first time in 25
years, and that Derry staged a round of the Triathlon World Cup for the very
first time, and you can see that the 'Peace Dividend' extends to major sporting
events. The ceasefires have created amazing amounts of interest from outside
and the future is full of exciting possibilities, from hosting the British Open at
Royal Portrush to a new all-purpose stadium in Belfast, while those with long-
term vision want the Commonwealth Games to come here. And why not?
Northern Ireland is a beautiful country with natural resources and an excellent
sporting infrastructure. I feel it can become a leisure centre to the world.

CitySport

One of the first indications of how good causes like sport and education could
benefit from the ceasefires, came in the release of one million pounds of
government money from the law and order programme in February. Most of the
money was allocated to the GAA and the IFA in Belfast, with £600,000 to be
divided equally under a project entitled 'CitySport'. David Bowen felt the
allocation was fully justified, "I'm delighted for the GAA and soccer. Everyone
can see that they are the two biggest and most popular sports in the province,
with the widest support, so it's only right that the money should start there".

Within months, the three-year scheme was up and running, with
development officers/coaches appointed in both sports. Former Northern Ireland
international Ian Stewart led youngsters onto Windsor Park at half-time in the
European Championship tie with Latvia in June to give an exhibition of 'mini-
soccer' skills, while former All Ireland gaelic football winner Brian McCormick
spent the summer passing on his knowledge to children at schools and clubs
throughout the city. Ian and Brian are members of highly-qualified 'CitySport'
teams (see picture on next page).

Sport For Young People Strategy

The money for the CitySport scheme was made available through the Making Belfast Work project, though its roots are to be found in a 'Sport for Young People Strategy' fashioned by the Sports Council. For many years, the need for a dramatic and sustained increase in quality, extent, and availability of sporting opportunity for all young people of school age in Northern Ireland, irrespective of class, religion, sex, and ability, had been identified by the Council. This became a key issue in the nineties and led to the 'Strategy', which challenges all those involved in the provision of sports for young people, in schools and clubs, to work in partnership, as part of a province-wide framework which encourages every child to participate to their desired level of personal ability, and to promote sporting excellence. In other words, everyone can have a go, whether they are able or disabled, good or not so good, boy or girl, and there is still room for talent to come to the fore. In the past, the emphasis was on the latter, as Ian Stewart recalls, "When I started playing football, I was one of the smaller kids who got pushed aside by stronger boys who inevitably were picked out, but now, the introduction of mini-soccer allows everyone to show and develop their skills. The Dutch and Norwegians have had mini-soccer for years, and I feel it is the vehicle for the next century. The 11-a-side game is dead for kids football".

Above: CitySport GAA and Soccer Development Officers and Co-ordinators. Back, L-R: Paul O'Hare, John Crossey, Brian McCormick, Shane McCullough, Jim Grattan, Ronnie Smyth, Director of Sport. Front: Ian Stewart, Jim Darragh, Danny O'Connor (Sports Council), Spike Hill, Paul Kirk, Maurice Crabbe (S. Council).

Next page: Willie Anderson, Dungannon RFC Director of Rugby, and Fintan Colgan from St Patricks Academy, with pupils from Royal School Dungannon and St Patricks. "I've introduced the game to schools with no rugby tradition and the response has been excellent", explains Anderson. "Rugby has been played on an All Ireland basis for well over a century, partition and civil unrest notwithstanding".

The Future

England is to host the 1996 European Football Championship, and Wales will stage the 1999 Rugby Union World Cup. What about Northern Ireland as the venue for some of the matches? Also, what about Belfast hosting the semi-finals of the All Ireland gaelic football championship? These suggestions may seem far-fetched, but we need to be adventurous and we need purpose-built stadia in order to become a serious contender for huge sporting events. We also need a 50 metre swimming pool to help our swimmers compete internationally, and we need more quality coaches and training facilities. I feel that the time is now right for us to start demanding that these dreams become reality. Why should we be denied access to large international events? The troubles were always a 'good excuse" for steering attention away from Northern Ireland, but now there is no excuse. It will take years of careful planning, so we must start right away. Let's build partnerships with business, commerce and tourism, and let us also explore the sharing of resources with the various governing bodies within sport. The Lottery Sports Fund will also help, It is managed and distributed by the Sports Council, and I feel the money from it can make a huge impact on sport here, from schemes at grass roots level to a proper, national stadium.

I believe that sport stood up remarkably well to the practical difficulties of 25 years of troubles, in that it remained important as a channel of communication between the two communities. International sports stars and teams may have reluctant to come here, but when they did, they were pleasantly surprised by how normal the situation was. In terms of funding, sport in Northern Ireland was largely neglected, yet it brought and continues to bring enjoyment to many thousands of people here, and now I hope that the progress of the last year and the announcement of events-to-come (We have been confirmed as hosts for the 1999 World Athletics Championships), will act as a catalyst to greater things ahead. The world is beginning to realise that Northern Ireland is finally back in business.

Above: James McCartan appeals for help, but Matt Gallagher is happy to sit around.

Below: An irate Conor Deegan makes his point.

1

"A Year Of Surprises"

Bank of Ireland Ulster SFC Preliminary Round, May 21, Clones
Donegal 1-12   Down 0-9

BBC Radio Ulster summariser Brian Canavan warned us just before the off in Clones: "I feel this could be a year of surprises in Ulster and I tip Donegal to start the trend today by beating the All Ireland champions". Both predictions proved to be correct, with the latter particularly bold as it ignored Donegal's injury problems, their defeat in the National League Final only seven days previously, and the bookies!

As early as March, Down were installed as 5/2 favourites to retain the Ulster Championship. Derry were second favourites and Donegal fourth, yet only one of the "three D's" would reach the semi-finals. It was to be an extraordinary championship, with reputations earned through Ulster's glorious revival now ruthlessly dismantled by hungry, emerging counties who simply wanted a piece of the action. "One of the main factors", explains Brian Canavan, "was Derry and Donegal's progress to the league final. In May, everyone was tipping Derry for the All Ireland, but it's very hard to keep a team going for so long. They probably were the best team in Ulster but there always comes a game when your form dips. Unfortunately for Derry, that's what happened when they ran into a motivated and talented Tyrone side.

"I'm also a great believer in form guides and therefore didn't fancy Down for the simple reason that no county has retained the Ulster title since 1976. As for the rest of the championship surprises, I anticipated a good run from Cavan after their league performances, but Monaghan's defeat of Donegal was one I honestly did not expect. They had no real form guide, from playing in Division Four, and I think even their own people were surprised that day in Ballybofey. In the semi-finals, I fancied Cavan but they shouldn't have won on the day. That's the unpredictability of the Ulster Championship!"

Donegal sprang the first surprise at Clones in May, yet the defeat of Down was to be the peak of their year. It was some reward for their considerable efforts in reaching the league final, and importantly, it restored lost pride. On the pitch at Croke Park Martin Shovlin's words were uttered with the dismay that would provide the inspiration for seven days later: "If we perform the way we did today I don't think we'll have an errant at all. We have to lift it by at least eighty to ninety per cent". "The difference between the league final and the Down game was the fear of losing", explained Brian Murray. "The team

BOOKIES TIPS TO WIN ULSTER CHAMPIONSHIP	
March 1995	
5/2	Down
3/1	Derry
5/1	Tyrone
11/2	Donegal
8/1	Armagh
12/1	Monaghan, Cavan
20/1	Fermanagh
25/1	Antrim

just couldn't contemplate losing and had to prove that they were better than the league final suggested". Donegal manager PJ McGowan whispered the word "Sweet" into Martin Gavigan's ear as they embraced on the steps outside the commentary box after the match. "I felt a sense of relief at the finish, we had played ten competitive games in eleven weeks and now we had achieved something". Donegal's busy period had included seven league games, two in the McKenna Cup and one in the Ulster SFC, all from the start of March. On their only "free" Sunday, they played Leitrim in a challenge at Burt.

In contrast, Down had no competitive fixtures since defeat by Cavan in the McKenna Cup on March 12. "Down were caught out by their lack of match practice", views former captain Paddy O'Rourke. "Gary Mason's free-kicks were off and Conor Deegan wasn't catching as he can. You could see the team hadn't played many matches and for me, the biggest thing was that Donegal looked more comfortable on the ball". Some of the Down players later revealed that they had known things weren't right from six weeks before Clones. The manager knew too. Peter McGrath had utilised his full panel in the league but following relegation he once more turned to his faithful fifteen. However, too many of the All Ireland team were struggling to recover from injury and the desire was not the same as before. "We just didn't have the edge, the deep hunger. You might try very hard to get that edge but if it's not there, then there's not much you can do about it".

For the first 31 minutes Down and Donegal traded scores, but the signs were ominous for the champions. PJ McGowan pulled a masterstroke by switching Martin Gavigan to midfield. "Rambo" gave the unfit Deegan a torrid time, while Noel Hegarty moved back to blunt the threat of Greg Blaney. In the half-forwards, Eamonn Burns and Barry Breen looked uncomfortable on the wings when faced by Paddy Hegarty and Mark McShane, while James McHugh's speed of foot and mind proved a handful for DJ Kane. There were problems in the full-back line as well, with Michael Magill starting the game despite hamstring trouble. Down warmed up Brian Grant after only twenty minutes but Magill remained for the 70 minutes and was unable to stop Manus Boyle helping himself to 1-5 and the Man of the Match Award.

Early in the contest, Ross Carr struck two classic free-kicks and a rasping drive by James McCartan rebounded off Gary Walsh's crossbar. Donegal responded with great purpose, Gavigan fielding a kick-out and finding Tony Boyle who turned Brian Burns before scoring. The tempo rose still further with a succession of classy scores in the wet conditions from Greg McCartan, Manus Boyle, Mickey Linden (with a brief glimpse of his 1994 best), James McHugh at the end of a four-man move, and Gary Mason with a left-footed kick. The Down sideline urged it's defenders to "mark tighter" but Donegal still edged ahead with three late first-half points. As the excited crowd sensed an upset, tempers were lost on the pitch in a brief melee. Referee Pat McEneaney defused the situation beautifully by blowing his half-time whistle and then booking two of the offenders, Martin Shovlin and James McCartan, when they re-appeared for the second-half.

Manus Boyle and Paddy Hegarty drew first blood for a fiercely committed Donegal in the vital early stages of the second period. Three points behind, Greg McCartan thought he had levelled in the 47th minute when he got up quickly after winning a free-kick and blasted the ball past Walsh. The goal was disallowed even though a similar effort by James McCartan in a league game with Meath in 1994 was allowed to stand. Ross Carr pointed the re-taken free and Greg McCartan made it 9-8, but on 51 minutes Gary Mason was sent off. Most of the crowd in the main stand saw the Down player fall as he ran alongside John Joe Doherty and then get up, race after his marker and throw a right-hook which broke the Donegal man's nose. Paddy O'Rourke viewed that "both players should have gone" but Doherty stayed on and refused to come off until his manager made a substitution. Peter McGrath saw Down's titles slipping away: "To lose a player at a time when you're chasing the game, and when you're not playing as well as you can, is a fatal blow".

		Down	Dgal
6 mins	Carr (F)	0-1	
7 mins	M.Boyle		0-1
10 mins	Carr (F)	0-2	
16 mins	T.Boyle		0-2
17 mins	G.McCartan	0-3	
19 mins	M.Boyle		0-3
20 mins	Linden	0-4	
22 mins	McHugh		0-4
23 mins	Mason	0-5	
31 mins	Duffy (F)		0-5
32 mins	M.Boyle (F)		0-6
33 mins	Farrell	0-6	
34 mins	Murray		0-7
HALF-TIME			
40 mins	M.Boyle		0-8
43 mins	P.Hegarty		0-9
48 mins	Carr (F)	0-7	
50 mins	G.McCartan	0-8	
59 mins	P.Hegarty		0-10
62 mins	Gavigan		0-11
63 mins	M.Boyle		0-12
65 mins	G.McCartan	0-9	
66 mins	M.Boyle		1-12
FULL-TIME			

Down's desperate attempts to save the game only made matters worse. A mistake by Deegan was punished by the stylish Paddy Hegarty and Gavigan scored after a Down attack broke down, making it 11-8. When the champions did come close, Carr missed a couple of frees and Walsh saved at the feet of James McCartan, And, just to rub salt into their wounds, Manus Boyle diverted a rebound to the Down net before Ciaran McCabe had a goal disallowed in the last minute for over-carrying. Bad fortune for Down, but it should not cloud the outstanding impression of the overall contest - Down's inability to find a response to Donegal's aggression and motivation.

After-Match Quotes

"We weren't kidding when we complained during the week about injuries. Tony Boyle was very badly hurt from the league final but he had treatment three times a day and made a miraculous recovery" - **PJ McGowan.**

"Greg McCartan's goal should have been allowed and the sending-off was a blow, two things you could not predict, yet you have to admit they were hungrier" -
Peter McGrath.

"Savagely quick and sweetly sure-footed when his two point-taking opportunities arose" - The **Donegal Democrat** describing Paddy Hegarty.

DOWN

Neil Collins

Michael Magill   Brian Burns   Paul Higgins

Eamonn Burns   Barry Breen   DJ Kane (c)

Conor Deegan   Gregory McCartan 0-3

Ross Carr 0-3   Greg Blaney   Aidan Farrell 0-1

Mickey Linden 0-1   James McCartan   Gary Mason 0-1

Subs: Collie Burns for Deegan, Ciaran McCabe for Farrell. Squad: Eamonn Connolly, John Kelly, Brian Grant, Shane McMahon, Gerard Colgan, Gerard Deegan, Gavin Murdock, Paul McCartan.

DONEGAL

Gary Walsh

John Joe Doherty   Matt Gallagher (c)   Barry McGowan

Mark Crossan   Noel Hegarty   Martin Shovlin

Martin Gavigan 0-1   Brian Murray 0-1

Mark McShane   James McHugh 0-1   Paddy Hegarty 0-2

John Duffy 0-1   Tony Boyle 0-1   Manus Boyle 1-5

Subs: Declan Bonnar for Duffy, John Gildea for Doherty.

Referee: Pat McEneaney (Monaghan).   Linesmen: Gerry McClorey , Anthony O'Neill.

Bookings: Brian Burns, Martin Gavigan, Martin Shovlin, James McCartan.

Sending-off: Gary Mason   Man of the Match - Manus Boyle   Attendance: 23,000

John Joe Doherty, complete with broken nose and blood-stained shirt,
is asked to explain the surprise victory of his team.

Awful Armagh or Dazzling Derry?

First Round, May 28, Armagh
Armagh 0-10   Derry 1-17

"I expected Armagh to come at us like lions but it didn't materialise that way. The atmosphere is surprisingly quiet and really, the first-half was effortless for Derry". The injured Joe Brolly sounded almost disappointed from his role as spectator after watching his team-mates power their way to a 10-5 lead, despite playing uphill and into the wind. The second-half was even more one-sided. Armagh scored only once from play while Derry finished the contest with 1-12 from play and with no fewer than eleven different scorers. Impressive statistics but one question still hangs over this match - were Armagh very bad or were Derry very good? I suspect both conclusions are true, but the convincing nature of Derry's victory, and the fact they had won the National League only a fortnight before, probably counted against them in the long-term.

"We had no answer on the day, they steamrolled us and will win the All Ireland" - Neil Smyth. "We were left standing in awe of them at times. Some of their back-up play was phenomenal. I don't think Armagh are a bad team but we just couldn't get to grips with Derry. At this stage, you couldn't look past them for the All Ireland"- Cathal O'Rourke. "Derry were awesome and are All Ireland favourites"- Brian McEniff. Even the former Ireland rugby captain and Derry fan Willie Anderson joined the lengthening queue of admirers, though the players were trying hard to maintain a firm footing. "We played very well but we're only into the semi-finals"- Henry Downey. "I think this Championship is going to be as or more difficult to win this year than any other, with a number of teams throwing their hat in as pretenders, but time will tell" - Damien Barton.

After only six minutes play, the pattern of the game had been set. Derry scored three times into the breeze and were in control. By the 22nd minute, they led 7-2 after some mouth-watering attacking moves. The best score came from deep in the Derry defence. Pressure on the Armagh forwards won a free-kick against Neil Smyth for over-carrying. Henry Downey wrestled

		Armagh	Derry
3 mins	S.Downey		0-1
5 mins	Bateson		0-2
6 mins	Tohill (F)		0-3
8 mins	Mackin	0-1	
12 mins	Barton		0-4
17 mins	O'Rourke (F)	0-2	
19 mins	Tohill (F)		0-5
20 mins	Barton		0-6
22 mins	Bateson		0-7
24 mins	O'Rourke (F)	0-3	
28 mins	O'Rourke (F)	0-4	
32 mins	McQuillan	0-5	
33 mins	Gormley		0-8
35 mins	McGurk		0-9
35 mins	McGilligan		0-10
HALF-TIME			
36 mins	O'Rourke (F)	0-6	
38 mins	Gormley (F)		0-11
40 mins	O'Rourke (F)	0-7	
41 mins	Gormley (F)		0-12
45 mins	Gormley (F)		0-13
46 mins	O'Rourke (F)	0-8	
49 mins	H.Downey		1-13
51 mins	O'Rourke (F)	0-9	
52 mins	S.Downey		1-14
53 mins	Heaney		1-15
58 mins	Marsden	0-10	
60 mins	Cassidy		1-16
65 mins	McGill		1-17
FULL-TIME			

the ball from Smyth and immediately set up the forward move, playing a one-two with Tohill, holding possession despite a shoulder charge and then sending a low ball towards Gormley. Derry's "Man of the First Half", Damien Barton, supported the move by first finding Seamus Downey and then being fouled close to goal after taking a return pass from Downey. Tohill tapped over the free.

It was controlled, exhibition football by fifteen players operating as the perfect team. "We're all level-headed, we work well and think well as a group", explained Barton. Derry had in fact won twelve games in a row since the third game of the National League, and more importantly, had been together for several years. Fourteen of the team had played in the 1993 All Ireland Final; thirteen had played in the 1992 League Final. It showed. Armagh's game-plan had been to cancel Derry's midfield and to contain their half-back line, but McGurk, Downey and McCusker came forward in waves in the first twenty minutes, with the result that the Armagh half-backs, and their tactics, were in disarray. Barton was the link-man: "Our half-back line seems to think they're the best attacking force in the game, and it just rules out the half-forward line, but today playing into the wind meant the half-forwards were used more, so we had a better balance".

Des Mackin was the only Armagh forward to score from play in the first 35 minutes. Cathal O'Rourke, just back from Philadelphia, proved accurate from free-kicks, and McQuillan reduced the deficit to 7-5 before Derry stepped up a gear before the break. Again, perfect timing and movement saw Henry Downey and Barton set up Gormley for a point. McGurk and McGilligan made it seven different Derry scorers in the first half.

A water bottle was hurled across the Armagh dressing-room as the frustration of being outplayed boiled over. More effort was demanded, in the name of the famous jersey, but worse was to follow. After the first six scores of the second half (all free-kicks) were shared, Derry truly killed the game 21 minutes before the end with a super goal by Henry Downey. With his marker nowhere to be seen, the centre-half-back took the ball from Tohill and drilled it low past Tierney. "Anthony took two looks at me as I ran past. He was surprised to see me and I don't think he was too sure whether to pass to me or not!" Both Derry substitutes added to the total, with McGill scoring before the man he replaced (Henry Downey) had reached the sideline! Consider also the fact that Joe Brolly, Karl Diamond and Dermot McNicholl were either injured or not used, and you had to conclude that Derry looked formidable.

Armagh had nowhere to hide, and almost inevitably, signs of internal friction appeared in the media. Jim McCorry's resignation was greeted with some criticism of his performance in the build-up to the Derry game, from the Grimley twins. They claimed McCorry had erred in not using Oisin McConville, Armagh's top scorer in the league, and that John Grimley had been used "out of position" when introduced. McCorry replied that McConville had examinations in the weeks before the game and was not showing good form. "The whole management team does take some of the blame, but the poor performance of ten players was a factor also. As Ger Houlahan said on television, I am the fall guy

Damien Barton leaves the Armagh defence in his wake.

for the team. This was the best prepared Armagh team of the past four years, and yet it fared the worst. We had a specialist hill-running coach, a specialist speed trainer, an additional football coach and a sports psychologist!".

Cathal O'Rourke struggled to come to terms with Armagh's display. "We trained approxiamately 470 hours for this game. That's for one hour's football. We let ourselves down, we let our county down, we let our families down. There was a time when we were every bit as good as those guys, you have to ask what's happened since. Derry are the standard-bearers and we've got to find the spark that they've found. But God knows where". Captain for the day, Benny Tierney, offered a rational theory. "Up to a week before we had been showing great form, but then we got a trimming from Meath and our form was gone. That's what is really difficult to understand, but I guess it happens sometimes".

ARMAGH
Benny Tierney

Mark McNeill	Ger Reid	John Rafferty
Damien Horisk	Kieran McGeeney	Martin McQuillan

Mark Grimley   Paul McGrane

Diarmuid Marsden 0-1	Neil Smyth	Cathal O'Rourke 0-7
Des Mackin 0-1	Ger Houlahan	Jim McConville

Subs: John Grimley for Smyth (38), Martin Toye for Mackin (46). Squad: Eamon Fleming,
Dominic Clarke, Jarlath Burns, Barry O'Hagan, Oisin McConville, Colm McParland, Michael Hanratty.`

DERRY
Damien McCusker

Kieran McKeever	Tony Scullion (c)	Gary Coleman
John McGurk 0-1	Henry Downey 1-0	Fergal McCusker

Anthony Tohill 0-2   Brian McGilligan 0-1

Dermot Heaney 0-1	Damien Barton 0-2	Eamonn Burns
Declan Bateson 0-2	Seamus Downey 0-2	Enda Gormley 0-5

Subs: Damien Cassidy 0-1 for Burns (54), Gary McGill 0-1 for H.Downey (59)

Referee: Tommy McDermott (Cavan). Linesmen: Mick McGrath, Dessie Slater. Bookings: Neil Smyth,
Gary Coleman, John Grimley. Man of the Match: Henry Downey Attendance: 15,000

Brian Canavan's After-Match Assessment

"This was an absolutely pathetic Armagh performance. There was a great lack of motivation, commitment and grit, right from the outset. I know Derry are a super team but you expect a bit more from Armagh in a championship game at the Athletic Grounds. Teams used to fear coming here, now they want to come. Armagh chopped and changed too often with the result that players weren't confident and were too anxious, in contrast to Derry's settled team. Their half-backs were strong coming forward and they all ran for each other whereas Armagh were not. All Armagh's scores were individual efforts, Derry's were team efforts. Having said all that, they looked to be only in second gear".

Captain Peter Steers Tyrone Home

First Round, June 4, Irvinestown
Fermanagh 1-11   Tyrone 1-15

Rarely do you see one man having such an impact on the other 29 players, as Peter Canavan did in this game. Named just before the start as captain for the day in the absence of Ciaran Corr, the full-forward kept Tyrone on course in a first-half where his colleagues wasted a number of glorious opportunities. Then, with the game finely balanced at the start of the second period, Canavan moved outfield, directed the traffic all towards the Fermanagh posts and scored three points as Tyrone went from 0-7 to 1-5 behind, to 1-14 to 1-5 ahead.

True, Fermanagh lost the influential Paul Brewster with torn cruciate ligaments when the scores were level, but Tyrone were never going to lose, not with Peter Canavan on board. He was involved twice in the move for Stephen Lawn's goal, with the final pass across the goalmouth taking three Fermanagh defenders out of the play. On 48 minutes, Canavan floated a right-footed free-kick from his hands over the crossbar, despite a poor angle. For his next trick, a minute later, he kicked a brilliant point from play off his left foot! On 59 minutes, the Man of the Match practically stopped the play by standing wide on the left wing, soloing the ball to himself. With defenders afraid to commit themselves to a tackle, Canavan waited for his brother Pascal to run into space before releasing the ball. Pascal scored, as did McGleenan moments later to make it 1-7 to 0-0 for Tyrone for the second half by the 60th minute.

Incidentally, McGleenan's second point marked a notable statistical landmark - he became the third player in the game to score a point off both feet, the others being Peter Canavan and Shane King. Equally remarkable was a Fermanagh revival consisting of six points-in-a-row in as many minutes, to come within a goal of catching Tyrone. A double from Mark Gallagher, a brilliant effort from McCreesh and two frees from Shane King, brought a dying contest back to life. But a wasted free-kick was punished by Pascal Canavan as Tyrone breathed easily once more. Some of the blame for the issue remaining in doubt until the very end must be accepted by the Tyrone

		Ferm	Tyrone
6 mins	Pl Canavan		0-1
11 mins	Logan		0-2
13 mins	King (F)	0-1	
14 mins	McCreesh	1-1	
18 mins	Pr Canavan (F)		0-3
20 mins	King (F)	1-2	
25 mins	Pr Canavan (45)		0-4
27 mins	Gormley		0-5
30 mins	Pr Canavan (F)		0-6
32 mins	King (F)	1-3	
33 mins	King	1-4	
35 mins	Pr Canavan (F)		0-7
35 mins	King (F)	1-5	
HALF-TIME			
37 mins	Pr Canavan (F)		0-8
43 mins	McCallin		0-9
45 mins	S.Lawn		1-9
48 mins	Pr Canavan (F)		1-10
49 mins	Pr Canavan		1-11
55 mins	McGleenan		1-12
59 mins	Pl Canavan		1-13
60 mins	McGleenan		1-14
61 mins	King (F)	1-6	
63 mins	M.Gallagher	1-7	
65 mins	M.Gallagher	1-8	
65 mins	McCreesh	1-9	
66 mins	King (F)	1-10	
67 mins	Coyle	1-11	
69 mins	Pl Canavan		1-15
FULL-TIME			

forwards who squandered chances early in the game. Stephen Lawn struck the ball against the outside of the post after two minutes, Gerard Cavlan's drive was blocked by Cormac McAdam, and Adrian Cush was guilty of three misses. After the Donaghmore man saw his side-footer flash past the corner of the upright, his confidence visibly drained from him. Twice he got in behind the Fermanagh defence, but first he weakly fisted the ball across the goals, neither a point-scoring effort nor a pass, and was then blocked after finding space just six yards from goal. At the other end, Colm McCreesh rocked Tyrone with a dipping kick over McConnell's considerable reach on 14 minutes, after Mark Gallagher had shown Fay Devlin a clean pair of heels. Tyrone's other corner-man, Paul Devlin, was surprised by Shane King who enhanced his reputation with five excellent first-half points. Fermanagh manager Terry Ferguson had reason in his first Ulster SFC game to be proud of his team's performance, considering the loss through injury of Fergal McCann, Raymond Gallagher and, during the game, Paul Brewster.

After-Match Quotes

"We had a number of men playing their first championship game and two of them, Ronan McGarrity and Sean McLaughlin, gave magnifcent performances. Also, don't forget we missed Ciaran Corr, our workhorse and leader" - **Art McCrory**.

"Our attitude wasn't right, running through and going for goals when we should have taken points. We won't be able to do that against Derry" - **Mattie McGleenan**.

"Tyrone tried to put us away in the first fifteen minutes, which was a little bit arrogant of them, taking us for granted" - **Terry Ferguson** (below left).

Opposite page left: Terry Ferguson. Right/Above: Adrian Cush walks off after an off-day in front of goal.

FERMANAGH

Cormac McAdam

Raymond Curran   Paddy McGuinness   Martin Greene

Tommy Callaghan   Tony Collins   Kieran Gallagher

Paul Brewster   Brian Carty

Collie Curran (c)   Paul Greene   Malachy O'Rourke 0-1

Mark Gallagher 0-1   Colm McCreesh 1-1   Shane King 0-7

Subs: Colm Courtney for Brewster (38), Paul Coyle 0-1 for Curran (50), Justin Gilheaney for Callaghan (64). Squad: Dermot Feely, Pearse Collins, Simon Bradley, Mark Lunney, Bart O'Brien, Garvan Gallagher.

TYRONE

Finbarr McConnell

Paul Devlin   Chris Lawn   Fay Devlin

Ronan McGarrity   Seamus McCallan 0-1   Sean McLaughlin

Fergal Logan 0-1   Jody Gormley 0-1

Gerard Cavlan   Pascal Canavan 0-3   Adrian Cush

Matt McGleenan 0-2   Peter Canavan 0-7 (c)   Stephen Lawn 1-0

Subs: Ciaran Loughran for Cush (59).

Referee: Mick McGrath (Donegal).   Linesmen: Raymond Graffin, Kevin Brolly.

Bookings: Gerard Cavlan, Martin Greene.   Man of the Match: Peter Canavan.   Attendance: 16,000

Footnote: Since 1970, Fermanagh have played 33 championship games, won six. Tyrone have played 51, won 27.

Cavan Win The McHugh Way

First Round, June 11, Breffni Park
Cavan 2-11   Antrim 0-8

Peter Reilly's spectacular first-half goals may have made the difference on the day, but if you want to know why this confident Cavan side has emerged from the doldrums, then look no further than Martin McHugh. Everything Cavan did right had the mark of the Donegal man, from pre-match preparation to style of play, and even to dealing with the media afterwards. McHugh must have given more than a dozen interviews within an hour of the final whistle, on-the-pitch and in the press/radio box, ensuring Cavan benefitted fully from positive publicity. Meantime, his players took themselves back onto the playing arena for a "warm-down", one of the modern practices in sport where it is considered that post-match exercise can help prevent injuries. Cavan aren't the first to do this, and it may seem largely irrelevant, but in the wider scheme of things it has been important to the rehabilitation of the Breffni Blues.

Without a championship win since 1987, morale was at an all-time low when McHugh took over. Cavan had just suffered the humiliation of losing to neighbours Monaghan after leading by six points. The Donegal man immediately instilled his principles in Cavan - hard work (99 training sessions from his appointment to the Antrim game), a running, short-passing game (breaking the long-ball tradition in Cavan), and smart appearance (the squad looked like winners when they arrived for the match). The little things, like the warm-down, and the smart sweatshirts, allied to good results (four wins before Christmas), helped the players begin to believe in themselves once again. Promotion to Division Two followed, and now an end to the barren summers.

In the relief and excitement of victory, McHugh had words for the losers, the only county with a worse record than Cavan going into the championship. "I feel sorry for Antrim because it's hard to go back to your county and encourage young people". Antrim manager Paul O'Hare, who played in the 1982 team which won at Breffni, had high hopes of a repeat result, peeping out of the dressing-room during the minor game to say that his forwards were "on fire" and that it would be a good toss to win, given the strong breeze going straight down the pitch.

Antrim won the toss, but instead of building up a lead, they lost the first-half by 2-5 to 0-3. O'Hare's forwards failed to score from play in the entire half (midfielder Paul McErlean was the only Antrim man to do so) while Peter Reilly grabbed two glorious goals in the first quarter and his team-mates should have added another three. Quite simply, Cavan tore the Antrim defence apart, with Reilly carrying the ball through the middle unchallenged and scoring with either foot. His first strike was quite stunning, coming after only two minutes and executed with speed, power and style. Antrim showed naivety in defence, being dragged out of position instead of marking space in front of goals, and in marking the Cavan forwards from behind instead of alongside or in front of their man. Reilly therefore had no difficulty in gaining possession, and once he set off, Charlie McStravick simply didn't have the legs to catch the 20-year-old.

Terence McCrudden was switched onto Reilly after his second goal on 17 minutes, but the onslaught continued. Debut boy Dermot McCabe burst through on 19 minutes and saw his goalbound effort brilliantly diverted over the crossbar by Sean McGreevey. Next, McCabe over-hit a fist pass on the 14-yard line when another goal looked inevitable, and on 27 minutes, Ronan Carolan saw his drive cannon off the bar. Excellent fielding by Murphy and especially McErlean provided brief respite but Antrim's laboured approach play provided a stark contrast to Cavan's direct route to goal. They persisted with a short game when it looked easier to use the strong wind to get ball into the forwards. "We had a small team", explained Paul O'Hare, "big Donagh

		Cavan	Antrim
2 mins	Reilly	1-0	
7 mins	Kennedy (F)		0-1
8 mins	Carolan (F)	1-1	
15 mins	Kennedy (F)		0-2
17 mins	Reilly	2-1	
19 mins	McCabe	2-2	
26 mins	Lambe	2-3	
28 mins	Lambe	2-4	
32 mins	Carolan (F)	2-5	
33 mins	McErlean		0-3
HALF-TIME			
37 mins	Carolan	2-6	
42 mins	Kennedy		0-4
45 mins	Carolan (F)	2-7	
46 mins	A.Finnegan		0-5
48 mins	Kennedy (F)		0-6
55 mins	Carolan (F)	2-8	
56 mins	Carolan (F)	2-9	
60 mins	Heatley (F)		0-7
61 mins	Brady	2-10	
65 mins	Heatley (F)		0-8
68 mins	Carolan (F)	2-11	
FULL-TIME			

Finnegan was sidelined with injury and because of the lack of height, we felt we had to develop the openings". Credit must also go to Man of the Match Aidan Connolly for a fine performance at Number Six, and, directly behind him, Damien O'Reilly. The captain had been more recognised as a full-forward, but his move to full-back looked to be a masterstroke by McHugh.

Antrim did penetrate the Cavan backline on one notable occasion towards the end of the opening period, and were very unfortunate not to score a goal. Mickey Boyle's shot deflected off a post and across the goal-line into the path of the in-running Donal Armstrong. All he had to do was touch the ball over the line but at the crucial moment, the full-forward lost his footing and stumbled over the ball. It could have been 2-4 to 1-3 at the break but instead Ronan Carolan increased the difference to eight points, 2-5 to 0-3. The same Carolan scored all but one of his team's six scores in a low-key second-half, including a mighty effort out of his hands and from near the sideline. Cavan however went from looking like championship contenders in the first-half to looking like an ordinary team. Martin McHugh, who continued to circle the field right to the end of the game, encouraging his players, couldn't complain too much as the game had been won in the first 35 minutes. "The pressure was on us to win this match. It's a good achievement to get over the first hurdle, and important to me after all the work we've put in". There were no crumbs of comfort for Antrim. They had been unlucky once more in the closing stages when Conal Heatley almost charged down a clearance into the Cavan net, but by then the small Antrim support either cared little or had already left the ground.

Paul O'Hare resigned during the week, lamenting the worst result of his four years in charge and Antrim's thirteenth consecutive first-game defeat in the championship. The statistics also show that O'Hare is the sixth manager to have come and gone since 1982, which would indicate that there may be a wider problem in the county. As an outsider, I can't pinpoint the exact reason, but factors that have been raised by others include the fact that Antrim is a dual county, that the club infrastructure is flawed (too many clubs?), and that the various managers have sometimes been unable to command unanimous support from both the clubs and the County Committee. No players from Cargin were made available to the county team for the Cavan game, and it was reported in the Sunday Life that as few as eight players had attended a training session four weeks before the match. Perhaps there is not the same pride in playing for the county as there is elsewhere, partly because of years of defeat but also perhaps it is a "city" problem. Antrim have an effective structure for young players up to the start of their teens, but then they seem to lose them to other sports. "We have to start competing again at MacRory Cup level", suggests the outgoing manager. Paid or outside coaches are often not the answer, but Antrim must have envied the impact Martin McHugh has had in Cavan.

CAVAN

Paul O'Dowd

Aidan Watters	Damien O'Reilly (c)	Finbar Reilly
Bernard Morris	Aidan Connolly	Gerry Sheridan
	Stephen King	Pat Shields
Dermot McCabe 0-1	Peter Reilly 2-0	Ronan Carolan 0-7
Adrian Lambe 0-2	John Brady 0-1	Fintan Cahill

Subs: Fergal Harton for Shiels (50), Raymond Cunningham for Cahill (70), Ray Cole for King (71).

ANTRIM

Sean McGreevey

John Kelly	Martin Mulholland	Kieran Prenter
Terry McCrudden	Charlie McStravick (c)	Aidan Donnelly
	Chris Murphy	Paul McErlean 0-1
Frankie Wilson	Joe Kennedy 0-4	Anto Finnegan 0-1
Mickey Boyle	Donal Armstrong	Conal Heatley 0-2

Subs: Gearoid Adams for McStravick, Donagh Finnegan for A Finnegan, Colum McCabe for Armstrong.
Squad: Brian McNulty, Sean McArdle, John McManus, Tom Murphy, Paul McCabe, Locky McCurdy
Referee: Brian White (Wexford).   Linesmen: Michael Cranny, John Scully.
Bookings: Frankie Wilson, Bernard Morris.   Man of the Match: Aidan Connolly.   Attendance: 10,000

After-Match Quotes

"Cavan looked fit and very sharp in the first-half and are playing a new, attractive brand of football, different to previous years" - **James McHugh**.

"We gave away two goals that helped settle them down. Our main problem was our half-backs who gave too much room to their half-forwards" - **Paul O'Hare**.

"I have to revise my judgement now. Armagh aren't the worst team in Ulster, Antrim are!" - **Brian Canavan**.

Youth Knows No Fear

First Round, June 18, Ballybofey
Donegal 0-8   Monaghan 1-14

Pony-tailed Joe Coyle epitomised this most refreshing and significant performance for Monaghan football. A 20-year-old medical student at UCD, the debutant centre-half-back showed no signs of nerves as he negated Donegal playmaker James McHugh and took every opportunity to stride forward with confidence. Coyle's youthful dynamism was reflected throughout a team which comprehensively upstaged the hot favourites in their own backyard, and helped Monaghan rise from their slumber to overhaul one of the "three D's" for the first time in the nineties.

Manager Michael McCormick only handed Coyle his chance when first-choice Gerard McGuirk was injured, but the man from Monaghan Harps re-paid his boss with interest. In fact, McCormick's wider gamble on youth (which had come in for pre-match criticism) was a primary reason for the defeat of a vastly more experienced Donegal team. Alongside Coyle, John Conlon and Martin Slowey were 20 and 23-years-old respectively and playing their first senior championship game. "You can't get experience if you don't get on, so we decided to start today by giving them experience. I knew we had unbelievable talent right through the side and they worked tirelessly for the whole seventy minutes. They showed that the hunger is back in Monaghan football".

Declan Loughman was the only member of his team to have played in an Ulster Final, but was delighted to be surrounded by younger men. "This is the

Declan Smyth, in the company of Barry McGowan, looks to set up a Monaghan attack.

greatest display by a Monaghan team in the last six or seven years", he proclaimed as hundreds of their supporters swarmed onto the Ballybofey pitch at the final whistle. Team captain Frank McEneaney added, "Youth knows no fear. The young lads weren't nervous in the dressing-room before the game; sometimes inexperience can be a good thing". Joe Coyle however admitted to one or two butterflies, "I was a bit apprehensive going into the game, especially as I was marking James McHugh. These are players you have grown up watching on television". Coyle would also have watched Donegal playing in the National League Final only five weeks earlier, and again when they defeated Down at Clones. His own team had spent the winter in Division Four of the National League, but they had a gameplan which worked to perfection, albeit after a shaky start. Coyle himself was caught cold as James McHugh bore down on goal within 30 seconds before being taken out by David King. But, strangely enough, John O'Connor's first-minute penalty save from Declan Bonnar was arguably the turning point of the match, as an inspired Monaghan team grew in confidence and dictated the play. In defence, they closed down their opponents; in midfield, they pounced on every breaking ball with total commitment, and their forwards worked back to disrupt Donegal's short game. "You can stop Donegal by stopping the man who passes the ball from getting a return pass. Crowd them out, in other words", revealed Brian Canavan, who played against eleven of this Donegal team in the 1990 Ulster Final.

Donegal regularly ran into trouble with forward moves appearing slow and laboured in stark contrast to Monaghan's energetic and direct raids upfield. The clash in styles, one of the enduring memories of this contest, was most evident in the final quarter when the Farney men struck six unanswered points. Still, Donegal attempted to run the ball out of defence with short kick-outs and free-kicks, but invariably the rampant Monaghan forwards hustled the home defenders off the ball and belted it over the bar, to roars of approval from their support. Declan Smyth appropriately kicked the last of the six spectacular points in the final minute, for it was his accuracy which settled Monaghan early in the game. Despite surviving the penalty scare, his young team-mates took a while to adjust to the pace and atmosphere (Michael Slowey badly mishit a scoreable free-kick), but then Smyth took over, scoring Monaghan's first three points and adding a free-kick out of the hands from beyond the 45 metre line on 22 minutes. However, the single most important score

		D'gal	M'han
3 mins	M.Boyle	0-1	
6 mins	Smyth (F)		0-1
7 mins	Gavigan	0-2	
12 mins	Loughman		1-1
14 mins	Smyth (F)		1-2
15 mins	Smyth		1-3
17 mins	Murray	0-3	
18 mins	P.Duffy		1-4
19 mins	Conlon		1-5
21 mins	M.Boyle (F)	0-4	
22 mins	Smyth (F)		1-6
26 mins	P.McShane		1-7
28 mins	Bonner (F)	0-5	
36 mins	N.Hegarty	0-6	
HALF-TIME			
40 mins	Smyth (F)		1-8
46 mins	M.Boyle (F)	0-7	
47 mins	M.Boyle	0-8	
51 mins	McGinnity		1-9
60 mins	P.Duffy		1-10
61 mins	McGinnity		1-11
63 mins	P.Duffy		1-12
66 mins	P.McShane		1-13
70 mins	Smyth		1-14
FULL-TIME			

was a fortunate goal by Declan Loughman, when a speculative lob dropped over a stunned Gary Walsh.

"Donegal's living in the past, on beating Down", declared a supporter from behind the wire. Certainly, their performance dropped considerably from Clones, with Paddy Hegarty, Martin Gavigan and even Tony Boyle much less effective. Monaghan full-back David King fielded impressively above Boyle, more than once, while Loughman dropped into midfield to direct much of the play towards the Donegal goal. At half-time, Monaghan led by four points, but the manager urged his players to imagine the score was nil-nil. "I told the boys to treat the second-half as a new game. Donegal looked tired and if we worked as

Martin "Rambo" Gavigan

hard as we had done, then I knew we would win". The underdogs did as instructed, and refused to relinquish their grip on the match, even when Manus Boyle struck twice for Donegal (their only scores of the half). Brian Murray might have been awarded a penalty but equally, Declan Smyth's lovely ball inside the Donegal defence nearly resulted in a goal for Gregory Flanagan.

On 51 minutes, Stephen McGinnity upped the pace with a marvellous point after a one-handed catch and surging run. Donegal responded but Paddy Hegarty's flick came back off the post when a goal would have reduced the arrears to one point. The game effectively ended in the 60th minute when Manus Boyle's short free-kick was intercepted and the ball was worked up to Peter Duffy for another point, 1-10 to 0-8. With Pauric McShane, and even corner-back Edwin Murphy, bursting forward, McGinnity and Duffy added further exhibition scores, while Barry McGowan blasted Donegal's last chance straight at O'Connor. The rebound was cleared off James McHugh's boot for a 45 which became wide number ten. It was a frustrating day for PJ McGowan's men, Clones in reverse. "Monaghan played against us today the way we played against Down. That was the difference. It wasn't a characteristic Donegal performance at all."

Footnotes: Monaghan's victory was only the second time in five seasons that one of the "three D's" had been put out of the championship by a team other than one of themselves. Tyrone were the only other county to break the monopoly when they beat Donegal in 1994. Monaghan also became the first team to beat Donegal at Ballybofey in the championship since 1987.

DONEGAL (above): Gary Walsh, John Joe Doherty, Matt Gallagher (c), Barry McGowan, Mark Crossan, Noel Hegarty 0-1, Martin Shovlin, Brian Murray 0-1, Martin Gavigan 0-1, Mark McShane, James McHugh, Paddy Hegarty, Declan Bonner 0-1, Tony Boyle, Manus Boyle 0-4. Subs: John Duffy for McShane (34), John Gildea for Bonner (46). Squad: Paul Callaghan, Tommy Ryan, John Cunningham, Gerard Kelly, Eamon McMenamin, Charles O'Donnell, John Ban Gallagher.

MONAGHAN

John O'Connor

Edwin Murphy	David King	Noel Marron
Martin Slowey	Joe Coyle	John Conlon 0-1
Pauric McShane 0-2		Frank McEneaney
Gregory Flanagan	Michael Slowey	Declan Loughman 1-0
Stephen McGinnity 0-2	Peter Duffy 0-3	Declan Smyth 0-6

Sub: Ray McCarron for Flanagan (67).

Referee: Jim Curran. Linesmen: Damien Campbell, Brendan Gorman. Bookings: Martin Slowey, Brian Murray, Noel Marron, David King. Man of the Match: Declan Smyth. Attendance: 12,000

After-Match Quotes

"We came up here as complete outsiders, with nothing to lose, and showed pure grit and determination. They're a better football team but we were better prepared and more tuned in" - **Declan Loughman**.

"We played poorly for 55 minutes. It was over long before the end" - **PJ McGowan.**

"We won playing good football with lots of points from open play. We're a young team and deserved the victory. I'm fifth oldest and I'm only 24!" -

Stephen McGinnity.

"It's been a season of highs but not high enough. We got to the league final and beat Down but were well-beaten today. We've just got to take it on the chin" -

Matt Gallagher.

Escape From The Darkness

Semi-final, June 25, Clones
Derry 0-10   Tyrone 0-11

"What a great tilting roller coaster of a game. The sun beating down relentlessly. Legs weakening and spirits soaring. Bad temper and fine football in equal measure. Spleen vented and scores settled. Two Tyrone men and one Derry man dismissed. Seventy minutes of turmoil, chaos and fevered football. Enough arguments to last us to eternity ... and Derry, the All Ireland favourites, lay slain".

Tom Humphries' assessment in the Irish Times did not understate the case. This has to be viewed alongside the greatest games of the nineties - Dublin v Meath and Down v Meath in 1991, Donegal v Derry in '92, Derry v Dublin in '93, and Derry v Down in '94. Another classic, and like all those games, memories of the day are precious. You try to recollect every thought, every image, for fear they may be fading away, and so that you can relate your own personal version to your children. "I was there". Most of the excitement derived, as it did in all of the classic games listed above, from the fact that the underdogs won. Tyrone had lost to Derry (yet again) in their league semi-final and had then struggled to overcome Fermanagh; Derry were everybody's tip for the All Ireland after their annihilation of Armagh. Yet, when I met Art McCrory a week before the game, at an appreciation dinner for Derry great Jim McKeever, he was supremely confident. Here's the way Art saw it - Tyrone could and should have put five

The Tyrone bench celebrate at the final whistle.

Derry v Tyrone in the 90s				
1991	Derry 1-7	Tyrone 1-6	NFL	
	Derry 1-9	Tyrone 1-8	Ulster SFC	
1992	Derry 1-10	Tyrone 1-8	NFL Final	
	Derry 1-10	Tyrone 1-7	Ulster SFC	
1993	Derry 1-16	Tyrone 1-4	McKenna Cup	
1995	Derry 1-13	Tyrone 1-11	McKenna Cup	
	Derry 1-8	Tyrone 2-3	NFL Semi	
	Derry 0-10	Tyrone 0-11	Ulster SFC	

goals past Fermanagh, but he was glad they didn't. What purpose would that have served? Tyrone were happy to be written off because they felt they were capable of scaling the heights while Derry had peaked and were ripe for a fall. Also, most importantly, Tyrone had lost an Ulster Final and had taken too many beatings from their neighbours to endure another. It was time for this young, talented outfit to finally arrive, and they did.

"Release. This is what escape from darkness means. If Tyrone go on to win three All Ireland titles in a row they won't experience joy of a more pure, distilled variety than that which they drank in at full-time ... shirts whipped off for swapping, shoulders red from the slapping, breath still short from the running, they embraced each other and danced around in tiny crazy knots". Tom Humphries once again captured the mood perfectly. One Tyrone player refused to swap his jersey, because for Fay Devlin, this was a special day. "It means a lot to beat Derry. It's been nine years since I was on a Tyrone team that beat them. We would have taken a lot of stick if we'd failed again, especially where I'm from, on the Derry border." Tyrone stopped at nothing to win this game, from early in the year. "Ever since January it's been Derry, Derry, Derry for eighty training sessions", revealed McCrory. His team's level of fitness, as evidenced in a second-half played in almost unbearable heat, with fewer men and coming from behind, was astonishing. Mind you, the players were helped by regular water supplies from Tyrone helpers strategically placed behind each goal and on each side of the pitch. The management had gone to the lengths of contacting the Football Association of Ireland in Dublin to ask how Jack Charlton's team had coped with playing in high temperatures at the 1994 World Cup in America.

Before the game, injury rumours emanated from both camps, and for a change, they all had foundation. Tyrone's Ciaran Corr and Mattie McGleenan would be replaced at half-time, while Brian McGilligan, troubled by a groin strain sustained the previous Monday, was withdrawn five minutes into the second-half. Art McCrory was content to "trade" two of his men for one of Derry's, for he knows the worth of McGilligan. In fact, at a Chat Show in 1993, the Tyrone manager chose the Dungiven man when given an imaginary one million pounds to buy a player. "We need a work-horse in our team, someone as powerful and influential as McGilligan, to drive us on", McCrory told the audience. He also needed a midfield, and found a reasonable one, with Jody Gormley plucked from nowhere during the league and Fergal Logan converted from centre-half-back. Seamus McCallan then assumed the number six shirt, to bring Tyrone's quota of All Ireland Under-21 medallists on the starting line-up at Clones to seven (two more came on), and to make it eight changes from the team that played in the 1994 Ulster Final. "Tyrone teams don't generally bow

Tyrone out in front. Seamus McCallan beats Damien Barton to the ball.

out gracefully, so for this year we had to isolate players that had commitment. The training was stepped up, I've heard the word 'brutal' used, but we did what had to be done in order to compete with the more successful teams".

Tyrone started impatiently, fouling Johnny McGurk in the first minute and then throwing him to the ground when the free-kick was awarded. The defence would go on to play well, apart from reckless fouls which gave Derry nine of their ten points. Anthony Tohill punished Tyrone, as Enda Gormley did in the third minute when another foul followed a brilliant save by McConnell, from Bateson. At 3-2 to Derry, Peter Canavan announced his presence by collecting the ball fifty metres out and taking on the entire Derry defence single-handedly. Twenty metres from goal, they thought they'd stopped him when he went to ground, but instead, Canavan bounced up, changed onto his left foot and popped the ball over the bar (see front cover). Derry responded with three quick-fire points. Tohill, doing the work of two men, won a free and converted one, while Eamonn Burns added his team's only score from play. Their supporters began to raise a chant of "Derr-ree, Derr-ree", but before they could reach full voice, Peter Canavan had the ball over the bar at the other end, with a lovely shimmy and a kick from a tight angle.

Canavan closed the gap further with a mighty kick from outside the 45, but again Derry were handed a score as McCallan fouled McGurk. A minute later, the same Tyrone defender caught Seamus Downey with a high tackle. Two bookings meant he was sent off. Pascal Canavan switched to centre-half-back, but within minutes he too was ordered off. Already booked, he had to go after swinging punches at Damien Barton. Another Tohill free concluded a crazy five minutes and sent Derry in at half-time with a 8-5 lead and a two-man advantage. "Those two boys should be ashamed of themselves", gasped Brian Canavan. "You can't throw punches these days, and they could have cost Tyrone the game". Eugene Young made for the Derry dressing-room with these comments, "Our boys set out to control their discipline and they've done that, but as far as I'm concerned Tyrone are trying to rough us up. We have to re-focus, but it could work to their advantage with 13 men. The game's not over yet by a long shot."

How right he was, for while Derry urged caution and even more control, so as to avoid a "evening-up" sending-off, Tyrone pledged to die for one another in the second half. Their management dramatically changed the game-plan to bring on two runners in Paul Donnelly and Adrian Cush, playing with four men up. "We knew they would put two men on Peter so there was not point in using the long ball. We had to hold on to it for as long as we could, carry it up to him and make them chase us". However, it also has to be said that the referee was approached at half-time. Damien Barton later claimed the official had been intimidated, and immediately after the game he referred to "reckless comments" made to Tommy McDermott by Tyrone players during the game. Whatever was said, the 35 minutes that followed was quite astonishing. Tyrone defied the conditions to play a possession/running game, falling deep into their own defence with short passes, challenging Derry to "come and get it", before bursting upfield in numbers. Paul Donnelly, who would not play again until the All Ireland final, was the "Man of the Half". Peter Canavan

		Derry	Tyrone
1 min	Tohill (F)	0-1	
4 mins	E. Gormley (F)	0-2	
5 mins	Ptr. Canavan (F)		0-1
9 mins	Tohill (F)	0-3	
10 mins	Corr		0-2
12 mins	Ptr.Canavan		0-3
16 mins	E.Gormley (F)	0-4	
18 mins	Tohill (F)	0-5	
20 mins	Burns	0-6	
21 mins	Ptr. Canavan		0-4
27 mins	Ptr. Canavan (F)		0-5
29 mins	E. Gormley (F)	0-7	
36 mins	Tohill (F)	0-8	
HALF-TIME			
36 mins	Ptr. Canavan (F)		0-6
42 mins	Ptr. Canavan (F)		0-7
45 mins	Ptr. Canavan		0-8
48 mins	Tohill (F)	0-9	
52 mins	McLaughlin		0-9
54 mins	E. Gormley (F)	0-10	
59 mins	Ptr. Canavan (F)		0-10
63 mins	J. Gormley		0-11
FULL-TIME			

got the first, crucial score, and would add three more, but this time he was assisted brilliantly by his team-mates. Stephen Lawn won the free-kick for the score, then selfless runs from Cush, Donnelly, and Lawn again, set up the rest. Within ten minutes, the 13-men were level and Derry had failed to score. In a strange way, they had too many men and too much time on the ball. Defenders were able to come forward, but they could only get so far and their shooting was wild and erratic. Coleman, Downey and McGurk all missed the target in the second half, while the forwards, badly missing Joe Brolly, lost races all afternoon. Worse was to follow, with the dismissal of Fergal McCusker for allegedly striking Peter Canavan off the ball. The linesman reported the incident, but I have to say, from my position just behind the said linesman, it looked to be worse than it actually was, and the Derryman, who had not previously been booked, was unlucky to be sent off. Tohill edged the fourteen men in front, but the super-fit thirteen men were winning the exchanges. Fay Devlin and Ciaran Loughran combined down the left wing to create Sean McLaughlin's equaliser, and when Enda Gormley again scored for Derry, Canavan made it 10-10. The latter followed a superb piece of running by Stephen Lawn, anticipating Damien McCusker's attempted short kick-out and covering the ground to make the ball his. Jody Gormley watched the '94 final from the Stand, but this time he would

Whoosh! Finbarr McConnell is relieved after Geoffrey McGonigle's shot has gone wide.

Paul Donnelly sets off on a determined run.

score the winner with a left-footed kick seven minutes from time. Tyrone were ahead for the first time and would survive a couple of scares, when McGonigle's snapshot came back off a post and Eamonn Burn's tame shot was deflected into McConnell's grateful arms. Derry could have won or drawn the game, but as Art McCrory commented, "It was time we had a bit of luck against Derry".

While Tyrone rejoiced at the end, the 1993 All Ireland champions looked in disarray. What had happened to the young, talented team which had so competently secured the Sam Maguire for their county for the first time? Amid the mayhem at Clones, substitute Dermot McNicholl (not used) stared blankly across the scene, while his father had words with Mickey Moran. Later, criticism would be levelled at the manager from some of his own players, with Karl Diamond and Gary Coleman the most vociferous. Diamond insisted he wouldn't play again under Moran, while Gary Coleman, who suffered more than any of the players from the controversy which saw his father replaced by Moran, laid the blame with both the management and the County Board. "I have been sickened by the Board, and I believe the team will rot away to nothing. There's been a bad feeling in the camp, and it's still there. It won't go away until the present management has gone". Gary Coleman's wish came true when Moran resigned in September, after only a dozen players turned up for the first night of training for the league, though the outgoing manager made counter-criticisms of some players and the media. "Certain players have acted dishonourably..... it is common knowledge that a prominent player phoned other players asking them not to attend training. Others were harassed because they did attend.... my family has been subjected to malicious phone calls from persons obviously influenced by unfounded press reports." No-one condones the phone calls, but I have to say that if 'player power' had a role in Moran's downfall, it's hardly surprising. First, the players were deprived of the manager they liked and with whom they were successful. Then, Moran declared he would step down if he did not have their support. He stayed on, even though most of the All Ireland team boycotted the start of the 1994-95 league. At Christmas, senior players told me that the 1995 effort would "come from the players", and after losing to Tyrone, they told me that, "the day we missed Eamonn Coleman was the day we were beaten". Put simply, they respected Moran as a coach, but not a manager. They do accept a large slice of the blame for the Tyrone defeat, but they have been dismayed at how the world (or at least the dressing-room) has collapsed around them since their finest hour. Moran should never have become manager after the "dishonourable" treatment of Eamonn Coleman, but in fairness, he was the choice of the County Board and they ultimately must be held responsible. It is clear that Derry's problems began in late 1993, when certain members of the Board became determined to oust Coleman, after he stood by his players over a dispute with the Board. When Coleman then made well-publicised complaints about his "inadequate compensation" for managing Derry, the wedge became even more firmly rooted. It was later claimed that his sacking was to do with money requests and other matters, and not about personalities, but surely it was a combination of these factors, at best.

DERRY: Damien McCusker, Kieran McKeever, Tony Scullion (c), Gary Coleman, John McGurk, Henry Downey, Fergal McCusker, Brian McGilligan, Anthony Tohill 0-5, Dermot Heaney, Damien Barton, Eamonn Burns 0-1, Declan Bateson, Seamus Downey, Enda Gormley 0-4.   Subs: Ollie Collins for McGilligan, Damien Cassidy for Bateson, Geoffrey McGonigle for Barton.   Squad: Jonathan Kelly, Gary McGill, Sean McGuckin, Dermot McNicholl, Karl Diamond, Dermot Dougan

TYRONE: Finbarr McConnell, Paul Devlin, Chris Lawn, Fay Devlin, Ronan McGarrity, Seamus McCallan, Sean McLaughlin 0-1, Fergal Logan, Jody Gormley 0-1, Ciaran Corr (c) 0-1, Pascal Canavan, Ciaran Loughran, Matt McGleenan, Peter Canavan 0-8, Stephen Lawn.   Subs: Paul Donnelly for McGarrity (h-time), Adrian Cush for Corr (h-time), Gerard Cavlan for Loughran.
Referee: Tommy McDermott.   Linesmen: Mick McGrath, Damien Campbell.
Bookings: Pascal Canavan (2), Seamus McCallan (2), Ciaran Loughran, Eamonn Burns, Tony Scullion.
Sendings-off: McCallan, Pl Canavan, F. McCusker.   Man of the Match: Peter Canavan.   Attendance: 30,000

After-Match Quotes

"That was the finest half hour of football any Tyrone side has ever produced"
Eugene McKenna

*"You never have Tyrone beat. Like a terrier, no matter how big the dog,
they never let go"* - **Paddy O'Rourke**

"What was said at half-time was totally irrelevant. The players had been preparing for six months with Derry in mind, they had done too much bloody work to lie down to this lot" - **Art McCrory.**

"We kept two men in defence and lost it in the first ten minutes of the second half"
Anthony Tohill

"Tohill apart, I can't name a Derry man who played well. Every wide they hit in the second half was like a score for Tyrone." **- Brian Canavan.**

"I've never seen a comeback like this in all my life"   **Paddy O'Hara, BBC**

Fintan's Smash & Grab Act

Ulster SFC Semi-final, July 2
Cavan 1-9   Monaghan 0-10

Monaghan should have won this game. They failed for a number of reasons - because they missed a penalty, didn't score for the last 21 minutes of the first half, shot nine wides in the second half, and because of Fintan Cahill. The Cavan full-forward poached four match-winning scores against the run of play. His goal, after twelve minutes, undermined the good start Monaghan had made, and his second-half points were executed with the directness that was painfully missing from the Farney attack.

"Everything seemed to go for Cavan today", moaned Joe Coyle. "Every shot they took seemed to go in off the post or whatever. Up front, the space wasn't there, because of the Cavan backs and our hurried shooting. It just didn't click like it did against Donegal". Credit must also go to Martin McHugh for doing his homework from the Donegal game, and for instilling confidence in his forwards to take scores when their backs were against the wall. "There was never a lack of commitment in Cavan football, but now we're playing a better brand of football", explained Ronan Carolan. "Martin preaches at us not to give the ball away, so we carried the ball out of defence, and his great self-belief in himself is rubbing off on us. Join these factors together and you'll see why we're in our first Ulster final since 1983. The performance wasn't great, but we showed great spirit".

Fintan Cahill bursts through for his goal.

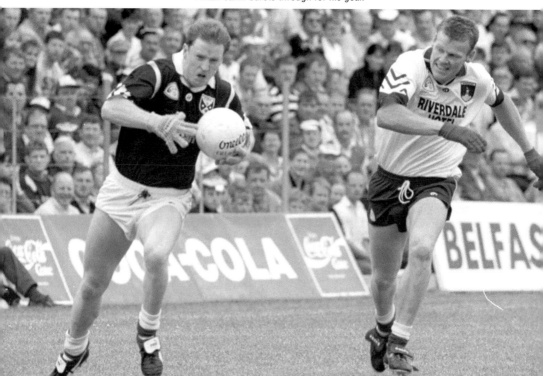

Cavan goalkeeper Paul O'Dowd saves Declan Smyth's penalty.

Cavan supporters were still celebrating on the Clones pitch and chanting 'We want McHugh', half an hour after the end of the game. They had lost to their neighbours in each of the previous three years in the championship, and had not caught sight of the Anglo-Celt since the sixties, yet Stephen King, a veteran of many Ulster battles, uttered words of caution. "We'll need to improve by one hundred per cent to win the title". Cavan started the semi-final poorly, after arriving late from their warm-up at Newtownbutler, and conceded five points in fourteen minutes. Peter Duffy grabbed the first two, and Declan Smyth two others, but Fintan Cahill responded with a brilliant goal. Collecting the ball wide on the right, he cut inside David King and struck a low drive which hit both posts before entering the net. With Damien O'Reilly showing his fellow backs how to mark closely and attack the ball, and with Stephen King lording midfield, Cavan owned the second quarter. McCabe, Lambe, Carolan (2), and Reilly took them from 1-1 to 0-5 in arrears, to 1-6 to 0-5 in front. Monaghan had one golden chance, when Pauric McShane was upended in the square, but Paul O'Dowd acrobatically touched Declan Smyth's penalty onto a post.

		Cavan	M'han
26 secs	Duffy		0-1
4 mins	Duffy		0-2
8 mins	Cahill	0-1	
9 mins	Smyth (F)		0-3
12 mins	Cahill	1-1	
13 mins	Slowey		0-4
14 mins	Smyth (F)		0-5
15 mins	McCabe	1-2	
20 mins	Lambe	1-3	
23 mins	Carolan (F)	1-4	
28 mins	Reilly	1-5	
35 mins	Carolan (F)	1-6	
HALF-TIME			
38 mins	Loughman		0-6
47 mins	Reilly (F)	1-7	
51 mins	Cahill	1-8	
55 mins	Duffy (F)		0-7
57 mins	Duffy (F)		0-8
58 mins	McEneaney		0-9
68 mins	Cahill	1-9	
69 mins	Smyth		0-10
FULL-TIME			

CAVAN (above): Paul O'Dowd, Aidan Watters, Damien O'Reilly (c), John Donnellan, Gerry Sheridan, Aidan Connolly, Bernard Morris, Stephen King, Pat Shiels, Dermot McCabe 0-1, Peter Reilly 0-2, Ronan Carolan 0-2, Adrian Lambe 0-1, Fintan Cahill 1-3, John Brady.   Sub: Fergal Harton for Shiels (66).

MONAGHAN: John O'Connor, Edwin Murphy, David King, Noel Marron, Michael Slowey, Joe Coyle, John Conlon, Pauric McShane, Frank McEneaney (c) 0-1, Peter Duffy 0-4, Michael Slowey 0-1, Gregory Flanagan, Stephen McGinnity, Declan Loughman 0-1, Declan Smyth 0-3.   Subs: Gerard McGuirk for Conlon (27), Ray McCarron for Loughman (42), Eoin Meegan for McShane (69).   Squad: Glenn Murphy, Brian Morgan, Conor Mone, Kieran Lavelle, Ian Larmer, Colin McCaul, Seamus Mullan, Peter McLaughlin, D.McKiernan, B.O'Brien.   Referee: Mick McGrath   Man of the Match: Fintan Cahill

The withdrawal of Declan Loughman early in the second half was surprising, considering he had just scored a point, and the fact that other, younger heads, were starting to drop. The suggestion after the match was that he was injured and "not on his game", but the latter could have been applied to the whole forward unit. Michael Slowey's shot rolled wide, Peter Duffy missed a close-in free, and Frank McEneaney's goal-bound drive was superbly blocked by O'Reilly. "We had them pinned well down, but panicked a bit and went for goals", lamented Michael McCormick. Cavan defended in numbers, and at times in desperation, but held on to reach their 59th Ulster final when Fintan Cahill burst through in the last two minutes for a brilliant individual score.

After-Match Quotes

"I thought the second half would never end. We only scored three points, but we had things covered at the back - **Damien O'Reilly.**

"It was one of those days. Luck deserted us, but this is a young Monaghan team with a big future, and they'll learn from this" - **Michael McCormick.**

"The defence was the best part for us. The pace in the first half was great, and we decided to go man-to-man in the second half. They coped well."- **Martin McHugh.**

Red Hot McBride Cools the Breffni Blues

Bank of Ireland Ulster SFC Final, July 23, Clones
Cavan 0-10   Tyrone 2-13

Two minutes into the game, Ciaran "Dinky" McBride fielded a ball above his marker and slotted it over the Cavan crossbar. It was a score of stunning simplicity, from a player who would go on to play a significant part in Tyrone's bid for All Ireland glory, even though the Ulster Final was his championship debut. He wasn't even in the squad for the semi-final with Derry, and had been on the injury list at the outset of the campaign. But, just a week before the final, McBride scored three goals in a challenge game with Meath at Irvinestown, to win a place on the team ahead of Mattie McGleenan."He's red-hot", whispered Art McCrory before the Clones decider. The Omagh man was also Tyrone's surprise packet, providing the perfect foil for Peter Canavan and adding a new dimension to the Tyrone attack. His height, scoring ability and effectiveness as a target man, were exactly what was needed. McBride's second score came on 22 minutes, after a superb fetch and swivel in a crowded goal-mouth, and he set up Stephen Lawn for another score shortly after. It was a vital contribution in

what proved to be a match-winning period for Tyrone, scoring eight points without reply from the 9th-34th minute.

Cavan had made the better start, with a Peter Reilly point after 27 seconds, and two more from Carolan and Smyth. They were unlucky not to add a couple of goals, as incisive runs by Dermot McCabe and Fintan Cahill were stopped by Finbarr McConnell. The rest of the Tyrone defence had been caught cold, with Seamus McCallan watching the ball instead of his man, and Chris Lawn unsettled by finding Dermot McCabe by his side from the start. He had prepared for Fintan Cahill. Lambe and Carolan had also switched, as part of Martin McHugh's successful early tactics. Tyrone countered with Pascal Canavan dropping back to fill the glaring gaps, and with

Ciaran "Dinky" McBride

		Tyrone	Cavan
1 min	Reilly		0-1
2 mins	McBride	0-1	
4 mins	Carolan (F)		0-2
6 mins	Smyth		0-3
9 mins	McLaughlin	0-2	
12 mins	Pr Canavan (F)	0-3	
18 mins	Pr Canavan (F)	0-4	
22 mins	McBride	0-5	
25 mins	Corr	0-6	
26 mins	S.Lawn	0-7	
31 mins	Pr Canavan	0-8	
34 mins	McCallan	0-9	
35 mins	Reilly (F)		0-4
Half-time			
36 mins	McCabe		0-5
40 mins	Pr Canavan (F)	0-10	
42 mins	Carolan (F)		0-6
43 mins	Carolan (F)		0-7
47 mins	Loughran	0-11	
52 mins	Pr Canavan	0-12	
55 mins	Carolan (F)		0-8
57 mins	McCabe		0-9
63 mins	McGleenan	1-12	
67 mins	S.Lawn	1-13	
69 mins	Carolan (F)		0-10
70 mins	Cush	2-13	
Full-time			

their midfield taking control. Jody Gormley caught a few high balls, and Fergal Logan began to pick out Peter Canavan, who scored three times. The hard-working Corr fisted another, after Reilly's kick was intercepted by Pascal Canavan, and McCallan pointed from distance, unchallenged. Crucially for Cavan, Ronan Carolan missed two scoreable free-kicks in the middle of the Tyrone onslaught. McHugh made a switch just before the half-time whistle, but he admitted later that Cavan's chance had gone. "We lost it in the second half of the first half. We lost it in the middle of the field by allowing them to overrun us. You can't let anyone get eight points in-a-row if you seriously want to win a match".

Cavan opened the second half with another move straight from the training ground, with four passes ending in a point by McCabe, though his team would score only once more from play. Tyrone defended in numbers, with men behind the ball, and with a water-tight full-back line holding their men (including First Round hero Fintan Cahill) scoreless. McCallan also settled to have a fine game. Cavan came close twice in the half, at 10-7 and 12-9, but both times Tyrone responded. First, Ciaran Loughran scored at the end of a determined run down the left, after Carolan had pointed back-to-back frees for Cavan. Second, Mattie McGleenan came off the bench to thump a high, bouncing pass from fellow substitute Adrian Cush to the Cavan net, seven minutes from time. At the other end, Cahill had been guilty of two wides from play , though credit to the likes of Loughran, Corr, and even Canavan for helping the defence. The forwards covered a lot of ground by proceeding to burst upfield with the ball. As Art McCrory observed later, "We adopted this style of play in the Derry game and it worked so well it's been difficult to shake off since".

McGleenan's goal ended the contest, but for good measure, Lawn pointed after a pinpoint pass from Pascal Canavan and Cush took advantage of the area vacated by Damien O'Reilly (sent upfield as Cavan gambled) to announce his return to form with a goal, after a pass from Lawn. Amazingly, the score triggered an invasion of the playing surface by high-spirited Tyrone supporters, engulfing Cush and the referee who was whistling furiously and waving his arms to indicate that the game had not yet ended. Fortunately, they retreated quickly and formed a human perimeter around the pitch for the closing moments.

Mattie McGleenan was besieged by fans when the final whistle did go, and he left the ground without any of his playing gear. "They're mad for the gear and why not? They put a lot into it too and we haven't much to give them", said Mattie, who was to be married the following Thursday. "The stag night is tonight, and you can all come", he told a packed dressing-room, though his wife had mixed feelings. A honeymoon holiday in Tunisia had to be cancelled the next day!

In his victory speech, Ciaran Corr insisted that Tyrone weren't finished yet, and were intent on adding the Sam Maguire to the Anglo-Celt. On paper, his team had an excellent chance of reaching the All Ireland final, though Eugene McKenna expressed reservations about playing a tall, physical Galway team in the semi-finals. The Dublin press and Martin McHugh went further, with the former suggesting that Tyrone's "rather messy display" meant a lengthening of the odds of another All Ireland for Ulster, and the latter predicting that Tyrone would not beat Dublin because of their smaller physical make-up. It was true that Tyrone had been rather "messy" early in the Ulster Final, and that they had scored just three times in the second half before McGleenan's goal, but their winning margin was also the biggest in the provincial final since 1989.

After-Match Quotes

"The common perception of Tyrone is that we're a one-man forward line, with no midfield, and a crowd of little leprechauns at various places around the field. The truth is, we are giving away size and height, but we compensate in other areas, and we have reached the stage where we feel we can cope without" - **Art McCrory.**

"Art's an awful man for setting goals but the players reach them. The players know he's done so much for Tyrone football, so whatever Art says, goes" - **Ciaran Corr.**

"I think when we sit down and think about it, we may come to the conclusion that we didn't do too bad this year" - **Martin McHugh.**

"We're going to have to improve by 50/60 per cent, but today is only the beginning. Greater things and tasks lie ahead for us" - **Mattie McGleenan.**

"We showed we're not a one-man forward line" - **Peter Canavan.**

Finbarr McConnell with his son Ciaran
and the Anglo-Celt Cup

41

CAVAN: Paul O'Dowd, Aidan Watters, Damien O'Reilly (c), John Donnellan, Gerry Sheridan, Aidan Connolly, Bernard Morris, Stephen King, Tommy Smyth 0-1, Dermot McCabe 0-2, Peter Reilly 0-2, Ronan Carolan 0-5, Adrian Lambe, Fintan Cahill, John Brady. Subs: Fergal Hartin for Lambe (35), Anthony Forde for Brady (53). Squad: Declan McCarthy, Pat Shiels, Seamus Donohue, Raymond Cunningham, Raymond Cole, Joe McCarthy.

TYRONE: Finbarr McConnell, Paul Devlin, Chris Lawn, Fay Devlin, Ronan McGarrity, Seamus McCallan 0-1, Sean McLaughlin 0-1, Fergal Logan, Jody Gormley, Ciaran Corr (c) 0-1, Pascal Canavan, Ciaran Loughran 0-1, Ciaran McBride 0-2, Peter Canavan 0-5, Stephen Lawn 0-2. Subs: Adrian Cush 1-0 for McBride (49), Mattie McGleenan 1-0 for Gormley (60). Squad: Joe Cassidy, Brendan Mallon, Paul Donnelly, Gerard Cavlan, Damien Loughran, Damien Gormley, Danny Barr.

Referee: Pat McEneaney
Linesmen: M. Cranny, A. O'Neill
Bookings: Lambe, O'Reilly, McCallin.
Man of the Match: Ciaran Corr
Attendance: 33,000

Chris Lawn feels the force of Fintan Cahill's challenge.

ULSTER SFC TOP SCORERS

	Total	Games	Average
Peter Canavan (Tyrone)	0-20 (20)	3	6.66
Ronan Carolan (Cavan)	0-14 (14)	3	4.66
Manus Boyle (Donegal)	1-9 (12)	2	6.00
Peter Reilly (Cavan)	2-4 (10)	3	3.33
Enda Gormley (Derry)	0-9 (9)	2	4.50
Declan Smyth (Monaghan)	0-9 (9)	2	4.50
Cathal O'Rourke (Armagh)	0-7 (7)	1	7.00
Shane King (Fermanagh)	0-7 (7)	1	7.00
Peter Duffy (Monaghan)	0-7 (7)	2	3.50
Anthony Tohill (Derry)	0-7 (7)	2	3.50

Note: Peter Canavan is the first player to finish the Ulster SFC Top Scorer in successive years for three decades. (Brendan Kelly (Derry) shared the top spot in 1976 and was the clear winner in 1977). Canavan's 1994 total was 1-17.

Step One:
Peter goes left.

Step Two:
Peter goes right.

Step Three:
Peter goes left again and scores a point, despite the attention of Gary Fahy.

"Wrap Peter up in Cotton Wool!"

All Ireland Semi-final, August 13, Croke Park
Galway 0-13 Tyrone 1-13

In both 1986 and 1995, Tyrone defeated Galway to reach the All Ireland final, and on both occasions the Ulstermen defied their favourites tag to win by just three points. "Both games were similar", reckoned '86 star and '95 fan, Damien O'Hagan, "Tyrone failed to play to their full potential both times, and required crucial goals from Kevin McCabe nine years ago, and Peter Canavan today. However, comparing the two sides overall, I would say the '95 team has more strength in depth than we had, and they depend a lot on Canavan. I feared for Tyrone when he took a knock on his ankle at the end of the first half, but he came out and did more in the first two minutes of the second half than the whole team had done up to then. Tyrone need Canavan, and if I was Art and Eugene, I would wrap Peter up in cotton wool and put him away until the next day!"

Canavan totalled 1-7 and his best score was the second point of the second half, where he turned his marker inside out before levelling the game at 1-5 to 0-8 (see opposite page). Galway restored their two-point advantage soon after, but another burst of brilliance from the full-forward inspired Tyrone's best spell, between the 49th and 55th minutes. He scored three times as his team established the three-point cushion with which they would end the contest. A vital factor in Tyrone's second half revival was the better quality of ball played towards Canavan, mainly from his brother, Pascal, and Adrian Cush. Pascal, switched to midfield at half-time, picked out Peter with a pinpoint pass for the equaliser, while substitute Cush held the ball up before placing the target man for the next score (1-6). The Donaghmore man also won a free-kick in front of the posts after a darting run through the heart of the Galway defence on 63 minutes, while fellow sub Mattie McGleenan (right) made another telling impact with two points. His first was angled beautifully from wide on the right, and his second came a minute from the end, when the huge Tyrone support finally breathed a collective sigh of relief. Back in the dressing-room, the mood among the winning team was subdued. Players took their time changing and they

muttered to one another that they had nearly blown a whole year's work. Art McCrory thought he had walked into the wrong dressing-room when he returned from giving media interviews, and tried to lift his player' spirits with some straight-forward logic. "It doesn't matter how we played today. What might have happened might have happened, but it didn't. We're in the All Ireland final, for only the second time in our lives, and it's how we play on that day that matters. We can play better, and we will".

		Tyrone	G'way
4 mins	McBride	0-1	
5 mins	Logan		0-2
7 mins	Finnegan		0-1
12 mins	Silke		0-2
14 mins	Finnegan (F)		0-3
18 mins	Finnegan (F)		0-4
20 mins	Wilson		0-5
23 mins	Pr Canavan (F)	0-3	
26 mins	Pr Canavan	1-3	
28 mins	Fallon (F)		0-6
30 mins	Gavin		0-7
31 mins	Finnegan		0-8
Half-time			
36 mins	Pr Canavan (F)	1-4	
37 mins	Pr Canavan	1-5	
41 mins	Finnegan (F)		0-9
48 mins	Finnegan (F)		0-10
49 mins	Pr Canavan	1-6	
50 mins	Pr Canavan	1-7	
51 mins	McLaughlin	1-8	
53 mins	McGleenan	1-9	
55 mins	Pr Canavan (F)	1-10	
62 mins	Finnegan (F)		0-11
63 mins	Daly		0-12
64 mins	Pr Canavan (F)	1-11	
69 mins	Cush		1-12
69 mins	McGleenan	1-13	
71 mins	Finnegan (F)		0-13
Full-time			

Tyrone had played particularly poorly in the first half, and would have been in serious trouble but for Peter Canavan's 26th-minute goal. Ciaran McBride had a hand in the build-up to the goal, and was involved in the three points his team added (scoring one and making two). He recalls the mood in the Tyrone dressing-room at half-time being worse than at full-time, "We just sat there like zombies for a while, until we started talking among ourselves and worked out what we had to do". Peter Canavan explained to McBride why it was sometimes better to pass the ball instead of shooting from a bad position, and the corner-backs, Paul and Fay Devlin (who required a pain-killing injection to an injured shoulder), urged the half-back line not to caught upfield, as they were allowing the fast Galway wing-men to race through almost at will. Tyrone had also lobbed too many wind-assisted high balls into the forwards, and were struggling at midfield, mainly because Fergal Logan had suspected glandular fever! The Stewartstown man took a chance, and lasted until ten minutes into the second half. He also scored Tyrone's second point of the game, to give them a 2-0 lead, but Galway replied with five straight points. "Galway caught us by surprise with their tactics", recalls Finbarr McConnell. "We easily beat them in the league (2-13 to 0-4), but this time they were very fit and played a fast, running game. We expected long balls in to Val Daly, but they dictated the pace for forty minutes and put us on the back foot". Tyrone sorted themselves out and won the second half, though their performance was compared to Donegal's poor showing against Mayo in the 1992 All Ireland semi-finals. Some argued that this was the best thing to happen to Tyrone, as it would keep their feet firmly on the ground, but others would have been happier going into an All Ireland final with a morale-boosting, confident display.

Above: Tyrone captain Ciaran Corr leads from the front.

Below: Peter Canavan watches the ball drop over the Galway goal line.

Tyrone supporters celebrate with Peter Canavan.

After-Match Quotes

"We were terrible in the first half but we had that extra little bit when it counted. Ciaran Corr and Pascal and a few others started to play in the second half, and Peter produced a few outstanding points which you can always rely on him to do. When you give it to him, he delivers. He's the icing on the cake" - Fergal Logan.

"1986 was the first time, and maybe the first time is the best time, but I can assure you that this too is very sweet" - Art McCrory.

"We had to carry the burden of four All Ireland champions going into this match, and the pressure of being expected to beat the Connacht champions, but we're a young, learning team" -Finbarr McConnell.

"Tyrone are the best eighteen-man team in Ireland" - Jim Carney, Tuam Herald.

Pat McCartan in radio contact with Art McCrory in the Hogan Stand.

"We knew in January that we had the talent to win an All Ireland, so we set our stall out for this year because there's only one All Ireland each year" - Art McCrory.

TYRONE : F.McConnell, P.Devlin, C.Lawn, F.Devlin, R.McGarrity, S.McCallan, S.McLaughlin 0-1, F.Logan 0-1, J.Gormley, C.Corr (c), Pl.Canavan, C.Loughran, C.McBride 0-2, Ptr.Canavan 1-7, S.Lawn.
Subs: M.McGleenan 0-2 for S. Lawn (35), A.Cush 0-1 for Logan (45), Brian Gormley for Loughran (63).
GALWAY : Cathal McGinley, John Kilraine, Gary Fahy, Kevin Fallon, Raymond Silke 0-1, Damien Mitchell, Sean Og de Paor, Fergal Gavin 0-1, Kevin Walsh, Jarlath Fallon 0-2 (c), Thomas Mannion, Tommy Wilson 0-1, Niall Finnegan 0-7, Val Daly 0-1, Fergal O'Neill.

Referee: Brian White (Wexford)   Linesmen: Pat Casserly, J.Bannon

Bookings: Logan, Mitchell   Man of the Match: Peter Canavan   Attendance: 37, 053

Pantomime Season Comes Early

Bank of Ireland SFC Final, September 17, Croke Park
Dublin 1-10   Tyrone 0-12

The morning after the final, I listened to the Joe Duffy show on RTE radio, while travelling home. Jason, Dessie, John O'Leary, and the rest of the Dublin lads, told Joe how they had won the All Ireland, and how great it was for the city. Charlie Redmond also gave his version of the sending-off farce. "Ah, poor Charlie. Sure the ref had an off-day", was the gist of the reaction, and when they came to discussing the incident that led to the sending-off, sure that wasn't Charlie's fault either! The hero was allowed to claim, unchallenged, that "Fergal Logan tried to injure me. He came in with the boot and then with his elbow. I got up and ran into him with my head down, but I didn't head-butt him". With three minutes of the programme remaining, the presenter announced that Fergal Logan was joining him "on the line" from the Burlington Hotel. "Did Charlie actually connect?" says Joe. "Och, not really, no...", replied the voice on the other end. Redmond was absolved, and in return, he said he hoped "they could have a pint together sometime". And so, the controversy was put to rest, except for one thing..... the northern voice on the phone was NOT that of Fergal Logan.

The Tyrone midfielder heard the interview but could not get through to RTE until the programme had ended. They explained that they had asked for Fergal by name at the hotel, and that the person who took the call had claimed to be Fergal Logan. Apparently, it was a Tyrone fan, but goodness only knows

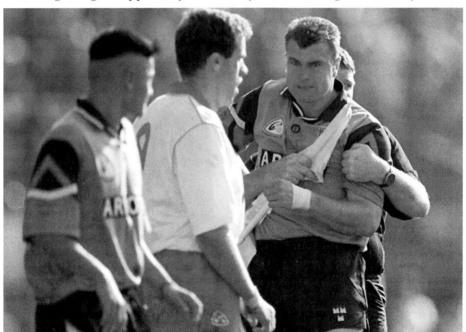

Charlie Redmond snarls at Fergal Logan after their clash.

49

why he pretended to be Fergal. Neither the Dublin players, nor anyone involved in the show, realised the mistake, but I suspected something, especially as an angry Fergal Logan had told me the previous evening that he wanted to "have his say", after seeing Charlie Redmond and Colm O'Rourke criticise him on 'The Sunday Game'. The Evening Herald followed up on Monday, by describing Logan's part in the incident as "the worst foul in the game", even though it was not called as a foul. Later that week, the Tyrone Times carried Logan's story, though with all due respect to the newspaper, it did little to balance the controversy outside the losing county. 'Fergal was the villain and Charlie was the hero', was the version the Dublin media appeared happiest with, even though Logan had not attempted to exaggerate the situation by complaining to the referee or by feigning injury, and even though Redmond had been outrageously critical of the referee (he told Paddy Russell that if he sent him off, he wouldn't be given another final) and was later suspended for three months. Tyrone Chairman Declan O'Neill branded the Dublin player "a thug" and said it was clear that he had made an intentional head gesture towards Logan, while former All Ireland referee John Gough praised Paddy Russell and criticised Pat O'Neill for adding to the confusion, "he shouldn't have been anywhere near the touchline. It wasn't the ref's fault the player stayed on the field". Logan himself was bitterly disappointed with the damage done to his reputation, and with the prevailing attitude in the South. He protested that "there was absolutely no malice in what I did. I was running over to tackle Redmond and he went down. I made slight contact as I was finishing my run, but he seemed to turn and bundle me over the top of him. Yet, he was guilty of one of the lowest acts in any form of violence you can imagine, attempting to head-butt an opponent, and he's been treated as an heroic figure. The situation is that he's been propped up for another year. Year in, year out, he makes some sort of blunder, and the bigger it is, the more they seem to love him for it".

All in all, the farcical Redmond/Logan aftermath added insult to injury, from an Ulster perspective. Sam was not going to spend a fifth successive winter in the province, and Tyrone were denied the first ever All Ireland title they craved for. "My immediate reaction is that Dublin needed to win an All Ireland, but I didn't think they needed to win it that badly", blasted Art McCrory after the final whistle. "Pantomime would be a good word to describe the second half. Dublin repeatedly contrived to stop the play from developing, which resulted in only 12-15 minutes play for the whole half. They held up the play and then took a minute to take a free. It was deliberate time-wasting. The referee would have been entitled to play ten minutes extra time. Dublin and the scribes will call it control, but it was nothing more than time-wasting". The Tyrone manager's attitude may have appeared ungracious in defeat, but he has been angered by what he sees as a 'pro-Dublin bias' on more than one occasion down the years. Indeed, he and I are both open to accusations of 'Ulster paranoia', but we are not alone. Didn't Eamonn Coleman lambast the Southern media for under-rating Derry in 1993, "Youse boys know nothing"; didn't the same media write off Down and Donegal's chances before the 1991/92 finals; weren't Down told in

Hands up! Keith Barr lets Peter Canavan go past him.

1994 that Dublin deserved to win the All Ireland and that they "didn't know what it takes to win an All Ireland"; and haven't Ulster's sensational successes been undermined by the decisions of the Dublin media-dominated All Stars scheme? For example, why was Tony Boyle ousted from the full-forward position in 1992? Also, what justification was there for Peter Canavan not being selected at full-forward in 1994, and how on earth was Neil Collins omitted the same year, after saving a dramatic penalty from "darling Charlie", with only minutes to go in the final, and right under Hill 16?

Having said all this, Tyrone did not play well enough to deserve to win the 1995 All Ireland final. Dublin played better, though not much, in the worst final in years. The second half in particular left observers frustrated, and almost disinterested, as the play stopped, started, and stopped again. There was no score between the 44th and 66th minutes, while the winners scored only two points in the entire half, and the losers scored only twice from play in the entire game. It has to be admitted that Dublin might have won by more, if Redmond had been fit enough to take free-kicks, and if Tyrone did not have the amazing Peter Canavan. His eleven points were a testimony to his brilliance, but also an inditement of his colleagues, who simply didn't supply enough ball for the full forward to do further damage. Questions must be asked of the Tyrone team selection, easy to do in hindsight of course, but all three substitutes performed better than most of the starting line-up. Mattie McGleenan had shown the management what he could do as a sub in the two previous matches , though

Adrrian Cush sits out training.

admittedly he had not always produced the goods when on from the start; Brian Gormley made a huge difference, simply because he looked up whenever he got possession and used the ball intelligently, whereas others ran into trouble; and Paul Donnelly's determined runs gave Tyrone momentum and hope in the frantic closing stages. Surely, he should have been introduced much earlier, though he was the last sub available and the managers had to stall when McCallan became injured.

Some argue that Tyrone lost the All Ireland on the Monday night before, when Adrian Cush slid into a tackle he was never going to win. From the scream he gave out, it was feared he had suffered a broken ankle. He hadn't, but the ligament damage was still bad enough to rule him out. Cush was instructed to sit out training two days later, but to hide the injury as best he could from the media. It's likely he was going to be named in the first fifteen, especially as Stephen Lawn was a slight injury doubt, though any announcement was to have been delayed until close to the game. With this indecision in the air, Cush made a rash challenge, but again in hindsight, should there have been a training match six days before the final? Cush's admirers feel that his running and ball skills would have made all the difference in the last quarter. Tragically for Cush and Tyrone, we will never know.

As one of the Tyrone supporters in the Cusack Stand, I have to say that I winced with embarrassment when our team broke away from the pre-match parade, just as it reached Hill 16. The move was planned, but I couldn't help feeling that the incident helped the Dublin players, left to complete the parade alone, focus on the job in hand. Still, Tyrone made a perfect start, by taking a 3-0 lead. Peter Canavan held his nerve to kick the first two from free-kicks into the Dublin end, after Paddy Moran had over-carried and Stephen Lawn had been fouled. Canavan set up Jody Gormley for the third, as the Tyrone midfield began to answer its critics. Gormley and Logan went on to win the battle, with the highly-rated Brian Stynes moved to corner-back to mark McGleenan. At times, their distribution was hesitant and mis-directed, but the suggestion made after the match by Colm O'Rourke, that Tyrone still need to find two good midfielders, was surely a harsh judgement on their performance, especially Logans'.

After Tyrone's whirlwind start, Dublin recovered to win the rest of the half by 1-8 to 0-3. Their control in this vital period was down to close-marking in the full-back line (making delivery to the Tyrone full-forwards difficult), superb tackling and counter-attacking by the half-backs, and a lively half-forward line which scored five times before the break. Also, with Redmond restricted, Keith Barr, Paul Clarke, and Dessie Farrell all pointed excellent frees, from long-distance and from ackward angles. And then, there was the goal, on 25 minutes. Somehow, a low ball got through a forest of legs and fell into the path of Jason Sherlock. The speed of the little fellow in reaching the ball first was telling, though Finbarr McConnell, so central to Tyrone's year, will forever regret his split-second indecision when faced with the one-on-one situation. The ball trickled across the goalmouth for Redmond to kick to the net. Man of the Match Paul Curran raced through for the next score, to give Dublin a five-point lead, and Tyrone replaced his marker, Ciaran Loughran, with McGleenan. At half-time, John O'Leary reminded his players that 'Tyrone are a

		Tyrone	Dublin
2 mins	Pr Canavan (F)	0-1	
4 mins	Pr Canavan (F)	0-2	
5 mins	Gormley	0-3	
6 mins	Barr (F)		0-1
9 mins	Redmond (F)		0-2
10 mins	Clarke (F)		0-3
15 mins	Farrell		0-4
18 mins	Pr Canavan (F)	0-4	
21 mins	Farrell (F)		0-5
22 mins	Pr Canavan (F)	0-5	
25 mins	Farrell		0-6
25 mins	Redmond		1-6
32 mins	Curran		1-7
34 mins	Pr Canavan (F)	0-6	
35 mins	Gavin		1-8
Half-time			
37 mins	Pr Canavan (F)	0-7	
39 mins	Pr Canavan	0-8	
42 mins	Pr Canavan (F)	0-9	
44 mins	Farrell		1-9
66 mins	Pr Canavan (F)	0-10	
67 mins	Clarke		1-10
68 mins	Pr Canavan (F)	0-11	
71 mins	Pr Canavan (F)	0-12	
Full-time			

second half team', but they didn't appear to have heeded his warning as three points from Canavan brought the Ulster side back into the contest. McBride, who struggled all afternoon to get free of Paddy Moran, was fouled for the first;

Jason Sherlock squeezes the ball past Finbarr McConnell and Chris Lawn for Redmond to goal.

Above: Paul Donnelly forces his way past Mick Galvin.

Below: The point that never was. Sean McLaughlin kicks the ball over the Dublin bar.

Canavan played a one-two with Corr for the second, and McGleenan was fouled for the third. But, after working up a head of steam, Tyrone failed to score again for 24 minutes. The Redmond debacle began after Farrell put Dublin three in front, and then further delays were caused by a catalogue of free-kicks, bookings, and injuries. Dublin were certainly guilty in this period of slowing the game down and of over-protesting to the referee, who at one point appeared to give Tyrone a sideline ball and then changed his mind just as the players had made their way into the Dublin half. In between the stoppages, Tyrone did attempt to engage their hitherto successful running game, but Dublin's half-backs tackled effectively, and their full-backs were usually first to the ball whenever it was released, which was simply not often or quickly enough. Ciaran Corr and Pascal Canavan were drawn into their own half, leaving Peter Canavan and Co isolated and hard to pick out. Dublin couldn't score either, with several frees missed and Logan blocking bravely at the feet of Sherlock, though Clarke eventually found the target with a fine long-distance point in the 67th minute. It was Dublin's last score, and a vital one.

"Everybody panicked in the closing stages", views former Down captain Paddy O'Rourke. "Tyrone panicked at the thought of winning, Dublin panicked at the thought of losing. The referee panicked too, though it's not that surprising, considering the stakes are so high. It was there for the taking for Tyrone, but they didn't have enough players who were prepared to have a go. In 1991, when we needed a score, Ross Carr thumped a 50-yard free-kick ten yards over the bar. In 1993, Johnny McGurk had a go with his left-foot in Derry's semi-final against Dublin, and it came off. Paul Donnelly was the sort of player with the right conviction and he had a go, but overall, Peter Canavan was on his own". Ciaran Corr revealed after the game that he did 'have a go' in the last minute, but his effort at a point dropped short of the Dublin goal. John O'Leary punched the ball clear, towards Peter Canavan, and Tyrone supporters held their breath as the man who could do no wrong lost his footing when trying to control the ball.

Canavan still managed to pass the ball to Sean McLaughlin, who kicked it over the bar and raced away thinking he had levelled the scores. Paddy Russell, who was well-positioned, judged that Canavan had played the ball illegally off the ground. At the time, I agreed with the referee though I was shocked five weeks later when I watched the television replay from behind the goals and viewed that the ball was clearly off the ground. It was a cruel way to lose an All Ireland final. Tyrone fans stood silently on the Croke Park pitch for some time after the final whistle, in pure disbelief. Their feeling of injustice was not eased by after-match replays showing Paddy Moran clearly lifting the ball off the ground earlier in the game.

Back in the Tyrone dressing-room, Peter Canavan brought his first down on the table and summed up the day in just thirty seconds. "We were awful and Dublin were awful. We beat ourselves, but we came very close and I got a taste of what it would be like to win an All Ireland final. I hope you did too, because I want one of those medals. If we work harder, we can come back. Remember the Under-21s lost an All Ireland before winning two." Later that evening, at the

Tyrone banquet, Ciaran Corr made an impassioned plea to "all 28 players in the squad to come back next year and put the record straight". Corr also won many plaudits for his dignity in defeat, and for his insistence the following day that Tyrone should not appeal for a replay, on the grounds that Charlie Redmond broke the rules. "When you're beat, you're beat', he said. But will this young Tyrone team (average age 23) be back? The experts are divided, with former Dublin boss Kevin Heffernan optimistic: "Tyrone have the basis of an All Ireland win within maybe two or three years", and former Kerry boss Mick O'Dwyer pessimistic: "Tyrone are clearly three or four players short of an All Ireland winning team". Personally, I feel there are seven or eight teams capable of winning the All Ireland, and Tyrone are one of them. They are very young and maybe they froze a little against Dublin, giving the impression of being unfit even though they had trained relentlessly since January (they had also frequently been led through Drum Manor Forest, near Cookstown, by Northern Ireland runner Donal Gallagher, on a punishing ten-mile course, during the summer). Tyrone will benefit from the experience of losing, but they must also find an alternative route to goal, other than Peter Canavan. The night before the 1995 final, Eugene McKenna told the players that if one or two of the other forwards could contribute two points each, then Tyrone would win. In his five matches, Canavan scored 1-38, to finish top of the national chart, and a massive 34 points clear of his team-mates (none of whom found the target more than five times). The full-forward also accounted for 1-18 of Tyrone's total of 1-25 in the games with Galway and Dublin.

ALL IRELAND SFC TOP TEN SCORERS			
	Total	Games	Average
Peter Canavan (Tyrone)	1-38 (41)	5	8.2
Colin Corkery (Cork)	0-36	4	9.0
Charlie Redmond (Dublin)	1-31 (34)	5	6.8
Maurice Fitzgerald (Kerry)	4-20 (32)	3	10.6
Damien Delaney (Laois)	2-17 (23)	3	7.6
Niall Finnegan (Galway)	0-22	5	4.5
Colm O'Rourke (Meath)	3-8 (17)	4	4.25
Brian Stafford (Meath)	2-10 (16)	4	4.0
Evan Kelly (Meath)	3-7 (16)	4	4.0
Ronan Carolan (Cavan)	0-15	3	5.0

TYRONE SCORERS	
Peter Canavan	1-38
Matt McGleenan	1-4
Stephen Lawn	1-2
Adrian Cush	1-1
Ciaran McBride	0-4
Pascal Canavan,	
Sean McLaughlin	0-3
Ciaran Corr, Jody Gormley,	
Fergal Logan,	
Seamus McCallan	0-2
Ciaran Loughran	0-1
Total - 4-64	

Teams in All Ireland Final

TYRONE

Finbarr McConnell

Paul Devlin	Chris Lawn	Fay Devlin
Ronan McGarrity	Seamus McCallan	Sean McLaughlin

Fergal Logan   Jody Gormley 0-1

Ciaran Corr (c)	Pascal Canavan	Ciaran Loughran
Ciaran McBride	Peter Canavan 0-11	Stephen Lawn

Subs: M.McGleenan for Loughran (31), B.Gormley for S.Lawn (35), P.Donnelly for McCallan (60). Squad: Joe Cassidy, Damian Loughran, Adrian Cush, Gerard Cavlan, Stephen Conway, Danny Barr, Damian Gormley.

DUBLIN

John O'Leary (c)

Paddy Moran	Ciaran Walsh	Keith Galvin
Paul Curran 0-1	Keith Barr 0-1	Mick Deegan

Paul Bealin   Brian Stynes

Jim Gavin 0-1	Paul Clarke 0-2	Dessie Farrell 0-4
Charlie Redmond 1-1	Jason Sherlock	Mick Galvin

Subs: Pat Gilroy fo Galvin (50), Robbie Boyle for M.Galvin (60), Vinnie Murphy for Farrell (71). Squad: David Byrne, Brian Barnes, John O'Callaghan, Sean Cahill, Enda Sheehy, Brian Whelan.

Referee: Paddy Russell (Tipperary).   Linesmen: W.O'Mahony (Limerick), F.Finan (Sligo).

Bookings: McCallan, Deegan, McConnell, Clarke, Sherlock   Sent Off: Charlie Redmond

Man of the Match: Paul Curran.   Attendance: 65,600

After-Match Quotes

"We were hanging on at the end. It was horrible out there. Peter Canavan is an awesome player, but, fortunately for us, he was the only one they had. Tyrone are a one-man team" - **Brian Stynes.**

"We didn't deserve to win, but we deserved a draw. There was a lack of strength shown by the referee. It was very different to Ulster refereeing, though the referee didn't beat us" - **Art McCrory.**

"I can fairly say that this was the worst All Ireland final I have ever seen. It is time to look at the option of a sin-bin to provide a fitting punishment for persistent offences" - **Mick O'Dwyer.**

"There was a lot of talk before the game about how the GAA needed and wanted a Dublin win, and there was a few things that happened which would make you wonder whether that was right" - **Ciaran McGarvey.**

"I'm retiring from inter-county football after the final" - **Mattie McGleenan**

"Next year, I'll be standing beside Jack Boothman after the final" - **Ciaran Corr.**

Find what you're looking for!

You know what you want.
And you know what makes
you happy... in your life,
and in your bank.

It's all about choice.

And personal banking at
Bank of Ireland gives you
just that. Options that suit
your pocket and your plans.

So choose the bank you'll be
happy with.

And ask yourself, would you
really settle for anything less?

Bank of Ireland

PERSONAL BANKING

Irish News/Guinness Ulster All Stars

Back, L-R: Paul Devlin, Sean McLaughlin, Finbarr McConnell, Anthony Tohill, Ronan Carolan, Tony Scullion.
Front: Fergal Logan, Ronan McGarrity, Henry Downey, Fay Devlin, Stephen Lawn, Peter Reilly.
Missing from the photocall were Peter Canavan and Mickey Linden.

Jim McKeever All Stars

Back, L-R: Pat King, Art McCrory, Danny Quinn, Matt Trolan, Peter McGinnity, Liam Austin, Paddy Diamond,
Jimmy Smyth, John Rafferty. Front: Mickey Darragh, Ray Morgan, Jim McKeever, Leo Murphy,
Seamus Downey, Peter Canavan. Missing from photo: Colm McAlarney. This team was announced at a
Tribute evening for Jim McKeever, to mark his 35 years at St Josephs/St Marys. The selection was based on
playing ability, in-house contribution at the college, and on spreading the "McKeever gospel".

ULSTER ALL STARS 1972-95

1
Paddy Linden ('88)
Gary Walsh ('92)

2
Donal Monaghan ('74)
Nudie Hughes ('79)
John Joe Doherty ('93)
Michael Magill ('94)

3
Paddy Kennedy ('81)
Conor Deegan ('91)
Matt Gallagher ('92)
Tony Scullion ('93)

4
John Lynch ('86)
Tony Scullion ('87,'92)
Paul Higgins ('94)

5
Brian McEniff ('72)
Peter Stevenson ('75)
Kevin McCabe ('80)
John McGurk ('93)

6
Anthony McGurk ('75)
Paddy Moriarty ('77)
Ollie Brady ('78)
Ciaran Murray ('85)
Martin Gavigan ('92)
Henry Downey ('93)

7
Gary Coleman ('93)
DJ Kane ('94)

MIDFIELDERS

Colm McAlarney ('75,'78)
Joe Kernan ('77)
Colm McKinstry ('80)
Liam Austin ('83)
Eugene McKenna ('84)
Plunkett Donaghy ('86)

Brian McGilligan ('87,'93)
Barry Breen ('91)
Anthony Molloy ('92)
Anthony Tohill ('93)
Gregory McCartan ('94)

10
Gery McElhinney ('75)
Peter McGinnity ('82)
Ray McCarron ('86)
Ross Carr ('91)
Anthony Tohill ('92)
Peter Canavan ('94)

11
Jimmy Smyth ('77)
Joe Kernan ('82)
Eugene McKenna ('86)
Greg Blaney ('91,'94)
Martin McHugh ('92)

12
Greg Blaney ('83)
Joyce McMullen ('90)
James McHugh ('92)
James McCartan ('94)

13
Andy McCallin ('71)
Martin McHugh ('83)
Tony Boyle ('92)
Mickey Linden ('94)

14
Sean O'Neill ('71,'72)
Frank McGuigan ('84)
Damien O'Hagan ('86)
Eugene McKenna ('89)
Ger Houlahan ('93)

15
Paddy Moriarty ('72)
Anthony McGurk ('73)
Dermot McNicholl ('84)
Nudie Hughes ('85,'88)
James McCartan ('90)
Enda Gormley ('92,'93)

WHO WILL BE NEXT? WATCH OUT FOR THE NEW...

POWERSCREEN
G.A.A. ALLSTARS

More Power to the All Stars

Dungannon-based Powerscreen International has saved the GAA All Stars scheme from going to the wall. Several months had gone by since the withdrawal of previous sponsors 'Bank of Ireland' when the successful Tyrone company came to the rescue with a deal which will keep the scheme afloat for at least five years, and revolutionise the much-criticised selection process.

No longer will journalists decide who are the fifteen best hurlers and footballers in the land. Instead, the players themselves will pick the teams, with every player involved in the championship having a vote. Auditors will organise the nominations as they come in, and a steering committee will finalise the selections. Players will not necessarily win places in which they have played during the year, as the process has been simplified to reward those with the most nominations. Therefore, the six defensive positions will simply go to the defenders with the most nominations, even if there are three full-backs in the six, and so on. GAA fans will undoubtedly welcome the transfer of power, as there can not now be accusations of bias levelled at the selectors. In the past, the journalist panel of selectors was considered by some to the too Dublin-based, and criticism came from Ulster on more than one occasion. Some memorable examples have been: 1) the preference of Mick Lyons over Ciaran McGarvey in 1986, 2) the omission of Neil Collins in 1991 and 1994, 3) Tony Boyle being selected at corner-forward in 1992, and 4) Peter Canavan being selected at right-half-forward in 1994. Hopefully, such controversy will now be avoided. "I want the scheme to finish up with the best fifteen players getting places on the team", explains Powerscreen Chief Executive Shay McKeown, "the main thing is that the players will select the team".

There will also be a new Players Player of the Year Award, and all the awards will be presented at a banquet at the Burlington Hotel on December 1. One further point - the "sportsmanship rule", so much a part of the previous selection scheme, will not be a factor this year. Therefore, players sent off and suspended for more than the minimum period during the year will not be disqualified.

Powerscreen have been long-time supporters of the GAA, from sponsoring Tyrone in the early nineties, to McKeown's personal involvement in turning around the fortunes of Dungannon Clarkes after it appeared to be on the verge of closing. At the end of his three-year stint at club chairman, their finances were healthy and the ground had been transformed into one of the best in Ulster. Similarly, the company, manufacturers of quarrying machinery, has grown in stature and now has an excellent worldwide reputation. It has also taken over smaller companies throughout Ireland and employs Tyrone footballers Adrian Cush, Joe Cassidy, and Adrian Kilpatrick.

Tyrone may not have won the All Ireland, but it can certainly claim to have revived the GAA All Stars, thanks to Powerscreen International.

Player Of The Year
Peter Canavan, Tyrone

Willie Anderson reckons he would make a superb out-half, Frank McGuigan estimates his worth on an imaginary GAA transfer market at ten million pounds, Peter McGrath says he'd swop him "in a couple of years time" for Mickey Linden if he could, and Tyrone supporters ask for the letters "GOD" to be imprinted on the back of their replica jerseys, directly above the number 14.

Of all these compliments, Peter Canavan will probably take most pleasure from the one paid by the man they call "The King" in Tyrone, Frank McGuigan. His eleven points from play in the 1984 Ulster Final is now gaelic football folklore, and not just in his own county. No fewer than eight out of nine leading figures in the game selected the Ardboe man on their All-Time Ulster Football teams in my first book, "The Path of Champions". Jim Reilly recalled his "pure genius", Peter McGrath referred to his "sleek brilliance", and Jimmy Smyth said McGuigan had "beautiful balance ... he could do everything".

Canavan didn't need to read these informed comments to discover the regard with which his fellow Tyrone man is held. He's old enough to remember 1984 (he was fourteen years-old) and his memory is constantly refreshed by Tyrone supporters. "All I ever hear, wherever I go, is McGuigan this and McGuigan that!", protested Peter earlier this year, though it was a protest with a smile. He accepted the comparisons as part of life, there was nothing he could do to prevent them ... or was there? Man of the Match performances in the defeats of Fermanagh and Derry drew the ultimate praise, from "The King" himself.

"Canavan is the only player I would specifically go to a game to watch", McGuigan told the Tyrone Times. "I would dearly love to have played with Peter, that's the only way I think I could see how good he really is. I believe we would have known what one another was trying to do, for, like myself, I can sense Canavan suffers a bit sometimes from the inability of others to read his game. I can understand that, however, because he doesn't really know himself what he's going to do when he gets the ball. Everything is instinctive, watch him and you'll see that his actions are intuitive. He just does what comes naturally. His talent is verging on genius. It is something you're either born with or you're not. They say Anthony Tohill is the complete footballer but he's limited in his versatility. Canavan has everything. He just oozes class and if Tohill was worth a million pounds on the transfer market, Canavan would be in the ten million pounds category."

Ulster's Team of the 90s

Neil Collins
(Down)

Kieran McKeever
(Derry)

Tony Scullion
(Derry)

Fay Devlin
(Tyrone)

John McGurk
(Derry)

Henry Downey
(Derry) (c)

DJ Kane
(Down)

Anthony Molloy
(Donegal)

Anthony Tohill
(Derry)

Ross Carr
(Down)

Greg Blaney
(Down)

Martin McHugh
(Donegal)

Mickey Linden
(Down)

Peter Canavan
(Tyrone)

James McCartan
(Down)

This team has been selected by the man who led Down and Ulster out of the doldrums in 1991 - Paddy O'Rourke. He was the first captain from this province to raise the Sam Maguire in the nineties, and has been delighted, if not surprised, to watch three others follow suit. He made this prediction after Down's win in 1991: "I firmly believe Ulster can go on to dominate the All Ireland Championship over the next ten years. Tyrone have a crop of brilliant Under-21s coming through, Derry and Down are still quite young and Donegal have a great depth of talent within their county". Paddy was spot on, though he admits he didn't expect Ulster to win the All Ireland continuously, "perhaps three or four over ten years". In 1992, he was surprised Donegal won the All Ireland after losing the 1991 Ulster Final to Down, but understands why they came back, "They were like the rest of the Ulster teams who felt that if Down could do it, then so could they. Before '91, teams from here thought the Sam Maguire was for others, but now, players feel that if they can get into the county panel, they will have a chance of winning an All Ireland. As a result, the standard has improved greatly, and I don't think we'll ever go back to the drought of 23 years".

Paddy rates the Down '94 team as the best-balanced of the four All Ireland winners from Ulster, though he acknowledges that Derry were stronger in some

ULSTER FINALS

1990 - Donegal	0-15	Armagh	0-14
1991 - Down	1-15	Donegal	0-10
1992 - Donegal	0-14	Derry	1-9
1993 - Derry	0-8	Donegal	0-6
1994 - Down	1-17	Tyrone	1-11
1995 - Tyrone	2-13	Cavan	0-10

ALL IRELAND FINALS

1991 - Down	1-16	Meath	1-14
1992 - Donegal	0-18	Dublin	0-14
1993 - Derry	1-14	Cork	2-8
1994 - Down	1-12	Dublin	0-13
1995 - Tyrone	0-12	Dublin	1-10

All Stars 1990-94: Down 12, Derry 10, Donegal 9, Armagh, Tyrone - 1

sections. "Down had brilliant forwards, which is why I have picked four of them on my team, as well as the fact that they won two All Irelands, and I have four Derry defenders. Overall, Derry get five selections, three more than both Donegal and Tyrone. They nearly always beat Tyrone and have won two National Leagues, though I feel they have only themselves to blame for not winning a second All Ireland. Eamonn Coleman was a good manager for them and I feel Derry did little wrong in 1994, but they had problems off the field. In any county, it's important to have good links between the Chairman, the manager and the team captain, so that any small problem cropping up can be nailed before it becomes a big problem".

The man from Burren also reckons the two best individual performances of the nineties contributed to denying Derry a second All Ireland. "Mickey Linden was absolutely superb at Celtic Park in '94. The whole atmosphere was tense, yet he spelt danger every time the ball came near. He turned right, then left, and couldn't be stopped, while at Clones in '94 ,Tyrone got a score from everything Peter Canavan did, and he, more than any one player, stopped Derry. Another outstanding display came from Greg Blaney in the '91 Ulster Final. I was concerned by him getting married a few days before the game, but it did him no harm at all. In fact, he got better, while Anthony Tohill was untouchable for Derry against Down in Newry in '93, and Henry Downey showed superb leadership in Derry's defeat of Dublin in the same year. Henry was always pushing forward, making fifty-yard runs, taking balls, giving passes, and scoring points". Paddy makes the Derryman captain of his "Team of the 90s", while Anthony Molloy and DJ Kane are selected. "I am very reluctant to leave

ULSTER RECORDS, 1990-95

			Championship					League	
	P	W	D	L	UFs	UCs	All Ires	Finals	Wins
Donegal	21	14	2	5	4	2	1	2	-
Derry	19	12	2	5	2	1	1	2	2
Down	18	13	2	4	2	2	2	1	-
Armagh	15	5	4	6	1	-	-	1	-
Tyrone	13	6	1	6	2	1	-	1	-
Monaghan	12	4	2	6	-	-	-	-	-
Cavan	10	2	2	6	1	-	-	-	-
Fermanagh	9	2	1	6	-	-	-	-	-
Antrim	6	-	-	6	-	-	-	-	-

UFs - Ulster Finals, UCs - Ulster Championships

PLAYER OF THE YEAR - PETER CANAVAN, TYRONE

Above: The Tyrone star evades Galway's Gary Fahy to score another point.
Below: My Ball! Canavan beats two Cavan defenders in a race for possession.

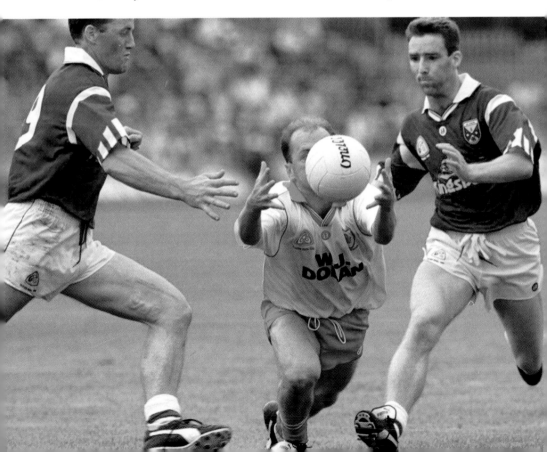

BEFORE AND AFTER

Above: Relief! Tyrone Chairman Declan O'Neill is engulfed by supporters at the end of the All Ireland Semi-final.
Below: Tyrone manager Art McRory addresses the crowds in Dungannon the evening after the final.

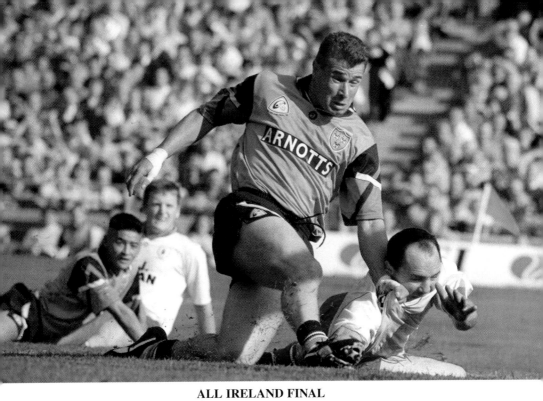

ALL IRELAND FINAL

Above: **Charlie Redmond holds off Paul Devlin to score Dublin's goal.**

Below: **Ronan McGarrity gets to grips with Dessie Farrell.(right).**

ULSTER SFC

Above: **Near Miss. Cavan goalkeeper Paul O'Dowd has the ball after an Antrim attack.**
Below: **Cavan's Stephen King leaves Tyrone's Seamus McCallan empty-handed in the Ulster Final.**

ULSTER SFC

Above: Derry have a last-minute team talk before their perfect performance against Armagh.

Below: Monaghan's John Conlon comes away with the ball as Donegal take a tumble in Ballybofey.

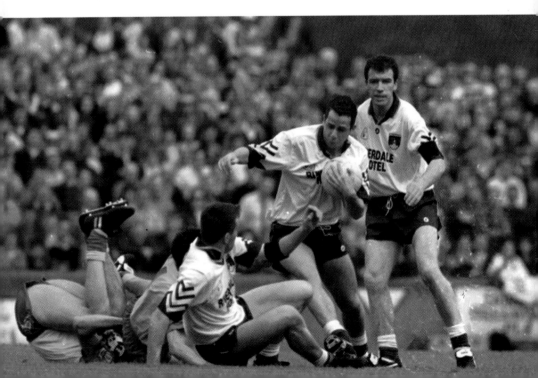

MINORS

Above: **Antrim captain Kieran Kelly receives the Ulster MHC cup from Ulster President John Vesey.**
Below: **Delight and despair for Derry minor footballers, after the Ulster Final (left) and the All Ireland final (right).**

HURLING

Above: Down goalkeeper and captain Noel Keith holds the Ulster SHC Cup after his team's win over Antrim.
Below: Dermot Woods grips the sliothair as Terence McNaughton closes in.

CLUBS

Above: Bellaghy, All Ireland Finalists, in close-up. Back, L-R: Kevin O'Neill, James Mulholland, Mark Kearns, Ciaran Donnelly, John Mulholland, Gerry McPeake. Middle: Karl Diamond, Jude Donnelly, Damian Brown, Danny Quinn (c), Louis McPeake, Eunan Cassidy, Ciaran Doherty. Front: Gareth Doherty, Declan Cassidy, Cathal Scullion.

Below: Derrygonnelly Harps, Guinness SFC winners in Fermanagh. Back, L-R: Colm Carroll, Niall Smyth, Martin Greene, Paul McGrady, Gary Smyth, Paul Greene, Martin Hamilton, Michael Glynn. Front: Donal Corrigan, Francis McKenna, Kevin Casidy, Sean Flanagan, Dermot Feely, Eoghan Cassidy, Kevin McGrath.

Brian McGilligan out, as you could argue that he nearly made Tohill and was badly missed against Tyrone this year, but I feel Donegal wouldn't have won their All Ireland without Molloy. He was very influential and had a good final. DJ was superb in '91 and a great motivator and leader in '94. In goals, Neil Collins gets the nod for his all-round game and his penalty save from Charlie Redmond. Neil would have thought that he was going to save it. A confident keeper, good in one-on-ones and unlucky not to get an All Star in both years. Kieran McKeever, a wee man with a big heart, gets the number two shirt, alongside Tony Scullion, who reads the game so well and performs on the big day. In the left corner, Fay Devlin, who did well at times when Tyrone were struggling this year, like late in the Derry game and early in the Ulster Final". Paul Higgins came close to making Paddy's team, as did Donal Reid, just losing out to Johnny McGurk, scorer of Derry's famous winner against Dublin in '93.

The half-forwards are Ross Carr, Greg Blaney, and Martin McHugh, with the latter selected on the wing. "Ross has been the best half-forward in Ireland. He can win ball, has a good shot, is skilful on the ball, and thrives on difficult free-kicks. He's the sort of player a captain doesn't have to worry about, and who wins All Irelands. Greg had the marvellous ability of being able to sense which of his colleagues was playing well, and could then direct his service accordingly. 1991 was his best year, while Martin McHugh was a class above in '92. He had a superb Ulster Final in the comeback against Derry, and ran the show in the final with Dublin. Tony Boyle was another outstanding Donegal forward that year, but I can't find room for him in a full-forward line of Linden, Canavan and McCartan. Mickey has been the best corner-forward for five or six years, had two great finals and was consistently brilliant in '94. Canavan picks himself, and James was Man of the Match in the '91 final. He hasn't always performed, but if there's a score needed on the big day, he'll get it. Others in contention for the last position were Joe Brolly and Enda Gormley".

Looking to the future, O'Rourke predicts a return to power for either Down or Derry in 1995, "if they can get their respective houses in order. I wouldn't read too much into the upsets by the likes of Monaghan and Cavan this year, as I don't think they have improved enough to surprise the big names again. Down should come back to beat Donegal, who still have to replace some of their retired men, but men like DJ Kane and James McCartan are central to our chances. Something had to give in Derry, and they will hope to move forward now under Brian Mullins. Tyrone are still short a few more players, most notably a big, strong forward, and although I feel they can win an All Ireland, it may take a couple of years".

As for the loss of the Sam Maguire, which Paddy proudly carried North in 1991, he doesn't see any need to despair, "It doesn't mean too much from an Ulster point of view. We weren't going to hold on to it forever, and our champions will continue to be strong contenders".

Nice Guys Do Win

Church & General National Football League Final
Derry 0-12   Donegal 0-8

Tony Scullion pulled a piece of paper from a pocket in his shorts, unfolded it and began to deliver his acceptance speech as Derry captain. He had taken the time to write down what to say and who to thank, and had played the whole match with the note in his shorts! And, as Tony began to deliver his carefully-worded speech, everybody listened to his every word, because they respect his attitude to playing football, and because everybody likes Tony Scullion. He's a real, nice guy.

Nobody begrudged the proud Ballinascreen man the joy of raising the New Ireland Cup before the Derry supporters, though the fact that the previous captain to have the honour was still on the team, tells part of the story behind a remarkable turnaround in events. Way back at the start of the league, Henry Downey was joined by most of the Derry panel in a boycott of the team, in protest at the removal of their friend and manager, Eamonn Coleman. Scullion also liked the former boss, but he could not refuse the jersey and would not stay away.

Laois destroyed a makeshift Derry fifteen at Celtic Park, 1-17 to 0-8. Two weeks later, Donegal beat Derry in Ballybofey, 0-15 to 2-6, but the strike was nearing an end. Brolly, Tohill, McNicholl and McKeever had already returned, and they were followed by most of the first-team for the next match against Kerry on November 13. Derry won by two points and remained undefeated throughout the rest of the league. The unusual nature of their title success threw up a unique statistic - Derry's scoring aggregate over their ten games amounted to 7-94, while their "scores against" total was just one point less, 7-93. Kerryman John O'Keeffe was impressed by a re-united Derry. "I'll be very surprised, even at this early stage, if they are not back in Croke Park in the third Sunday in September". Derry indeed looked capable of proving to themselves and others that there was another All Ireland title in them. With the line-out almost identical to the '93 team, they had improved in their last three games and re-captured the unity of purpose that had swept them to the Sam Maguire.

"Our corner-forwards are defenders and our defenders are attackers", explained Joe Brolly. "Eamonn instilled that in us. If one man goes forward, then the other covers back. The system broke down briefly in the semi-final when Gerard Cavlan was left unmarked to score a goal for Tyrone, but you know we [the team] discussed what went wrong in that one instance, for a full hour. When we do get it right consistently, it gives us a certain predictability in our play, and we become very hard to beat. The fact that we have won trophies also helps. Tyrone haven't, and in their eagerness they tend to panic when they get the ball and don't look up."

Indeed, Tyrone did waste a number of good scoring chances while Derry were able to step up a gear when it was required. They responded to Tyrone's early second-half revival with a goal and a point, and again to Cavlan's goal with three points in three minutes to open up a five-point lead. True, Tohill's goal did owe something to good fortune, but Derry had built the foundation for victory in a first-half in which they held Tyrone's feared forwards to a solitary point.

In the quarter-finals, Derry had struggled to overcome Cavan while Tyrone had blasted Kerry out of Croke Park with a flamboyant 3-7, yet it was Derry who might have scored goals early in this game. Finbarr McConnell first saved low to his left from McGonigle and then spectacularly deflected a Barton rocket over the bar. Peter Canavan apart, the nervy Tyrone forwards failed to sparkle. Several of their nine first-half wides came from free-kicks (in contrast to the in-form Enda Gormley who converted five from six), though credit must also be paid to the defensive work of the likes of Downey and Scullion. The latter even managed to get on the scoresheet, a most irregular occurrence!

Donegal meanwhile resembled a runaway train, gathering speed from high-scoring victories over Kildare, Clare and Laois, and unable to stop themselves from reaching a final they had reason for not wanting to be part of. The fixture book showed that they would have to play All Ireland champions Down only a week after the league decider, yet Donegal defied the warning signals and thoroughly enjoyed their winning run ... until they collided with Derry. Within 17 seconds, Anthony Tohill had fired the ball over the Donegal bar. The same midfielder would add four more points, including three expertly-taken second-half free-kicks, while his partner, Brian McGilligan, strengthened Derry's grip on the game with his best performance since returning from a career-threatening injury. Donegal's best spell reaped four consecutive points

"Our ambitions in the league were very modest. The team was badly hit, morale-wise before Christmas with the Eamonn Coleman affair, though we enjoyed playing in the league ... but ultimately, when you've won the Sam Maguire, the league pales into insignificance".

Joe Brolly

DERRY RESULTS - 1994-95 NFL

Derry	0-8	Laois	1-17
Donegal	0-15	Derry	2-6
Derry	1-11	Kerry	2-6
Meath	0-8	Derry	0-9
Derry	1-10	Down	1-7
Kildare	0-9	Derry	0-10
Dublin	1-9	Derry	1-9

QUARTER-FINAL

Derry	1-11	Cavan	0-11

SEMI-FINAL

Derry	1-8	Tyrone	2-3

FINAL

Derry	0-12	Donegal	0-8

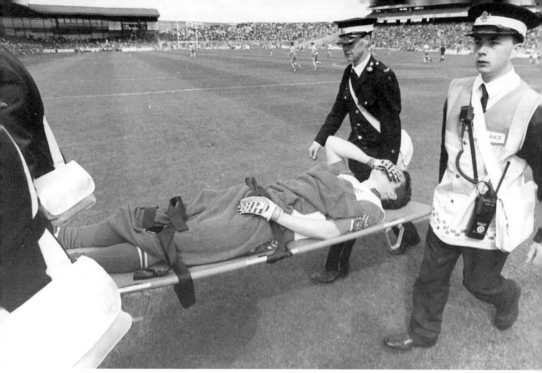
Joe Brolly is stretchered off Croke Park during the league final.

but when Derry replied with a similar burst of scoring to lead 6-4 at half-time, they were left to rue several missed goal chances.

FINAL		Derry	D'gal
17 secs	Tohill	0-1	
9 mins	Burns	0-2	
10 mins	Murray		0-1
11 mins	M.Boyle		0-2
13 mins	Duffy (F)		0-3
16 mins	M.Boyle		0-4
18 mins	Tohill	0-3	
22 mins	Gormley (F)	0-4	
25 mins	Burns	0-5	
30 mins	Coleman	0-6	
HALF-TIME			
32 mins	M.Boyle (F)		0-5
34 mins	Heaney	0-7	
40 mins	Tohill (F)	0-8	
43 mins	Tohill (F)	0-9	
46 mins	N.Hegarty		0-6
47 mins	Bonnar		0-7
52 mins	N.Hegarty		0-8
55 mins	Tohill (F)	0-10	
59 mins	Burns	0-11	
60 mins	S.Downey	0-12	
FULL-TIME			

Both teams lost key players early in the second-half, Tony Boyle with ankle trouble and Joe Brolly with a double fracture of his left wrist. The latter was stretchered to the Derry dressing-room and then to hospital, though he wouldn't leave the ground until he was given a radio in order to listen to the match. Brolly later travelled north for a late night operation, stopping along the journey at the Carrickdale Hotel where he met Peter McGrath and showed typical high spirits. "We beat Donegal, what more could we do for you! But, the only reason we beat them is because we want to beat you later!"

Back in Derry, there was little sign of joviality or high spirits. "I've never seen the people in Derry as quiet after winning something", recalled Anthony Tohill. "The league is a national title and national titles are scarce up here, but compared to '93 the celebrations were nothing".

DERRY

D.McCusker, K.McKeever, T. Scullion (c),
G.Coleman 0-1, J. McGurk, H.Downey,
F.McCusker, A.Tohill 0-5, B. McGilligan,
E.Burns 0-3, D.Heaney 0-1, D.Barton,
J.Brolly, S.Downey 0-1, E.Gormley 0-1.

Sub: D.Bateson for Brolly (40).

Squad Members: J.Kelly, D.Cassidy,
G.McGill, K.Diamond, S.McGuckin,
O.Collins, G.McGonigle, D.Quinn.

DONEGAL

G.Walsh, JJ Doherty, M.Gallagher (c),
B.McGowan, M.Crossan, M.Gavigan,
M.Shovlin, M.McShane, B.Murray 0-1,
P.Hegarty, N.Hegarty 0-2, J.McHugh,
J.Duffy 0-1, T.Boyle, M.Boyle 0-3.

Sub: D.Bonnar 0-1 for T.Boyle (33).

Squad Members: P.Callaghan, T.Ryan, John
Ban Gallagher, G.Kelly, J.Gildea, S.Boyle,
C.O'Donnell.

Referee: Paddy Russell (Tipperary).
Linesmen: Pat Casserly, Tommy McDermott
Booked: Murray, N.Hegarty,
McGurk, Barton, S.Downey.
Men of the Match: McGilligan/Tohill

Above: Dana and Brian McEniff at the final.
Below: John McGurk pursues Noel Hegarty.

Adrian Cush's penalty lifts the Kerry net in Tyrone's quarter-final victory.

NFL TOP SCORERS

Conan Daye (Wicklow)	5-41
Manus Boyle (Donegal)	1-48
Ronan Carolan (Cavan)	1-40
Damien Delaney (Laois)	1-37
Adrian Cush (Tyrone)	2-32
Ger Heavin (Westmeath)	3-25
Ian Larmer (Monaghan)	2-26
Damien Walsh (Kilkenny)	1-28
Oisin McConville (Armagh)	2-25
Pat Daly (Offaly)	0-30
Colin Corkery (Cork)	0-27
Aidan O'Keefe (Clare)	2-21
Stephen McGinnity (Monaghan)	3-18
John Duffy (Donegal)	0-25
Martin Daly (Clare)	6-7
Anthony Tohill (Derry)	2-18
Stefan White (Louth)	1-21
Pat Gavin (Limerick)	2-18

1995 NFL RESULTS

Play-offs

Donegal	1-16	Kildare	0-11
Tyrone	1-10	Louth	0-9

Quarter-finals

Derry	1-11	Cavan	0-11
Donegal	2-11	Clare	3-7
Laois	2-8	Monaghan	1-6
Tyrone	3-7	Kerry	0-10

Semi-finals

Derry	1-8	Tyrone	2-3
Laois	2-8	Donegal	1-14

Final

Derry	0-12	Donegal	0-8

The Magic Man

Railway Cup Football Final, Clones, Feb 26
Ulster 1-9   Leinster 0-8

When Greg Blaney won his fourth Railway Cup medal in 1991, he would have been forgiven for thinking that that was his lot. The Down forward had played in winning teams in 1983/84 and '89, and had enjoyed a interprovincial career spanning nearly a decade. He was not recalled by Brian McEniff for the claiming of the next three titles (1992-94), losing his place to younger, hungry men plucked from the Donegal and Derry All Ireland winners. But, after playing a central role in Down's resurgence, Blaney found himself back on the Ulster team and with a fifth winners medal. "I reminded the players of Greg's comeback in the dressing-room before the game", reveals McEniff. "He's a magic man and it's typical of him to come back a few years after I had dropped him". Another Down forward back in the team was Mickey Linden, three years after his last appearance. He was made captain (for the first time in his career) and, along with Blaney, took his place in an star-studded attacking unit.

"Look at the others - Carolan, Canavan, McCartan and Boyle, all good quality forwards. Four of us are current All Stars and five of us scored in the semi-final in the first 24 minutes. Carolan and Canavan went on to get five each, with Peter's scores all from play". Ulster won 16-8, but the final was a much closer affair, 4-3 at half-time. Then, James McCartan took a pass from Boyle and doggedly worked his way along the line to create a goal for Carolan.

Leinster closed the gap to two points, but once again the Ulster forwards provided that little bit extra. Carolan's long ball was brilliantly fielded by Linden who set up Canavan for a point. The Tyrone man also had to thank his team-mates for the build-up to Ulster's last score, as five of them had been involved, starting with the goalkeeper. Ulster are now unbeaten in the Railway Cup since 1988 (when Leinster won in Ballina by 2-9 to 0-12), they're the first province to win the cup six years in-a-row, and now head the Roll of Honour with a total of 23 successes (Leinster have 22, Munster 13, Connacht 9). Tony Scullion has played in the last six teams and treasures every medal. "The six medals have equal value. It's an honour to play for your province and I feel the Railway Cup is a very important competition".

ULSTER: Finbarr McConnell, Kieran McKeever, Tony Scullion, Matt Gallagher, Martin McQuillan, DJ Kane, Fay Devlin, Paul Brewster, Brian Murray, Ronan Carolan, Greg Blaney, James McCartan, Mickey Linden (c), Tony Boyle, Peter Canavan. Subs: Henry Downey for McQuillan, Anthony Tohill for Brewster, Ross Carr for Boyle. Squad: Brendan Tierney, Barry McGowan, Michael Magill, Gregory McCartan

LEINSTER: John O'Leary (c), Davy Dalton, Hugh Kenny, Paddy Moran, Denis Lalor 0-1, Glen Ryan, Paul Curran, Paul Bealin, Tony Maher, Hugh Emerson, Jack Sheedy, Niall Buckley 0-3, Dessie Farrell, Tommy Dowd 0-2, Colin Kelly 0-2.   Referee: M.Curley (Galway)

Note: Ulster were unchanged from the semi-final where the Substitutes used were: Gregory McCartan (Down) for Murray, Henry Downey (Derry) for Devlin, Ross Carr (Down) for J. McCartan. Ulster scorers in the semi-final were Carolan, Canavan 0-5 each, Brewster, Linden, Murray, Blaney, Kane, J. McCartan, Boyle, all 0-1.

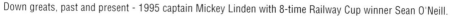

Down greats, past and present - 1995 captain Mickey Linden with 8-time Railway Cup winner Sean O'Neill.

Rory Adds to Derry Misery

McKenna Cup Final - Derry 0-11 Monaghan 1-12

19-year-old Rory Mone crowned a golden debut with the only goal of the game as Monaghan confirmed the potential they showed in the Ulster Championship. Most of the young team which steamrolled Donegal at Ballybofey were on show once more, unlike disjointed Derry who fielded just five of the side defeated by Tyrone at the same venue in June. Declan Smyth scored five points in a disappointing final to finish the McKenna Cup as joint top scorer along with Tyrone's Damien Gormley, who grabbed an impressive 2-2 on his senior debut against Armagh in the First Round. Eamonn Burns made an even better contribution of 1-6 in Derry's defeat of Tyrone in the semi-finals, while Ian Larmer brought his overall total to 0-12 with four points in the final, though the headlines from that day went to Mone, who further enhanced his reputation as a matchwinner (earned previously with Clontibret and Monaghan minors).

TOP SCORERS

Declan Smyth (Monaghan)	0-13
Damien Gormley (Tyrone)	2-7
Ian Larmer (Monaghan)	0-12
Eamonn Burns (Derry)	1-6
Geoffrey McGonigle (Derry)	0-8
Oisin McConville (Armagh)	0-7
Ray McCarron (Monaghan)	1-4

RESULTS

Cavan	0-13	Down	0-11
Fermanagh	0-12	Donegal	1-10
Tyrone	0-10	Armagh	0-9 (R)
Antrim	0-3	Derry	0-14
Monaghan	1-16	Cavan	2-5
Tyrone	1-11	Derry	1-13
Donegal	0-8	Monaghan	1-13
Monaghan	1-12	Derry	0-11

Monaghan, 1995

Back, L-R: Declan Smyth, Declan Loughman, David King, Joe Coyle, John O'Connor, Noel Marron, Gregory Flanagan, John Conlon, Pauric McShane. Middle: Michael Slowey, Peter Duffy, Martin Slowey, Frank McEneaney (c), Stephen McGinnity, Edwin Murphy, Ray McCarron. Front: Ian Larmer, Eoin Meegan, Conor Mone, Kieran Lavelle, Brian Morgan, Seamus Mullen, Colin McCaul, Glenn Murphy.

Note: Dermot Duffy, B.O'Brien and R.Mone are missing from photo but played in the McKenna Cup Final.

The New Donegal?

Ulster Under-21 Championship

The Donegal Senior team could hardly be labelled failures in 1995, after reaching the final of the National League and eliminating the All Ireland Champions a week later, but perhaps we were given a glimpse of the future for the county when their Under-21s beat Cavan to take the provincial title. Donal Buggy, James Ruane, Martin Coll and Damien Diver formed a formidable quartet and look capable of making the transition to senior football, though as Tyrone can testify, they will require patience and time to come through. Buggy finished top of the scoring charts with 2-21 from five games; Ruane's goal rescued Donegal in the drawn game; Coll was Man of the Match in the replay even though he sustained an injury in the first half, and team captain Diver was always inspirational from midfield.

Although fortunate to survive the first day against Cavan at Enniskillen, Donal Reid's boys produced a blistering 13-minute spell to kill the contest in the first-half of the replay. Trailing 3-1 after eleven minutes, Buggy took a pass from Adrian Sweeney and sent a superb shot to the net. Ruane added a long-range point before Buggy's 40-yard free-kick entered the Cavan net via a post. Buggy again, and 1-2 from Barry Ward, gave Donegal a 3-5 to 1-3 lead by the 24th minute, with Roy Brennan goaling for Cavan in the middle of the onslaught. The Irish News Cup was on it's way to Donegal for the first time since 1987, though the three-month gap to the All Ireland semi-finals seemed to blunt the Ulster champions as they went down to Kerry by 2-6 to 1-5 at Tuam.

Martin McHugh (left) congratulates former team-mate Donal Reid on Donegal's under-21 success.

DONEGAL (above): Darren Nash, Niall McCready 0-1, Eamonn O'Donnell, Sean McEwen, Peter McGinley, David Clarke, Dessie McNamara, James Ruane 0-1, Damien Diver (c), Barry Ward 1-4, Martin Coll 0-2, Pauric Gillespie, Adrian Sweeney 0-1, Donal Buggy 2-2, Brian Roper. Subs: A.McFadden for Gillespie, A.McGrath for Sweeney.

CAVAN: Aaron Donohoe, Adrian Oates, Kevin Brennan (c), Michael Reilly 0-1, Paul Brady, Johnny Graham, Brendan Dolan, Dermot McCabe, Christy Shiels, Roy Brennan 1-3, Peter Reilly 0-2, Paul Kinsella 0-1, Gerry McCrudden, Anthony Forde 0-3, Michael Lee 0-1. Subs: M.Graham for McCrudden, F.Lovett for Lee.

Martin McHugh's Cavan came close to taking the title for only the second time when they led by 1-7 to 0-5 early in the second half of the drawn game, and can also draw encouragement from clear victories over Antrim and Armagh in earlier rounds. Senior man Peter Reilly bagged 1-6 against Antrim while Frankie Lovett scored the only goal in the nine-point victory at the Athletic Grounds. Defending champions Fermanagh got past Derry, thanks to two goals from Tommy Maguire and nine singles from Shane King, but Brian Roper's goal for Donegal nine minutes from time decided their semi-final. Elsewhere, Declan Toner's goal gave Armagh a narrow victory over Tyrone.

TOP SCORERS		
Donal Buggy (Donegal)	2-21	(27)
Peter Reilly (Cavan)	1-12	(15)
Roy Brennan (Cavan)	1-8	(11)
Barry Ward (Donegal)	1-8	(11)
Brian Roper (Donegal)	2-5	(11)
Shane King (Fermanagh)	0-10	(10)
Frankie Lovett (Cavan)	2-4	(10)
Tommy Maguire (Fermanagh)	2-0	(6)

RESULTS			
Down	1-6	Donegal	1-9
Cavan	3-15	Antrim	0-8
Donegal	0-8	Monaghan	0-4
Fermanagh	2-14	Derry	0-10
Tyrone	0-10	Armagh	1-8
Armagh	0-4	Cavan	1-10
Donegal	1-12	Fermanagh	1-6
Donegal	3-11	Cavan	1-11
(R: 1-9 1-9)			

Jewel in Derry Crown
Minor Football Championship

Ballinderry boy Enda Muldoon emerged as the outstanding personality of the Minor Championship, primarily for his unerring accuracy from dead-balls almost anywhere withing 50 metres of the opposing goal. In Ulster, seven First Round points killed off a spirited title defence by Armagh, six more in the Semi-final wore down Tyrone, and 1-7 in the Final demoralised Down. At Croke Park, a last-gasp goal denied gallant Galway in the semi-final, though five points wasn't enough to overcome Westmeath. The Peter Canavan of Derry Minors, Muldoon's all-round play also offered more to his team than free-taking. He fielded superbly around the middle of the field and played a vital role in the Ulster Final, scoring the first goal and then helping to avert a potential crisis when Derry full-back Neil Farren had to retire injured in the second-half. "Johnny McBride moved to full-back and Enda to midfield where he had a stormer of a second half", recalls manager Chris Browne. "It definitely turned the game for us as Down had no answer to the man. He worked back and even fielded the last ball to fall into the Derry square. A great player and a great worker for the team".

Yet, Derry were not a one-man team. They had a fine goalkeeper in David Hopkins, a solid defence (including Emmett McGilloway from Derry city), a captain in the true sense of the word in Johnny McBride, and talented forwards where Number 14 Joe Cassidy (brother of senior star Damien) complimented Muldoon perfectly: "Very cool under pressure and another great player", adds Browne. Eight of the team won Hogan Cup medals earlier in the year. "Our team was built around the Maghera team. They're born winners and prepared brilliantly by Adrian McGuckin".

Tyrone's Paul Horisk holds off the challenge of Joe Cassidy (Derry).

The champions-to-be had their toughest game at Armagh. After leading by six points at half-time, thanks mainly to a Cassidy goal fashioned by Gary Coleman and Muldoon, Derry seemed powerless as the home side stormed back with five straight singles. In a nail-biting last quarter, Hopkins saved superbly from Sean O'Hare, Cassidy steadied the ship with a 57th minute point and Muldoon finally sealed victory three minutes into added time with his seventh score of the game (two of them had come from 45s). Adrian McGuckin Junior (below) grabbed two goals in the defeat of Tyrone, for whom his cousin, Brian McGuckin, lined out at Number 12. The losers could point to the loss of regular full-back Vivian Teague (injured in an Under-21 club game) as a factor, but in truth they could not cope with Derry's aerial power and slick running game. Tyrone were gifted a first-minute goal but Derry recovered with McBride lashing the Goal of the Championship to the Tyrone net later in the first half.

Down played three games to reach the final, but they had only been extended by Monaghan, for whom Rory Mone (Clontibret) scored a remarkable 1-8. The match was played at a damp and almost deserted Athletic Grounds on the evening of the Armagh-Derry games, and it really deserved a bigger

ULSTER FINAL

		Derry	Down
2 mins	Daly (F)		0-1
7 mins	Muldoon	0-1	
10 mins	Doran (F)		0-2
11 mins	Muldoon (F)	0-2	
15 mins	Caulfield (F)		0-3
17 mins	Muldoon	0-3	
19 mins	Matthews		0-4
20 mins	Greene		0-5
22 mins	Kearney	0-4	
23 mins	Muldoon (F)	0-5	
26 mins	Muldoon	1-5	
30 mins	Cassidy	1-6	
30 mins	Daly (F)		0-6
HALF-TIME			
31 mins	Cassidy	1-7	
33 mins	Muldoon (F)	1-8	
34 mins	McFlynn	1-9	
36 mins	Cunningham		0-7
41 mins	Muldoon (F)	1-10	
53 mins	Caulfield (F)		0-8
54 mins	Muldoon (F)	1-11	
56 mins	Cassidy	2-11	
60 mins	Cassidy	2-12	
FULL-TIME			

audience. A Stephen Caulfield goal gave Down a five-point start before a penalty and three points from Mone put Monaghan ahead. Gavin Hynds regained the lead for Down with a second goal and it was level pegging throughout the second period until Kieran Doran edged Down into a three-point lead. Even then, Mone replied with a brace of points to keep the issue in doubt right up to the final whistle. Conor Daly went on a semi-final scoring spree with 1-6 against Cavan. Down had 3-8 on the board within 16 minutes and won with ease, though the final against Derry was much closer. Corner-back Henry Greene fired Down into a 5-3 lead after 20 minutes but favourites Derry responded with a match-winning burst. Joe Cassidy found Muldoon running inside the Down defence for a cool finish to the net, and Cassidy added a point either side of the interval. Paul McFlynn came up from half-back for a fine score, Muldoon punished just about every indiscretion and Cassidy finished with another flurry, including a goal when the Bellaghy clubman outfielded Down goalkeeper Peter Travers who had come off his line.

Elsewhere in the competition, Fermanagh rallied from eight points down to almost catch Tyrone at Irvinestown. Sean Quinn was unfortunate not to find the net late in the game, though Tyrone were the better side overall and had the best player on view in Peter Loughran. Antrim rivalled Fermanagh for the "Comeback of the Championship" award, clawing back at half-time deficit of fifteen points (3-7 to 0-1) to come within two points of Cavan by the finish (3-8 to 2-9). Antrim conceded a goal to Declan Tighe ten seconds after the start of the game and looked doomed until big Joe Quinn and Ryan Dunlop both goaled in the second half. Cavan couldn't breathe easily until John Maguire pointed their first and only score of the period in injury-time.

Tyrone's Martin Early shows a clean pair of heels against Fermanagh.

Down Minors, Ulster Finalists 1995

MAY 21:   DOWN 2-14   DONEGAL 0-11

DOWN: Peter Travers (Bryansford) (c), Henry Greene (Teconnaught), Paul Shields (Clonduff), Lee Rooney (Banbridge), Malachy McMurray (Newry Bosco), Tom Morgan (Tullylish), Padraig M atthews (Clonduff), Anthony Gallagher (St Pauls, Lurgan) 0-1, Kevin Franklin (Warrenpoint), Conor Daly (Rostrevor) 0-4, Paul Cunningham (Ballymartin) 0-1, Kieran Doran (Loughinisland) 0-1, Shane Ward (Clonduff) 0-1, Gavin Hynds (Downpatrick) 0-1, Stephen Caulfield (Rostrevor) 2-5.

DONEGAL: David Greene (Aodh Ruadh), Eamonn Reddin (Muff), Martin McMenamin (Robert Emmetts), Raymond Daly (Bundoran), Rory Sweeney (Naomh Brid), Shane O'Donnell (St Eunans), Gerard Cannon (Naomh Columba), Dermot McColgan (Muff), Barry Monaghan (Four Masters), Conal Doherty (Ardara) 0-2, Ciaran Brown (Carndonagh), Charles Boyle (Glenties), James Boyle (Dungloe) 0-1, Brian McLaughlin (St Michaels) 0-6, David McGinley (St Eunans) 0-1. Subs: Kevin Winston (St Eunans) for C Boyle (26), Patrick McGrath (Aodh Ruadh) for Cannon (45).   Squad members: Conal McFadden, Stephen Ward, Raymond Sweeney, Don Monaghan, Aodh Brennan, Shane McArt, Kenneth McGarrin.

MAY 28:   ARMAGH 0-14   DERRY 1-12

ARMAGH: Karl Kimmons (Corrinshigo), Paul Watters (Killeavy), John McEntee (Crossmaglen), Barry Gordon (Pearse Og), Peter Quinn (Carrickcruppin), Tony McEntee (C'glen), John Toal (Keady), Barry Duffy (Killeavy), Philip Oldham (Clan na Gael) 0-3, Peter Loughran (C'cruppin) 0-3, Sean O'Hare (St Patricks) 0-5, Gary Donnelly (Ballymacnab) 0-1, Jason McGahan (Tullysarron), Alan O'Neill (Clan na Gael) 0-1, Shane McKeever (St Patricks) 0-1.   Sub: Anthony Bennett (C'cruppin) for O'Neill (50).   Squad members: Brendan Collins, Declan Fields, Adrian Doran, Liam Fegan, Martin Catney, Tony Hughes, Tony McParland.

DERRY: David Hopkins (Magherafelt), John Heaney (Glenullin), Neil Farren (Drum), Michael Kelly (Slaughtneil), Paul Diamond, Kieran McNally (Bellaghy), Declan McNally (Ballinderry), Johnny McBride (Loup) 0-1, Gary Doyle (Lavey), Gary Coleman (Loup), Enda Muldoon 0-7, Adrian McGuckin (Ballinderry), Gary Cushnahan (Lavey) 0-1, Joe Cassidy (Bellaghy) 1-3, Damian McErlean (Newbridge).   Subs: Emmet McGilloway (Doire Colmcille) for D.McNally (21), Paul Wilson (Ballinderry) for Doyle (28).

MAY 28:   MONAGHAN 1-13   DOWN 2-11

MONAGHAN: Derek McCarville (Aghabog), Paddy Hughes (Tyholland), Ronan Sheehan (Scotstown), Liam O'Neill (Aughnamullen), Ryan Treacy (Castleblayney), Gareth McElearney (Drumhowan), Padraig McKenna (Eire Og) 0-2, Gareth McAdam (Aghabog), Gary Meehan (Truagh), Paul O'Connor (C'blayney), Rory Mone (Clontibret) 1-8, Darren Swift (Monaghan Harps) 0-1, Johnathan Deery (Scotstown), Ciaran McKenna (Eire Og) (c) 0-2, Barry Conlon (Carrickmacross).   Subs: Fergal Shannon (Magheracloone) for McAdam, Francie Reilly (Eire Og) for Conlon.   Squad members: Michael Treanor, Ciaran O'Harte, Fergus Connolly, John McDaid, Dessie McGarry, Bernard Treanor.

DOWN: Unchanged. Scorers: C.Daly 0-4, K.Doran 0-3, G.Hynds 1-0, S.Caulfield 1-4. Subs: Eugene O'Hagan (Clonduff) for Morgan, Damien Smyth (Clonduff) for Ward, John Lavery (An Riocht) for Gallagher.

JUNE 4:   FERMANAGH 2-10   TYRONE 2-13

FERMANAGH: Shane Wilson, Clive Fitzpatrick (Newtownbutler), Rory McEnhill (Enniskillen), Shane Anderson, (Kinawley), Kevin Duffy (E'Killen), Peter Quinn (Teemore), Raymond Johnson, Sean McBrien (N'butler), Stephen Maguire (Belcoo) 0-1, Seamus Howell (Roslea) 1-1, Rory Gallagher (Erne Gaels) 0-3, Jonathan McCaffrey (Lisnaskea), Andrew Moohan 1-0, Tom Brewster (E'killen) 0-5, Sean Quinn (Teemore). Subs: Declan Campbell (Tempo) for Fitzpatrick (56).   Squad members: Peter Baird, Glen Monaghan, Ronan O'Reilly, Colm Shannon, Brian Hegarty, Ciaran Maguire, Stephen Ingram, Declan O'Reilly.

TYRONE: Stephen McCarron (Aghaloo), Ciaran Cox (Beragh), Vivian Teague (Coalisland), Damian Mullan (Dungannon), Michael Ferran (Coalisland), Paul Horisk (Errigal Ciaran), David McKenna (Omagh), Brian Meenan (Killyclogher) 0-1, Barry Eccles (Omagh) 0-1, Martin Early (Brackaville) 0-4, Peter Loughran (Carrickmore) 1-5, Brian McGuckin (Edendork), James Muldoon (Eglish) 1-2, Sean Douglas (Aghaloo) (c), Frank McGuigan (Ardboe).   Sub: Kevin Lynch (Aghyaran) for Teague.

JUNE 11:   CAVAN 3-8   ANTRIM 2-9

CAVAN: Charlie Clerkin (Castlerhan), Paul Lynch (Mullahoran), Raymond Maguire (Laragh United), Damien Foster (Kill), Raphael Rodgers (Knockbride) 0-1, Brian Donohoe (Ballymachugh) (c), Adrian McConnell (Butlersbridge) 0-1, Oliver Galligan (Cavan Gaels), Fergus O'Reilly (Killinkere), Michael O'Rourke (Crosserlough) 1-0, Brian Mulvey (Castlerahan), Brian O'Callaghan (Bailieboro) 0-1, Larry Reilly (Knockbride) 0-3, John Maguire (Bailieboro) 1-2, Declan Tighe (Drumalee) 1-0. Subs: Philip Galligan (Denn) for R. Maguire, Declan Flood (Drumalee) for L. Reilly, Finian O'Callaghan (Castlerahan) for O'Rourke.

ANTRIM: Barry McGreevey (St Pauls), Enda McLarnon (Creggan), Alistair McDonnell (Sean Stinsons), Steven Dowds (St Galls), Dultach Johnson (Cargin), Kieran Killyleagh (St Pauls), Kieran Stewart (Rossa), Ryan McAleese (Rasharkin) (c), Paddy Murray (St Galls), Brian McFall (St Johns), Ryan Dunlop (Rasharkin) 1-0, Kevin Madden (Portglenone) 0-7, Sean Kelly (Rossa), Joe Quinn (St Pauls) 1-1, Gavin Scullion (Cargin).   Subs: Conor McGinley (Sarsfields) for McDonnell, Kevin Doyle for Kelly, Sean Fynan (St Pauls) for McFall.   Squad members: John Paul Stitt, Darren Craig, Peter McGuigan, Conor McStravick, Jim McArdle, Owen Doherty, Cormac McKenna, Kevin Bradley.

SEMI-FINAL
JUNE 25:   DERRY 3-14   TYRONE 1-8

DERRY: D.Hopkins, J.Heaney, N.Farren, M.Kelly, P.Diamond, K.McNally, E.McGilloway, J.McBride(c) 1-1, P.Gormley, G.Coleman 0-2, E.Muldoon 0-6, G.Cassidy, B.Kearney 0-1, A.McGuckin 2-1, J.Cassidy 0-2. Subs: P.Wilson 0-1 for Cassidy (50), G.Doyle for Gormley (55), D. McErlean for Kearney (56).

TYRONE: S.McCarron, K.Cox, Kevin Lynch, D.Mullan, M.Ferran, P. Horisk, D.McKenna, B.Meenan, B.Eccles, M.Early, P.Loughran 0-5, B.McGuckin 0-1, J.Muldoon 1-0, S.Douglas (c) 0-2, F.McGuigan. Subs: B. Mallon for Douglas (46), R. Forbes for Muldoon (56).   Squad Members: Dermot Armstrong, Edward Daly, Martin Crozier, Damian McRory, Paul McVeigh.

SEMI-FINAL
JULY 2   DOWN 4-12   CAVAN 0-11

DOWN: P.Travers (c), H.Greene, P. Shields, L.Rooney, M.McMurray, T.Morgan, E.O'Hagan, P.Matthews 0-1, K.Franklin, C.Daly 1-6, P.Cunningham, K.Doran 1-2, G.Trainor, G.Hynds 1-0, S.Caulfield 1-3. Subs: D.Smyth for Cauflield, C.Kelly for Shields.

CAVAN: C.Clerkin, P.Lynch, D.Flood, D.Foster, R.Rodgers, B.Donohue (c), A.McConnell, O.Galligan, F.O'Reilly, M.O'Rourke 0-4, B.Mulvey 0-1, B.O'Callaghan 0-1, L.Reilly 0-2, D.Tighe 0-3, D.Keogh. Subs: Ronan Kiernan 0-1 for O'Callaghan, J.Maguire for Galligan, Finian O'Callaghan for Reilly. Squad members: Michael Boyle, Philip Galligan, Paul Cahill, John Farrelly, Finian McGovern, Raymond Maguire, Shane Maguire.

80

FINAL

JULY 23:   DERRY 2-12   DOWN 1-7

DOWN: P.Travers (c), H.Greene 0-1, P. Shields, L.Rooney, M.McMurray , E.O'Hagan, T. Morgan, P.Matthews 0-1, K.Franklin, C.Daly 0-2, P.Cunningham 1-0, K.Doran, G.Trainor, G.Hynds, S.Caulfield 0-3.

Subs: Shane Ward for Hynds.   Squad members: Enda McConville, Sean Devlin, Damien Smyth, Darra McLaughlin, Oliver Sloan, D.McCartan, G.Doran, S.Morgan, Michael Mulrine. Cathal Kielty.

DERRY: D.Hopkins, J.Heaney, N.Farren, M.Kelly, P.McFlynn 0-1, K.McNally, E.McGilloway, J.McBride (c), G.Doyle, Gary Cushnahan, E.Muldoon 1-7, A.McGuckin, B.Kearney 0-1, J.Cassidy 1-3, G.Coleman.

Subs: D.McErlain for N.Farren, Eoin Farren for Kearney, P.Wilson for Coleman

Squad members: Danny.McGrellis, Fergal Crossan, Paul Gormley, Gerry Cassidy, Cathal Grieve, Paul Diamond.

Referee: Martin McBrien.   Linesmen: Brian Crowe, Liam Browne

Derry Minors. Back, L-R: Enda Muldoon, Gary Doyle, David Hopkins, Michael Kelly, Danny McGrellis, Kieran McNally, Benny Murray, Emmett McGilloway. Middle: Adrian McGuckin, Paul McFlynn, Gerard Cassidy, Johnny McBride, Gary Cushnahan, Paul Diamond, Joe Cassidy, John Heaney, Gary Coleman. Front: Brian Lavery, Damien McErlean, Paul Wilson, Eoin Farren, Brendan Kearney, Fergal Crossan, Paul Gormley.

ULSTER MFC TOP SCORERS

	Total		Games	Average per game
Stephen Caulfield (Down)	4-15	(27)	4	6.75
Enda Muldoon (Derry)	1-20	(23)	3	7.66
Conor Daly (Down)	1-16	(19)	4	4.75
Joe Cassidy (Derry)	2-8	(14)	3	4.66
Peter Loughran (Tyrone)	1-10	(13)	2	6.50
Rory Mone (Monaghan)	1-8	(11)	1	11.00
Kieran Doran (Down)	1-6	(9)	4	2.25
James Muldoon (Tyrone)	2-2	(8)	2	4.00

Notes: Stephen "Ringo" Caulfield didn't look back after scoring 2-5 in a Preliminary Round game he might not have played in, but for a neighbour in Rostrevor called Peter McGrath. The Down senior team manager offered Stephen treatment for a niggling leg injury on the Thursday before the game with Donegal. Caulfield went on to top the charts though Derry's Enda Muldoon struck up a higher scoring average over his three outings. Both forwards easily surpassed last year's top scorer, Brian Dougherty (Down) with of 4-2, while Conor Daly (Down) bettered his 1994 tally of 1-9 but still dropped from second to third on the scoring list.

All Ireland Semi-Final

Derry 3-7   Galway 1-12

Enda Muldoon once again came to the rescue for Derry, though this time he left it very, very late. Galway led by point going into the closing minutes when McBride launched a high ball into their goalmouth. Four maroon shirts surrounded Muldoon but he still managed to gain possession, turn and slot the ball under the goalkeeper. Funnily enough, the star of the Ulster campaign had been relatively quiet up to his goal. He failed to score in the first-half and managed only two free-kicks in the second. This was a bizarre all-round performance by Derry, scoring as many goals as points in the first-half, and then letting slip a seven-point lead before Muldoon's saved the day.

Derry appeared to be troubled by Neil Farren's failure to make the starting line-up, and goalkeeper David Hopkins did well to keep a clean sheet in the opening period. His opposing number must take the blame for Derry's first goal, allowing McBride's lofted free-kick to drop into the net. Three minutes later, Joe Cassidy scored a classy goal to ensure a three-point lead at the break. Turning round with the wind behind them, Derry rattled over four quick points and that should have that. But Galway responded with 1-5 in eleven minutes to take the lead. The boys from the West looked intent on making up for losing the 1994 All Ireland minor final, and for the Hogan Cup semi-final defeat inflicted by St Pats Maghera on Tuam CBS. Substitute Gerard Cassidy steadied shaky Derry with a super equaliser, only for Reilly to put Galway back in front. Derry's dreams looked to be dashed, until Muldoon's rescue act.

		Derry	G'way
2 mins	Cloherty		0-1
10 mins	Conlisk		0-2
11 mins	J.Cassidy	0-1	
16 mins	McBride (F)	1-1	
17 mins	Moran		0-3
19 mins	J.Cassidy	2-1	
22 mins	Cloherty		0-4
28 mins	McGuckin	2-2	
30 mins	Moran		0-5
HALF-TIME			
31 mins	Muldoon (F)	2-3	
32 mins	G.Cassidy	2-4	
33 mins	McBride	2-5	
35 mins	Muldoon (F)	2-6	
38 mins	Moran (F)		0-6
42 mins	Reilly		1-6
44 mins	Moran		1-7
47 mins	Donnellan (F)		1-8
48 mins	Savage		1-9
49 mins	Moran		1-10
54 mins	G.Cassidy	2-7	
55 mins	Reilly		1-11
58 mins	Muldoon	3-7	
62 mins	Donnellan		1-12
FULL-TIME			

1995 TOP TEN SCORERS		
	Total	
Ian Fitzgerald (Laois)	5-39	(54)
Enda Muldoon (Derry)	2-28	(34)
Thomas Cleary (Westmeath)	2-26	(32)
Charlie Conway (Laois)	3-21	(30)
Stephen Caulfield (Down)	4-13	(25)
Joe Cassidy (Derry)	3-14	(23)
David Martin (Westmeath)	1-17	(20)
Derek Barrett (Cork)	0-20	
Conor Daly (Down)	1-16	(19)
Derek Reilly (Galway)	3-8	(17)

Note: Laois played seven games and Westmeath eight, including three meetings between the two teams in the Leinster final.

All Ireland Final

Derry 0-11 Westmeath 1-10

Nobody could deny Westmeath their moment of glory after winning the All Ireland Minor Championship for the first time, though Derry were left wondering where they had gone wrong. The most plausible reasons for Derry's defeat are six first-half wides, a below-par midfield, a fine opportunist goal by Thomas Cleary, and the grim determination of their opponents to hold out. A storming last-quarter brought the Oak Leaf boys within a point of Westmeath, but Joe Casey produced a stunning riposte, soloing out of his defence and scoring from forty metres. Then, in the last minute, Johnny McBride was crudely hauled to the ground as he raced towards the Westmeath goal. The resulting free-kick was of little use to Derry, as it was the lask kick of the game and they trailed by two. Muldoon sent the free wide. The same player had been moved back to help out, but the problems were too great for one man to solve. Joe Cassidy and Paul McFlynn did their best, with the latter having a goal disallowed for square ball, and both players accounting for four scores between the 45th-50th minutes, to take Derry within one point, but it wasn't enough.

		Derry	W'meath
3 mins	Muldoon (F)	0-1	
4 mins	Muldoon (F)	0-2	
6 mins	Cleary (F)		0-1
7 mins	Deehan		0-2
11 mins	Martin (F)		0-3
17 mins	Muldoon (F)	0-3	
22 mins	McGuckin	0-4	
26 mins	Cleary		1-3
29 mins	Cleary (F)		1-4
Half-time			
31 mins	Cleary		1-5
32 mins	Cushnahan	0-5	
38 mins	Cleary (F)		1-6
41 mins	Cleary (F)		1-7
44 mins	Muldoon (F)	0-6	
45 mins	McFlynn	0-7	
47 mins	Casey		1-8
48 mins	J.Cassidy	0-8	
48 mins	McFlynn	0-9	
50 mins	J.Cassidy	0-10	
52 mins	Casey		1-9
53 mins	Stuart-Trainor		1-10
56 mins	Muldoon (F)	0-11	
Full-time			

DERRY'S ALL IRELAND FINAL RECORD

1965	Derry	2-8	Kerry	2-4
1969	Derry	0-11	Cork	2-7
1980	Derry	0-11	Kerry	3-12
1981	Derry	2-7	Cork	4-9
1983	Derry	0-8	Cork	1-3
1989	Derry	3-9	Offaly	1-6
1995	Derry	0-11	W'meath	1-10

DERRY

David Hopkins

John Heaney Michael Kelly Emmet McGilloway

Paul McFlynn 0-2 Ciaran McNally Paul Diamond

Johnny McBride (c) Gary Doyle

Gary Coleman Enda Muldoon 0-5 Adrian McGuckin 0-1

Gary Cushnahan 0-1 Joe Cassidy 0-2 Gerard Cassidy

Subs: Danny McGrellis for Coleman (30), Paul Wilson for Doyle (40), Eoin Farren for Cushnahan (50).

Football Club Championships

Antrim

FIRST ROUND			
Ballymena	1-12	St Teresas	1-9
Creggan	2-5	Cargin	3-15
Dunloy	3-10	Rossa	6-10
Glenavy	0-7	St Pauls	2-8
Glenravel	1-7	Lamh Dhearg	0-12
O'Donnells	0-10	Tir na nOg	1-5
St Endas	1-9	Davitts	1-10
St Johns	3-13	St Galls	2-8
QUARTER-FINALS			
Ballymena	1-17	O'Donnells	0-5
Cargin	3-11	Lamh Dhearg	2-7
St Johns	1-13	Rossa	0-10
St Pauls	1-15	Davitts	1-5 (R)
SEMI-FINALS			
Cargin	0-15	St Pauls	0-7
St Johns	2-7	Ballymena	0-8
FINAL			
Cargin	0-8	St Johns	0-6

About time! Cargin's SFC triumph was their first in 21 years, and it followed five losing finals since 1987. They got it right this year, though not in convincing fashion. The early dismissal of St Johns Paddy Hannigan left Cargin with a numerical advantage, and they had a breeze on their backs in the second half, but their forwards looked to have lost their nerve with some poor shooting. That all changed in the 43rd minute, when Shennie McQuillan pointed from a dead-ball 55 metres from the St Johns goal. Brian Gribben quickly added a brace of points, to edge Cargin in front, and when corner-back Dermot McPeake kicked a glorious final score, the days of torment and frustration were all forgotten. Eight points was enough for victory, though it was much less than Cargin's average of 2-13 from the previous three games. In the First Round, they destroyed Creggan with two goals from JC Devlin and one from Adrian Craig, while Craig, McQuillan and Declan Gallagher, all goaled in the 3-11 to 2-7 defeat of Lamh Dhearg in the Quarter-Finals. Goalkeeper Scott

Cargin, Antrim champions, 1995.

McDonald saved a penalty from Frankie Wilson in the same game, and reigning champions St Pauls were easily dismissed in the semi-finals. The Belfast side had needed 1-5 from Joe Kennedy to get past Davitts after a replay. St Johns' path to the final (their first since 1988), included a First Round defeat of St Galls, when goals from Eamonn Blaney, Conal Heatley, and Paddy Nolan, cancelled out two from Billy Drake. Nolan found the net again in the win over Rossa, who had Jim Close sent off, and the Johnnies overcame Ballymena with goals from Blaney and Collie McKnight. Elsewhere, the highest-scoring game in Ulster was Rossa's 6-10 to 3-10 defeat of Dunloy. Collie Murphy, Jim Rogers (Both Rossa), and Chris Kearns (Dunloy), all grabbed two goals each. O'Donnells held on with thirteen men to beat Tir na nOg, while Enda McAtamney scored 1-6 in both Ballymena's victories over St Teresas and O'Donnells. The most dramatic finale was supplied by Davitts, who turned a two-point deficit into a narrow win over St Endas, with an injury-time goal from Paul McCartney.

Cargin in Final: Scott McDonald, Dermot McPeake 0-1, Michael Johnston, Martin McAuley (c), Matthew Gribben, Dessie McGuckin, Paul Craig, Eddie Quinn, Shennie McQuillan 0-1, Paddy Graffin, Ciaran O'Neill 0-1, Raymond McGuckin, Kevin Doyle 0-1, Brian Gribben 0-2, Declan Gallagher 0-2. Subs: Martin Logan for McAuley, Eamonn McCann for M.Gribben, Adrian Craig for Doyle.

Armagh

"Many may look upon this match as rubbish, but I can tell you it was hard going out there. Besides, winning is what matters, and we won". Evergreen Neil Smyth summed up the county final perfectly, after his Mullabawn team had won the SFC for the first time since 1964. They didn't shake off Armagh Harps until added time (of which there was five minutes), when frees from Declan Crawley and captain Fergal McDonnell sparked off the celebrations. Harps' goal had come in the first half, from Malachy Gribben, but they managed to score only five points in the contest. Mullabawn had no easy games on the route to success, as they faced the holders Clann na Gael in the First Round, then their local rivals Crossmaglen, and a dogged St Peters side also hungry for success, in the Semi-finals. The new champions came through each of these tests, partly thanks to their determination to wipe out memories of their final defeat in 1994, and partly thanks to five weeks of grafting on Slieve Gullion... in the heat of Summer! The scores were important too, of course, and against Crossmaglen they came mainly from Fergal O'Donnell (5) and Declan Crawley (4), while Patrick

FIRST ROUND			
Clan na Gael	0-6	Mullabawn	1-10
Collegeland	0-9	Carrickcruppin	0-5
Crossmaglen	1-7	Pearse Og	1-3
Harps	0-8	St Pauls	0-3
Maghery	0-14	Killeavey	0-11
Sarsfields	4-7	Madden	0-9 (R)
St Peters	1-10	St Patricks	2-3
Bye - Silverbridge			
QUARTER-FINALS			
Harps	0-8	Maghery	0-7
Mullabawn	0-12	Crossmaglen	0-10
Sarsfields	1-9	Silverbridge	1-6
St Peters	0-9	Collegeland	0-8
SEMI-FINALS			
Harps	1-13	Sarsfields	2-4
Mullabawn	1-11	St Peters	0-8
FINAL			
Mullabawn	0-11	Harps	1-5

McGeeney's superb solo goal was the only highlight of a poor Semi-final with St Peters. Harps meanwhile survived against Maghery in the Quarter-finals, despite having a player sent off and conceding a penalty in the last minute. With the scores at 8-7, Maghery's Dixie Robinson could have opted for a point to ensure a replay, but instead his shot rebounded off the upright. John Toner scored six of Harps' eight points in that game, and he added five in the Semi-final defeat of Sarsfields, who were stunned after only two minutes, when Harps' right-half-back James Toner sent a dipping shot past Brian McAlinden. Earlier in the competition, Eamonn Murray was Sarsfields hero with a hat-trick against Madden and 1-2 against Silverbridge.

Mullabawn in Final : Benny Tierney, Raymond Quinn, Colm Byrne, Gerard Larkin, Enda McNulty, Kieran McGeeney, Sean McDonnell, Justin McNulty, Neil Smyth 0-1, Declan Crawley 0-4, Fergal McDonnell 0-2 (c) , Patrick McGeeney 0-2, Kieran Grant 0-1, Shane Collins, Colm McParland. Sub: Paul McNulty.

Mullabawn, Armagh champions, 1995.

Cavan

Martin McHugh is not the only successful Donegal man in Cavan. Seamus Bonner played in two Ulster SFC finals for Donegal in the early seventies, and he was the man Bailieboro turned to this year, to guide their young team to a first county title in 31 years. Excited at the prospect of working with a number of Cavan's new senior stars, Bonner accepted the opportunity. Paul O'Dowd, John Donnellan, Gerry Sheridan, Aidan Connolly, and Adrian Lambe, all played important roles for their county, though Bailieboro also have Under-21 scoring star Roy Brennan (0-29 in the Meadowview Restaurant Cavan SFC), and promising midfielder Charles Clarke, Man of the Match in the final. Bonner's boys had to come from behind, after defending champions Gowna caught them with an early sucker punch. Sean Pierson converted a penalty after Dermot McCabe had been fouled in the 3rd minute. Interestingly, McCabe was set up by Bernard

Morris, who started at full-forward, but Bailieboro settled down and were in front by half-time, 0-9 to 1-4. With Morris recalled to midfield for the second half, Gowna stayed in contention as the game entered added time, but the important score came from a Roy Brennan free-kick. Gowna had lost the title they had been tipped to retain, though they were handicapped by the loss of Dessie Brady.

QUARTER-FINALS			
Cavan Gaels	1-8	Bailieboro	0-13
Crosserlough	1-8	Ballyhaise	0-8
Gowna	1-17	Killinkere	0-11
Mullahoran	1-16	Kingscourt	0-7
SEMI-FINALS			
Bailieboro	1-12	Mullahoran	1-9
Gowna	2-12	Crosserlough	0-3
FINAL			
Bailieboro	0-13	Gowna	1-8

Another county man, Ronan Carolan, was uncharacteristically sent off in the Quarter-finals, when his Cuchullains team lost to Cavan Gaels.

Bailieboro in Final: Paul O'Dowd, Glen Crossan (c), Jimmy Clarke, John Donnellan, Finbar Clarke, Michael Murtagh, Gerry Sheridan, Aidan Connolly, Charles Clarke 0-1, Paul Coleman, Roy Brennan 0-7, Sean Reilly, Kieran Clarke, Adrian Lambe 0-4, Adrian Larkin 0-1. Sub: Paul Cooney for Reilly.

Derry

The fact that a pair of seventeen-year-olds (Gerard Cassidy and Adrian McGuckin) shared the Man of the Match Award in the final, says much about Ballinderry's first title since 1981. At the start of the year, they opted for a youth policy in an attempt to take them from also-rans to champions, and it paid off in style. Cassidy took his goal in the final with all the coolness of a veteran, even though he only turned seventeen in August, while another Derry minor to excel throughout the senior club championship, was Enda Muldoon. In the First Round, the new kids compiled 6-12 against Greenlough; in the Quarter-finals, Muldoon and Cassidy accounted for eleven scores in the replay defeat of Glen; in the Semi-finals, Paul Conway top-scored with 1-2 to beat Loup, and in the

Men of the Match: Gerard Cassidy (left) and Adrian McGuckin with sponsor Patsy Forbes.

FIRST ROUND			
Ballinascreen	0-14	Newbridge	0-10
Bellaghy	1-13	Glenullin	0-11
Castledawson	1-9	Glen	1-10
Dungiven	1-5	Lavey	1-8
Drumsurn	0-5	Slaughtneil	1-23
Greenlough	2-9	Ballinderry	6-12
Loup	0-14	Kilrea	0-12
Magherafelt	0-5	Swatragh	0-11
QUARTER-FINALS			
Ballinderry	0-16	Glen	0-10 (R)
Bellaghy	1-11	Ballinascreen	0-11
Lavey	1-13	Swatragh	1-6
Loup	2-9	Slaughtneil	1-11
SEMI-FINALS			
Ballinderry	1-7	Loup	0-5
Bellaghy	1-6	Lavey	0-8 (R)
FINAL			
Ballinderry	1-8	Bellaghy	0-8

final, the only goal and six of Ballinderry's eight points came from Cassidy, McGuckin and Muldoon. Senior county man Declan Bateson grabbed the other two scores, and set up Cassidy for the goal, after a long pass from Queens student Ronan McGuckin. Still, Ballinderry required four late points to kill off a Bellaghy team reluctant to relinquish its title. At the final whistle, the most excited supporter in the 5,000 crowd was surely Adrian McGuckin Senior, "It was like winning three championships! Ronan and Adrian both played well, and Ballinderry were back as Derry's top team".

Unfortunately, the competition was marred by an unseemly brawl at the semi-final between Bellaghy and Lavey. Four players were sent off on the day, and fifteen individuals were later called to explain their actions. Ten suspensions, ranging from 2-3 months, were handed out to players and officials, and both clubs were fined one thousand pounds and banned from playing home games next season. Johnny McGurk, Danny Quinn, Ollie Collins, and Gareth Doherty, were among those banned. On

Ballinderry in Final: Robert Fitzpatrick, Martin Bradley, Barry McOscar, Dominic Rocks, Eugene Bradley, Ronan McGuckin, Sean Donnelly, Raymond Bell (c), Malachy Wilson, Gerard Cassidy 1-2, Terence McGuckin, Enda Muldoon 0-2, Declan Bateson 0-2, Adrian McGuckin 0-2. Paul Conway. Sub: Kieran Rocks for Conway.

appeal, the fines and some suspensions were halved, and the ban on home games reduced to three. The brawl had started after Bellaghy had gone into an 8-6 lead, but a Seamus Downey goal earned Lavey a draw. In the replay, Benny Lee eventually settled the argument with the only goal. Lavey had earlier beaten rivals Dungiven with a late goal and two points from Brian McCormick, after Eoin McCloskey had saved Johnny McGurk's penalty and Geoffrey McGonigle had goaled for the North Derry side. Gary Coleman also missed a penalty, as Magherafelt lost to Swatragh in the First Round, while Bellaghy required goals from Gareth Doherty and Joe Cassidy to get past Glenullin and Ballinascreen, respectively. Doherty's came very late, after Ruari Boylan has scored eight times for Glenullin, and Cassidy's was supplemented by ten points from Karl Diamond (nine frees) against Ballinascreen. Eamonn Burns bettered Diamond's total with eleven points in one game (ten frees). The last mention, most deservedly, goes to a Loup side which reached the semi-finals with an even more youthful look than that of Ballinderry. Only one of the team which beat Slaughtneil with a late Kieran Hegarty goal, was more than 21 years of age.

Donegal

Glasgow Celtic soccer player Declan Boyle came home for the weekend to watch his brother Mark and his old team-mates from Killybegs in the final of the Donegal SFC.... and ended up scoring the winning point! Manager Jimmy White, who admitted he didn't know Boyle was available to him, sent the versatile sportsman into the fray with ten minutes remaining. He responded with Killybegs' tenth point, which gave them a two-point cushion (0-10 to 1-5). Naomh Columba still had time to win the match, but Gregory Doherty sent his golden opportunity over the bar. Apart from

FIRST ROUND REPLAY			
Ardara	1-16	Glenties	3-15 (aet)
QUARTER-FINAL			
Aodh Ruadh	2-12	Kilcar	2-5
N.Columba	2-9	Red Hughs	2-8
Killybegs	2-13	Dungloe	3-9
St Eunans	1-14	Glenties	0-10
SEMI-FINALS			
Killybegs	2-5	Aodh Ruadh	1-7
N.Columba	1-5	St Eunans	0-4
FINAL			
Killybegs	0-10	N.Columba	1-6

Boyle, who Armagh fans will remember from the 1993 Ulster SFC, Killybegs had a goalkeeping hero in Ian Cunningham. He made some brilliant saves, while his outfield colleagues went to town in the first ten minutes of the second half. In this period, they turned a 4-2 deficit into an 8-4 lead, before Noel and Paddy Hegarty set up Paul O'Donnell for a goal, and that grandstand finish. However, it was to be Naomh Columba's third defeat in a final in four years, and Killybegs' fourth title since 1988. In the Semi-finals, the new champions eliminated the old champions (Aodh Ruadh), with two first-half goals decisive. Earlier, there was a remarkable series of games between local rivals Ardara and Glenties. Four games and extra-time was required to separate them.

Killybegs in Final: Ian Cunningham, Barry McGowan, Peter McGinley, Thomas McNairn, Jimmy White 0-1, John Cunningham (c), Francis Murray, Barry Cunningham, John Ban Gallagher, Mark Boyle 0-2, Conal Gallagher 0-1, Paul Callaghan 0-1, Conor White 0-1, Manus Boyle 0-3, Paul Murrin.
Subs: Eamonn Clancy for C.White, Declan Boyle 0-1 for Murrin.

Down

FIRST ROUND			
Ballyholland	0-9	Loughinisland	1-13
Ballymartin	1-9	An Riocht	0-10
Bryansford	2-16	Longstone	0-6
Castlewellan	0-12	Burren	0-10
Clonduff	0-12	Carryduff	0-7
Downpatrick	2-12	Drumaness	0-9
Mayobridge	3-8	Warrenpoint	2-4
Shamrocks	2-8	Rostrevor	1-13
QUARTER-FINALS			
Bryansford	1-12	Loughinisland	1-10
Castlewellan	1-18	Rostrevor	0-14
Downpatrick	1-14	Ballymartin	3-6
Mayobridge	2-6	Clonduff	0-7
SEMI-FINALS			
Castlewellan	1-12	Bryansford	1-11
Downpatrick	3-8	Mayobridge	1-11 (R)
FINAL			
Castlewellan	1-8	Downpatrick	0-10

"1994 was no fluke. This second title in-a-row proves we are the best in Down", exclaimed Maurice O'Neill after Castlewellan had survived one of the most nail-biting and longest county finals ever. Eight minutes of added time were played in the first-half, and ten more at the finish, making this a 78-minute contest! And, with Downpatrick the masters of late comebacks, Castlewellan had to call on all their reserves to hold out. Goalkeeper Mickey McVeigh denied Kyran Smyth a goal in the 73rd minute, as he had done earlier in the half, from a penalty. McVeigh revealed afterwards that he had studied Smyth's penalty technique in the Semi-final on video. Mickey Hawkins was another Castlewellan hero, with an excellent goal after just nine minutes. Ciaran McCabe had found Hawkins after a brilliant interception by Conor O'Neill, who was soon to be called up by Peter McGrath. Barry Breen scored six times as Downpatrick fought back, but the same player sent the last chance of the game wide, from a forty metre free. Overall, the green

90

and whites were left to rue the loss of Geoffrey Breen and Paul Moore, with suspensions from the drawn Semi-final with Mayobridge. Indeed, the Carrickdale Hotel SFC had a poor record this year in terms of discipline, with nine players dismissed in four First Round games, including three in the first nine minutes of the Warrenpoint-Mayobridge match. The Lower Mourne derby between Ballymartin and An Riocht also proved to be a poor advert, though the former team did go on to give a fine display in the Quarter-finals, against Downpatrick. A Charlie Doyle goal put them ahead late in the game, before the Deegan twins came to the rescue. Downpatrick escaped again in the Semi-finals, when Kyran Smyth sent over two injury-time points to earn a replay in which the same player scored the winning goal... again in injury-time! Castlewellan put out the much-fancied Burren in the First Round, in a tale of two penalties. Gavin Murdoch missed his when Burren trailed 9-6, and Conor O'Neill tapped his over the bar with the last kick of the game. In the Semi-finals, an Eamonn Burns-inspired Bryansford looked to be too good for Castlewellan, until a late goal from Colm McAlarney and a point from Ciaran McCabe, before 5,000 at Hilltown.

Castlewellan in Final: Mickey McVeigh, Rory O'Neill, Frankie Toner, Seamus McCartan, Donal Ward, Martin Laverty, Maurice O'Neill, Kevin Owens, Marty McKibben 0-1, Conor O'Neill 0-3, Colm McAlarney, Paddy Hardy (c), Ciaran McCabe 0-4, Dermot Hawkins 1-0, Audie McVeigh. Subs: Mickey Hawkins for Laverty, Brian O'Neill for A.McVeigh.

Fermanagh

The 'Year of the Youth' in Ulster Club football continued in the Guinness SFC with Derrygonnelly's first ever title success. Nine of their team in the final were aged between 17-22, with Francie McKenna the youngest (he still has another year at minor level). Managers Hugh Kelly and Donal Fee built their team around the outstanding Derrygonnelly minor side of the early nineties, though they did include a golden oldie at full-forward - 35-year-old Michael Glynn. Youth and experience blended superbly in the final, as they rocked Lisnaskea with early goals (inside a minute) from Kevin Cassidy and Paul Greene. A third goal, from Martin Hamilton, helped Derrygonnelly into an eleven point lead, though the defending champions reduced the gap to just two points in the closing stages, thanks mainly to a superb 1-5 from Shane King. However, Man of the Match Eoin Cassidy stood firm in the winners' defence, and there were new

FIRST ROUND			
Brookeboro	0-3	Lisnaskea	0-17
Derrygonnelly	1-10	Newtownbutler	1-9
Enniskillen	0-10	Devenish	0-11
Kinawley	1-7	St Josephs	2-11 (R)
Roslea	0-12	Aughadrumsee	0-8
Tempo	1-12	Erne Gaels	2-10
Byes - Irvinestown, Derrylin			
QUARTER-FINALS			
Derrygonnelly	2-13	Irvinestown	1-4
Devenish	1-13	Derrylin	0-7
Lisnaskea	1-7	Roslea	0-7
St Josephs	3-7	Erne Gaels	1-10
SEMI-FINALS			
Derrygonnelly	2-13	St Josephs	1-6
Lisnaskea	0-9	Devenish	0-7
FINAL			
Derrygonnelly	3-6	Lisnaskea	1-10

champions. On the way to the final, Derrygonnelly had scraped home against Newtownbutler, beaten Irvinestown with a goal from Manus O'Kane, and defeated Ederney with goals from Hamilton and Kevin McGrath. St Josephs did well to reach the Semi-finals, with a fine victory over Erne Gaels (goals from Ciaran Daly, Andrew Mohan, and Stephen Mohan), while Collie Curran scored nine points for Lisnaskea in the First Round defeat of Brookeboro. The same player accounted for Roslea with a super goal in the next round. Brian Carty's Devenish got past Enniskillen (with 14 men) and Derrylin, but lost to Lisnaskea.

Derrygonnelly in Final: Dermot Feely, Colm Carroll, Donal Corrigan, Eoin Cassidy, Niall Smyth, Paul McGrady, Francie McKenna, Sean Flanagan(c), Martin Greene 0-3, Kevin Cassidy 1-2, Paul Greene 1-0, Martin Hamilton 1-0, Gary Smyth 0-1, Michael Glynn, Kevin McGrath. Subs: Gabriel Jones for Corrigan, John McGovern for McGrath.

Monaghan

PRELIM ROUND			
Castleblayney	1-12	Scotstown	0-8
Donaghmoyne	0-6	Inniskeen	0-8
QUARTER-FINALS			
Carrickmacross	0-11	Aughnamullen	1-4
Castleblayney	5-18	Aghabog	1-5
Clontibret	1-11	Drumhowan	1-9
Inniskeen	0-7	Latton	0-5
SEMI-FINALS			
Clontibret	2-13	Carrickmacross	3-2
Castleblayney	0-12	Inniskeen	1-8
FINAL			
Castleblayney	0-14	Clontibret	0-8
(R: 0-11 0-11)			

Castleblayney have won more county titles than any other senior football club in Ulster. They took their total to 31 with this year's success in the ACC Bank SFC, and now lead nearest challengers St Johns, Belfast, by eight. In the modern era, Eamonn McEneaney and Nudie Hughes have done much to maintain Castleblayney's proud tradition, and once again they were to the fore, with the former managing the team, and Hughes adding his know-how to the attack. The former treble All Star scored four times against Aghabog, and twice against Inniskeen, though he was overshadowed in the replayed final with Clontibret by new county star Peter Duffy. Operating as a third midfielder, Duffy directed the play as Castleblayney recorded eleven unanswered points, to go from 7-5 in arrears to 16-7 ahead. Scotstown were in a position to sympathise with the losers, as they too had been 'blanked out' for 22 minutes fo their Preliminary Round meeting with an in-form 'Blayney. Five points from Duffy and a goal from Ciaran Connolly settled their tie, while winning captain Aidan Tavey scored 1-6 against Aghabog, 0-7 against Iniskeen, and 0-4 in the final replay. Clontibret reached the final with a late goal from Kieran Lavelle against Drumhowan, and 2-6 from Rory Mone in a one-sided Semi-final with Carrickmacross. Mone and Lavelle were also responsible for forcing the final into a second match, with the former scoring seven times and the latter grabbing a late equaliser.

Castleblayney in Final: Barry Kerr, Emmet Brennan, Declan Loughman, Derek Sullivan 0-2, Dermot McArdle, Edwin Murphy, Ray McArdle, Aidan Tavey 0-4 (c), Dermot Duffy, Pete McMahon, Keith Hanratty, Pauric McDonald 0-4, Eugene Hughes, Ciaran (Syd) Connolly, Peter Duffy 0-3. Subs: Mark O'Connor 0-1 for Connolly, Frank McBennett for Hughes, Paul Campbell for McMahon.

Tyrone

Moortown and Carrickmore have provided the main challenge to Errigal Ciaran's recent domination of the Tyrone SFC, but they have been beaten in the last two finals mainly because they have been unable to find an answer to the best player in Ireland - Peter Canavan. He led Errigal Ciaran to their first ever title in 1993 (beating Moortown), and followed up in 1994 by setting a new championship scoring record of 3-27 on the way to another success (beating Carrickmore in the final). This year, Canavan scored four times in the First Round win over Omagh, and added 1-9 in the defeat of Edendork. However, Danny Ball will tell you that his team is not just a one-man show, with some justification. In the game with Omagh, Peter had a penalty saved by Paul Logue and two of his team-mates (Eamonn McCaffrey and Colm McCann) were sent off, before Pascal Canavan arrived as a late substitute to dictate the play. Errigal Ciaran pulled away to win, with a goal from Eoin Gormley. Elsewhere, two goals from Conor McElduff helped Carrickmore beat Galbally in the First Round, and a double from Adrian Kilpatrick saw Dungannon beat Dromore. Justin Murray and Fergal Coyle starred for Moy and Cookstown respectively, but both teams were eliminated from the Quarter-finals. Newly promoted Edendork provided the shock result of the championship, when they ousted Coalisland with three points each for Brian McGuckin and Malachy McLarnon, but then they ran into Errigal Ciaran. Ardboe had two men sent off in their First Round defeat of Donaghmore, but won with goals from Paddy McElroy and Stephen Lynn. They reached the Semi-finals, where they lost to parish rivals Moortown, for whom Vinny Conway scored a vital goal.

FIRST ROUND

Ardboe	2-7	Donaghmore	0-9
Beragh	1-7	Cookstown	1-8
Carrickmore	3-10	Galbally	0-10
Dromore	0-10	Dungannon	2-11
Drumquin	1-7	Moy	0-11
Edendork	0-9	Coalisland	1-4
Moortown	1-16	Trillick	1-6
Omagh	0-3	Errigal Ciaran	1-9

QUARTER-FINALS

Ardboe	0-11	Dungannon	1-6
Carrickmore	0-10	Cookstown	1-5
Errigal Ciaran	2-17	Edendork	1-6
Moortown	1-10	Moy	1-5

SEMI-FINALS

Errigal Ciaran		Carrickmore	
Moortown	1-7	Ardboe	0-5

FINAL

Moortown		E.Ciaran/C'more

TO BE COMPLETED...

93

IN A COMPETITIVE WORLD

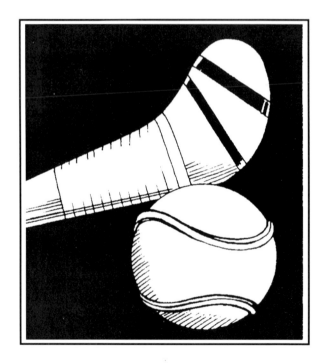

YOU CAN RELY ON OUR SUPPORT

Six Great Years With Sean

Guinness Senior Hurling Championship

When Sean McGuinness was appointed manager of the Down senior team in the Autumn of 1989, his immediate target was to consolidate their status in Division Two of the National League. It was a modest target for a modest team which had always lived in the shadow of the county football team. Six years later, Sean resigned after reaching and surpassing his initial goal. Down spent three years in Division One, and were Ulster Champions twice. Put simply, it was the greatest period in Down hurling history.

The 1992 Ulster triumph was the first in more than half a century, and the second ensured hurling immortality for McGuinness and his players on the Ards peninsula. "To come back three years after people said the team was finished, and to give the best performance in my time there, in the replay with Antrim, was a tribute to the lads. We had spent three nights practising long-distance shooting, and they went out and scored from everywhere. It went like a dream". McGuinness is also proud of the fact that Down beat every team in Leinster, including Kilkenny and Offaly when they were reigning All Ireland Champions. County Secretary James Keenan reckons the 1993 NHL victory in

Down's Paul McMullan and Dermot Woods put pressure on Offaly's Johnny Dooley during their All Ireland semi-final.

Nowlan Park was Down's greatest day under the Antrim man. "Motivating players is Sean's best quality, and against Kilkenny he lifted the Down team to a standard they didn't realise they could reach. To beat the Cats in their own back yard, in a game which they had to win to stay up, was a watershed for Down hurling".

The fact that McGuinness came from outside the Ards helped, partly because he was respected for what he had achieved with Antrim, and partly because he had no affiliation to either Ballygalget, Ballycran, or Portaferry. He made that clear on the day of his first league match, against Meath, when some players arrived later than the scheduled meeting time. McGuinness played without them, and although Down lost, the precedent was set - one set of rules for everyone. After that, the manager did not have to question the commitment of his players, especially the older ones. "The two 35-year-olds, Noel Keith and Gerard Coulter, led from the front in training this year, and never missed a night. They'll go down in folklore on the Ards, while another example of the character of the lads is Dermot O'Prey. He failed a fitness test before the replayed final, and although he knew he would miss out on lifting the cup as captain, he refused a place in the subs".

Midfielders John McCarthy and Danny Hughes were the stars of Down's 1-19 to 2-10 replay win, but the defence was the rock on which the success was built, as was so often the case over the years. Goalkeeper Noel Keith and five defenders played in the 1989 Ulster Final, and the average age of the first seven names on the Down team list was thirty. In contrast, Antrim's eldest player was Terence McNaughton (30) and the average age of their defence was 24. Both sets of defences played well in the drawn game, and ensured the half-time score was a lowly 6-4 to Antrim. The Saffrons raced into a 4-0 lead but could have went in a point behind, if Conor Arthurs' piledriver had not come off a post and back into play. Down were also denied early in the second half, when Gary O'Kane blocked Kevin Coulter's penalty, but two minutes later Dermot O'Prey found the net after a lovely pick-up in a crowded goal area. Antrim countered and looked to have sewn things up with a Joe Boyle goal

REPLAY		Antrim	Down
2 mins	McCambridge (F)	0-1	
4 mins	McKillop	0-2	
5 mins	McCarthy		0-1
7 mins	Ggy O'Kane	1-2	
8 mins	Gilmore (F)		0-2
10 mins	Gilmore (F)		0-3
12 mins	Ggy O'Kane (F)	1-3	
14 mins	Ggy O'Kane	1-4	
16 mins	Ggy O'Kane (F)	1-5	
17 mins	Hughes		0-4
20 mins	Woods		0-5
21 mins	Sands		0-6
25 mins	A.Elliott	1-6	
25 mins	McCarthy		0-7
26 mins	Mallon		0-8
28 mins	K.Coulter (F)		0-9
33 mins	K.Coulter (F)		0-10
35 mins	Sands		1-10
35 mins	Hughes		1-11
Half-time			
38 mins	P.Coulter		1-12
40 mins	McCarthy		1-13
43 mins	Sands		1-14
46 mins	Ggy O'Kane (F)	1-7	
54 mins	Ggy O'Kane (P)	1-8	
55 mins	McCarthy		1-15
60 mins	McNaughton	1-9	
61 mins	Hughes		1-16
63 mins	Arthurs		1-17
67 mins	Gilmore		1-18
68 mins	Carson (F)	2-10	
70 mins	K.Coulter (F)		1-19
Full-time			

seven minutes from time, 1-12 to 1-7, but a frantic and dramatic finish saw both Kevin Coulter's poorly struck penalty and his hopeful 65 enter the Antrim net. Gregory O'Kane equalised immediately, but the same player spurned the last opportunity of the contest when he passed instead of shooting. It was the first drawn final since 1944 (1-13 3-7), and surely a record for wides. Down had 14, and Antrim 23 (15 in the second half). "We have to learn to take responsibility to take scores", moaned Antrim boss Dominic McKinley, while Dermot O'Prey credited his manager for Down's comeback. "The hallmark of Sean's teams is how to fight and battle to the end. He told us at half-time that you don't play for 65 minutes, as Limerick did in the 1994 All Ireland final".

Antrim raced into an early lead in the replay, 1-5 to 0-3 after sixteen minutes, but they were to lose the rest of the match by 1-16 to 1-5. Dermot Woods, John McCarthy, Noel Sands, Marty Mallon and Kevin Coulter all put on an exhibition in long-distance shooting, while Sands also lashed a dropping ball to the Antrim net just before half-time. Revelling in the rain, Down extended their lead to six points after the break, and the contest was over long before the end. John McCarthy found the posts with consummate ease four times from midfield, in contrast to the Antrim forwards who tended to over-carry. They scored just once from play in the half and saw a penalty from Seamus McMullan deflected over the bar by Gary Savage. A week later, Down survived a difficult test in sweltering heat in Ruislip, overcoming London by sixteen points to nine. They led 12-4 at half-time, with Kevin Coulter grabbing three points to lead the way in the championship scoring charts, the first corner-back to do so.

Sean McGuinness has one disappointment from his time with Down... failing to reach an All Ireland Final. In 1992, they lost to Cork, and this year they were beaten by Offaly. "In '92, we worked in training on the Cork goalkeeper's quick, long puck-outs, yet when we scored our goal in the second half, the ball was in our net within seconds. This year, we had high hopes of beating Offaly,

Down, Ulster champions, 1995. Back, L-R: Gerard Coulter, Hugh Gilmore, Danny Hughes, Gary Savage, Noel Keith, Kevin Coulter, Michael Blaney, Conor Arthurs. Front: Martin Mallon, Dermot Woods, Dermot O'Prey, Paul Coulter, Paddy Braniff, Paul McMullan, Noel Sands.

as we had beat them in four of our previous five meetings, but we fell too far behind early on and couldn't come back". After losing by 2-19 to 2-8, McGuinness told his players that he had decided "take a rest" from management. Fresh offers have come his way since then, but he has been more than content to promote the game he loves as part of an excellent coaching scheme in Ulster.

ULSTER FINAL TEAMS AND SCORERS

ANTRIM: Shane Elliott (Dunloy), Eoin Colgan (Ballycastle), Eoin McCloskey (Loughgiel), Sean McElhatton, Seamus McMullan, Gary O'Kane 0-1 (all Dunloy), Ronan Donnelly (B'castle), Sean Paul McKillop 0-1 (Loughgiel), Nigel Elliott (Dunloy), Conor McCambridge, John Carson 0-2 (both Cushendall), Paul Donnelly 0-2 (St Pauls), Gregory O'Kane 0-5 (Dunloy), Terence McNaughton 0-2 (C'dall), Alastair Elliott (Dunloy). Subs: Joe Boyle (Rossa) for Carson, Jimmy Wilson (St Johns) for McCambridge, Paul McKillen (B'castle) for P.Donnelly. Squad: Paddy Nugent, Aidan McAteer, Colm McGuckian, Fergal Collins, Gary Maybin, Martin McClafferty, Ciaran McCambridge, Dominic Kearns, Frankie McMullan.

DOWN : Noel Keith (Ballycran), Kevin Coulter 2-1, Gerard Coulter, Paddy Braniff (Ballygalget), Marty Mallon, Paul McMullan (Portaferry), Dermot Woods, Danny Hughes, Gary Savage, Michael Blaney 0-1 (B'cran), Paul Coulter 0-1 (B'galget), Dermot O'Prey (c) 1-0, Conor Arthurs, Hugh Gilmore 0-4 (B'cran), Noel Sands (P'ferry). Subs: Sean Mallon (B'cran) for Blaney, Michael Braniff (B'cran) for McMullan, Gerard McGrattan (P'ferry) for Arthurs. Squad : Graham Clarke, Paddy Monan, John McCarthy, Conor Mallon, Brian McAleenan, John Brown, Barry Coulter.

Replay: Dermot O'Prey was replaced by Michael Blaney who had originally lost his place to John McCarthy. Antrim were unchanged. Scorers: Down:K.Coulter 0-3, M.Mallon 0-1, D.Woods 0-1, D.Hughes 0-3, J.McCarthy 0-4, P.Coulter 0-1, C.Arthurs 0-1, H.Gilmore 0-3, N.Sands 1-2. Subs: B.Coulter for Woods, M.Braniff for McMullan (36), S.Mallon for Gilamore (69). Antrim: S.McMullan 0-1, SP McKillop 0-1, C.McCambridge 0-1, J.Carson 1-0, Ggy.O'Kane 1-5, T.McNaughton 0-1, A.Elliott 0-1. Subs: J.Wilson for McKillop (15), C.McGuckian for McCambridge (35), F.McMullan for A.Elliott (52).

Down v London: N.Keith, K.Coulter 0-4, G.Coulter, P.Braniff, M.Mallon 0-1, G.Savage, P.McMullan, D.Hughes, J.McCarthy 0-1, P.Coulter, B.Coulter 0-1, N.Sands 0-2, C.Arthurs 0-3, H.Gilmore 0-3, M.Blaney 0-1. Subs: M.Braniff for P.Braniff, D.O'Prey for Sands.

Down v Offaly: Dermot Woods came in for the injured Paddy Braniff , and Dermot O'Prey replaced Michael Blaney .Down: N.Keith, K.Coulter 0-1, G.Coulter, D.Woods, M.Mallon, G.Savage, P.McMullan, J.McCarthy 0-1, D.Hughes 0-1, P.Coulter 1-0, B.Coulter, D.O'Prey (c), G.McGrattan, H.Gilmore 0-3, N.Sands 1-2. Sub: M.Braniff for Gilmore (60).

Offaly: D.Hughes, S.McGuckian, K.Kinahan, M.Hanamy, B.Whelehan 0-1, H.Rigney, K.Martin, D.Regan, J.Pilkington 0-1, Johnny Dooley 0-11, J.Troy 0-1, Joe Dooley 0-1, B.Dooley 1-2, P.O'Connor 0-1, M.Duignan 1-1. Subs: J.Errity for Rigney, D.Pilkington for Regan, B.Kelly for Troy.

GUINNESS SENIOR HURLING CHAMPIONSHIP

ULSTER

Antrim	2-10	Down	1-19
(R: 1-13 3-7)			

CONNACHT

Galway	2-21	Roscommon	2-12

MUNSTER

Kerry	0-12	Cork	1-22
Tipperary	4-23	Waterford	1-11
Clare	2-13	Cork	3-9
Limerick	0-16	Tipperary	0-15
Clare	1-17	Limerick	0-11

LEINSTER

Meath	1-13	Carlow	2-11
Westmeath	6-6	Carlow	3-14
Westmeath	1-7	Wexford	6-23
Kilkenny	2-14	Laois	2-12
Offaly	2-14	Wexford	1-10
Kilkenny	4-13	Dublin	2-10
Offaly	2-16	Kilkenny	2-5

ALL IRELAND QUARTER-FINAL

London	0-9	Down	0-16

ALL IRELAND SEMI-FINALS

Down	2-8	Offaly	2-19
Clare	3-12	Galway	1-13

ALL IRELAND FINAL

Clare	1-13	Offaly	2-8

Spreading the Hurling Gospel

Railway Cup Final, Croke Park
Ulster 1-9   Munster 0-13

The sight of Sean McGuinness pulling his hair out towards the end of the Railway Cup final told a story of frustration and great disappointment for the Ulster manager. If only Hugh Gilmore had converted a relatively straight-forward 35-yard free in the closing moments, the cup might have come north for the very first time. However, McGuinness can draw some encouragement from the fact that four Ulster counties were represented on his team, including Tyrone's first provincial player, Vinnie Owens. McGuinness has long recognised the need to capitalise on the breakthrough by Antrim in reaching the 1989 All Ireland final, and by Down in winning their first Ulster title in 51 years, in 1992. Spreading the hurling gospel has proved difficult, partly because of the success of the Ulster footballers, but it is hoped the appearance of Owens, along with Derry men Seamus Downey and Ollie Collins, and Armagh's Mattie Lennon in the substitutes, will help the development of the game. In their semi-final, Ulster trailed Connacht by seven points but came storming back with goals from Noel Sands and Hugh Gilmore. In the closing minutes, Gilmore added a couple of points to complete a famous comeback. After the game, the door to the losers' dressing-room remained closed for 45 minutes. In the final, Ulster staged another late show, but this time it was too late. Munster led 11-3 when Ollie Collins began the charge early in the second-half. Kevin Coulter reduced the arrears to three points with a goal 16 minutes from time, a 70 from Gary Savage and another score from Terence McNaughton gave Ulster hope, but Joe Quaid denied McCambridge a goal with a brilliant save, and then came Gilmore's miss.

Vinnie Owens, Tyrone and Ulster.

ULSTER: Noel Keith, Kevin Coulter (Down), Eoin Colgan (Antrim), Paddy Braniff, Martin Mallon, Gary Savage (Down) 0-1, SP McKillop, Paul McKillen 0-1, Conor McCambridge, Terence McNaughton (Antrim) 1-1, Ollie Collins (Derry) 0-4, Dermot O'Prey (Down), Vinnie Owens (Tyrone), Hugh Gilmore 0-2, Noel Sands (Down). Subs: Barry Coulter (Down) for Owens (41), Ronan Donnelly (Antrim) for Gilmore (60).

Antrim Regain Minor Title

Ulster Final - Antrim 2-17 Derry 1-4

Olcan McFetridge's young charges restored honour to their county by winning the Ulster crown for the first time since 1993, and more importantly, by putting up a good show on All Ireland semi-final day at Croke Park. Five of the team were especially determined to do well, after being part of the 1994 team so dramatically beaten in injury-time in the Ulster final by Down, who went on to lose at headquarters by 21 points.

This year, Down succumbed to Derry at Ballybofey in June, before the Donegal-Monaghan SFC game, 2-10 to 0-11. Johnny McGrattan was on target with 1-4, and minor footballer Padraig Matthews from Clonduff added two points, but Derry goaled through Raymond O'Hagan and, conclusively, through substitute Danny McGrellis. Peter McCloskey scored six points for Derry, but they were less prolific on Ulster final day, trailing by thirteen points by the time Eoin Farren found the net on the stroke of half-time. Antrim won with ease, and with goals from McMullan and Hamill.

Antrim have only ever won one All Ireland semi-final, against Laois in 1940, but they refused to lie down to Kilkenny, even when rocked by a goal on 19 minutes. Brian McFall grabbed three singles, including a brilliant sideline cut, to rival the Cats free-taking ace Raymie Cahill who amassed a personal tally of ten points in their 1-16 to 0-12 victory. In the All Ireland Final, Kilkenny lost to Cork, 2-10 to 1-2.

Antrim. Back, L-R: C.Hamill, J.Quinn, B.McFall, K.Kelly, M.McCloskey, K.McGaughan, L.Richmond, K.Killyleagh, S.McMullan. Front: P.Gillen, L.McMullan, A.Delargy, J.Flynn, C.Cunningham, K.Stewart. Mascot - Colm Cunningham.

Derry Minors, Ulster finalists.

McCambridge is Under-21 Star

Ulster Under 21 Final
Antrim 2-18   Derry 1-7

Conor McCambridge's personal tally of eleven points was more than the entire Derry team could muster in the Under-21 final at Ballinascreen. The Cushendall man scored seven times from frees, twice from 65s and twice from play, though Antrim still needed late goals from Colm McCloskey and Adrian Mort to kill off the contest. Leading 0-10 to 1-3 at half-time, they saw their advantage cut to two when Derry moved Geoffrey McGonigle out of his full-forward position. The dual player, who was used as a substitute in the Ulster SFC semi-final with Tyrone the following day, scored 1-4. McGonigle also contributed 2-5 to Derry's replay defeat of Down (3-9 to 0-10) in their Under-21 semi-final at Ballycran. Antrim had a smooth passage, beating Fermanagh by 11-18 to 0-1, with Paul Graham top-scoring on 4-3, but lost 4-12 to 1-8 to Tipperary in their All Ireland semi-final.

ANTRIM
Gary Agnew, Art Connolly, Anton Rogan, Mickey O'Neill, Seamus Bailie, Frankie McMullan, Chris McAuley, Joe Boyle, Colm McGuckian, Conor McCambridge 0-11, Malachy Molloy, Aidan McCluskey 0-1, Paul Graham 0-1, Colm McCluskey 1-1, Aidan Mort 1-3.
Subs: Stephen Ramsey, Robert Paul Laverty, Martin Crummey. Squad: Stephen Milligan, Mickey McCloskey, Darryl Fegan, Hugh McKay, Kieran Kelly, Liam McMullan.

DERRY
Kieran Stevenson, Shane Kelly, Paul McCloy, O.Young, Mark Heron, Shane McCartney, PJ Ward, Colin McEldowney (c) 0-1, Benny Ward, Michael Conway, Paddy Scullion, Gary Biggs 0-2, Gerard O'Mianain, Geoffrey McGonigle 1-4, M.McDermott. Subs: Danny McGrellis, Sean Lockhart Squad: P.McEldowney, Darren Doherty, Marty Lockhart, James Colgan, Kieran Higgins, P.McKaigue, M.McMullan, U.McCloskey, R.McEldowney, C.Leydon, C.McDaid, D.O'Kane.

101

Hurling Club Championships

Down

SEMI-FINAL			
Ballycran	1-13	Portaferry	1-12
Ballygalget	7-15	O'Rahillys	0-6
FINAL			
Ballycran	0-16	Ballygalget	1-7

County captain Dermot O'Prey played a vital role in both Ballycran's victories in the Carrickdale Hotel SHC, by scoring the match-winning point in the semi-final, from a penalty in injury time, and by top-scoring in the final with five singles. His stickwork was there to be admired as he grabbed the first three scores in the final, and set up an emphatic win. Goalkeeper Noel Keith, a solid half-back line, and a steady midfield, ensured Balycran led 8-3 at the break, and although Barry Coulter struck a late goal for Ballygalget, John McCarthy completed the scoring with his third of the match. Even without injured captain Paddy Dorrian, Ballycran won their 20th title, and their third in succession.

Ballycran in Final: Noel Keith, Stephen McAree, Bill Hughes, Hugh Torney, Michael Braniff, Dermot Woods, Gary Savage, Danny Hughes 0-1, John McCarthy 0-3, Kevin Blaney 0-2, Dermot O'Prey 0-5, Conor Arthurs 0-2, Seamus Mallon 0-1, Hugh Gilmore, Michael Blaney 0-2. Sub: Sean Masterson for Mallon.

Antrim

FIRST ROUND			
Cushendall	5-18	Glenariffe	1-6
Cushendun	1-19	Sarsfields	0-10
Gort na Mona	3-5	Armoy	4-11
Lamh Dhearg	1-4	St Johns	1-12
St Pauls	0-8	Ballycastle	3-9
Byes - Dunloy, Loughgiel, Rossa			
QUARTER-FINALS			
Dunloy	2-17	Cushendall	1-8
Loughgiel	2-13	Armoy	0-13
Rossa	2-9	Ballycastle	1-9
St Johns	4-9	Cushendun	1-10
SEMI-FINALS			
Dunloy	2-17	Loughgiel	0-9
Rossa	3-12	St Johns	0-12
FINAL			
Dunloy	0-14	Rossa	0-11

1995 All Ireland finalists Dunloy maintained their momentum to storm past North Antrim neighbours Cushendall and Loughgiel, but then found the city boys from Rossa a real handful in the final. They required a wonder save seconds before the final whistle from team captain Shane Elliott to protect what looked to be a fragile three-point cushion. Brendan Murray's effort was heading for the top corner of the Dunloy net when Elliott, who also saved a first half penalty, intervened. The reigning champions nearly paid for relaxing midway through the second half, as Ger Rogan inspired Rossa to a commendable fightback. Jim Connolly reduced the arrears to just two points near the finish, and his midfield partner Jim Close scored seven times in all, but Gregory O'Kane went one better as Dunloy held out. Earlier in the competition, the champions reached identical totals (2-17) in beating Cushendall by 12 points (Colm McGuckian was Man of the Match with 1-1) and Loughgiel by 14 points. Rossa's biggest win came over city rivals St Johns, when two goals from captain Collie Murphy, and one from Noel Murray, saw Aidan Hamill's team through. Elsewhere, Armoy'sOlcan McFetridge achieved a personal tally of 3-5 in the First Round defeat of Gort na Mona, two goals each from Danny McNaughton and Aidan Delargy helped Cushendall beat Glenariffe, Raymond McDonnell scored 1-4 for Cushendun against Sarsfields, and 2-3 from Ballycastle's Michael McShane was more than the whole St Pauls team could muster in reply.

Dunloy in Final: Shane Elliott (c), Niall McCamphill, Paul Molloy, Sean McIlhatton, Seamus McMullan 0-2, Gary O'Kane, Seamus Mullan, Nigel Elliott, Colm McGuckian, Jarlath Elliott 0-1, Tony McGrath, Frankie McMullan 0-1, Eamonn McKee 0-1, Gregory O'Kane 0-8, Alistair Elliott.

Derry

Dual stars Seamus Downey and Ollie Collins played key roles in Lavey's eighth title win in eleven years. The former scored a super solo goal in the semi-final defeat of Banagher, while Collins bagged no fewer than twelve points in the final. Lavey joined Dungiven on the Championship Roll of Honour with thirteen successes.

QUARTER-FINALS			
Banagher	2-15	Na Magha	1-3
Ballinascreen	2-4	Lavey	3-21
Kevin Lynchs	3-7	Slaughtneil	6-11
Drum (bye)			
SEMI-FINALS			
Lavey	1-6	Banagher	0-6
Slaughtneil	1-15	Drum	3-7
FINAL			
Lavey	1-22	Slaughtneil	1-6

Lavey in Final: Fergal McNally, PJ Ward, Joe Young, Kieran McGurk, Peter Doherty, Patrick McCloy, Benny Ward, Don Mulholland 0-1, Adrian McCrystal, Seamus Downey 0-3, Ollie Collins 0-12, Brian McCormick 0-3, Kieran Higgins 1-0, Michael Collins 0-1, Martin Collins. Subs: Henry Downey 0-2 for Ml Collins.

Fermanagh

Lisbellaw beat Enniskillen by 4-14 to 0-5 in the final of the Fort Lodge Hotel SHC to win their fifth title in-a-row. The team in the final was:

Stephen Hanna, T.Reihill, Seamus McCusker (c), D.Smyth, A.Watters, Rory O'Donnell 0-1, N.Murphy, Sean Duffy, Ollie McShea 1-2, Donal McShea 1-2, R.Timoney, Adrian McPhillips, Shane O'Donnell 1-5, John McCusker 1-4, G.Winterson. Subs: Paul Coogan for Smyth, S.Murphy for Watters, M.McGinley for Winterson.

Tyrone

Killyclogher retained their title the hard way, after giving Dungannon an eight-point start in the final. They managed to wipe out the 1-6 to 0-1 scoreline with goals from Owen McKenna, Gary Burns, and Brendan Hegarty, but then contrived to fall behind once more in a dramatic finale. Brian McIntosh shot Dungannon

QUARTER-FINALS			
Dungannon	3-11	Shamrocks	0-3
Killyclogher	4-11	Carrickmore	4-8
Naomh Colmcille	2-12	Clann na Gael	2-8
SEMI-FINALS			
Dungannon	2-5	Omagh	0-7
Killyclogher	5-10	Naomh Colmcille	0-5
FINAL			
Killyclogher	4-5	Dungannon	2-8

back into the lead with minutes remaining, before Killyclogher finally won the contest when Vinny Owens' 65 yard free sailed all the way to the net.

Killyclogher: Barry McCaul, Paddy Hutchison, Martin Hegarty, Brian Burns, Mark Kelly, Vinny Owens 1-3, Aidan McAleer, Damien McCallion, Pauric Quinn, Gary Burns 1-0, Colin Quinn, Sean Bradley, Brendan Hegarty 1-1, Terry McCann 0-1, Owen McKenna 1-0. Subs: Neil McDermott for McAleer, S.O'Kane for B.Hegarty.

Out of Africa … to Dunloy!

AIB All Ireland Club Hurling Championship

Father PJ McCamphill has one small regret about working as a missionary in Africa for the last 25 years - "They can't play hurling out there!". He had been a county player before he left and still holds the game close to his heart, as he showed on his return this year. "I was so pleased to witness Dunloy reaching the All Ireland final, because I know what it means to the people. Hurling is at the very heart of this small parish. I don't like to say it, but it's like a religion! In Church, I pray for the hurlers as I pray for someone who is sick". The thirteen-strong McMullan family is typical of this part of the Glens. Seamus, Frankie and Dominic are senior players, two more brothers play for the Under-16s, four sisters play camogie, mum washes the jerseys, and dad is the groundsman. Senior coach Seamus Elliott has two sons (Shane and Nigel), and two nephews (Alistair and Jarlath), on the team, and so on. Drawing on this 'family spirit', Dunloy humbled Athenry in their All Ireland semi-final at Clones, with a sensational late goal from substitute Jarlath Cunning, and then forced a replay in the final against Birr from Offaly with an injury-time score. Dunloy were facing a gale force wind and had conceded six points in-a-row when Tony McGrath equalised. "At half-time in both games, Mushy (Seamus McMullan) and Pappy (Gary O'Kane) told the boys never to lie down", recalls Club PRO Tony Chivers. The Pilkingtons and Daithi Regan ended the Dunloy dream, but their challenge was a reminder of the what the GAA is all about.

Concerned team-mate Shane Elliott inspects Seamus McMullan's head cut.

Gone With The Wind

Bellaghy's Bid for All Ireland Glory

A team-mate keeps the ball still as Karl Diamond takes a free-kick.

You had to feel sorry for all the players involved on the St Patricks Day All Ireland Club Finals. For many of them, it was the biggest day of their sporting lives, yet the winds were as bad as any of the 18,500 crowd could remember in Croke Park; Bellaghy's game with Kilmacud Crokes was even held up when of an advertising hoarding became airbourne! The Derrymen trailed 6-1 after playing into the wind, but then failed to score for 17 minutes of the second half. Cathal Scullion, Louis McPeake, Gareth Dougherty, and Damien Cassidy (outstanding in Bellaghy's run) all missed goal chances, the latter from a penalty 30 seconds from time. But Bellaghy have lots of young talent, and as Danny Quinn promised, "We'll be back".

Catherine Quinn comforts husband Danny.

105

Above: Athlone Town goalkeeper Shane Curran keeps out Stuart Gauld's penalty at St Mel's Park, to effectively deny Derry City the League Championship.

Below: Gauld makes amends with Derry's second goal in the 2-1 FAI Cup final defeat of Shelbourne.

3

The Tale of Two Penalties

League of Ireland
Athlone Town 1   Derry City 1
FAI Cup Final
Derry City 2   Shelbourne 1

"The main thing I remember about the season is not the winning of the cup, but walking off the pitch at Athlone and the scene in the dressing-room. We were gutted and there were tears shed. We could have won 6-0 but conceded a freak goal after thirteen seconds, missed a penalty and couldn't put the ball in the net. It was cruel thing to happen to anybody. Coming back from that to win the cup was superb, but I guess I'm like the actor on Broadway who received ten good reviews and one bad one. He only remembered the bad one".

Derry City manager Felix Healy is not alone in retaining vivid memories of the day his team lost the league title at St Mel's Park. Thousands of supporters had made the journey to the midlands, never stopping to think that their team might fail to get the three points needed to win the championship for the first time since 1989. The players, and in particular Stuart Gauld, will always reflect on the one-all draw as one of the blackest days of their career.

The League Championship dream had started just six games into Healy's reign, when a 3-1 home win over Cobh Ramblers took them level at the top of the Premier Division in January. From there, Derry went on a roller-coaster ride towards the title, scoring dramatic victories and suffering occasional setbacks over eleven games. Paul "the Dog" Doolin grabbed a last-minute winner against Shamrock Rovers at the Brandywell, and another home win over Galway put Derry three points clear, but eventual champions Dundalk wiped out City's advantage by beating them 2-0 at Oriel Park in midweek. Former Down All Ireland gaelic footballer, Peter Withnell, scored one of the goals. Felix Healy saw the defeat as a turning point, as his team defeated Monaghan and St Pats to regain a three point lead with just three games to go. But, before their next fixture, away to Cobh, Derry became embroiled in a cup marathon with Bohemians, meeting three times in seven days before Derry won 3-2 after extra-time. "One of the truly great FAI cup semi-final sagas of all-time", according to Gerry Thornley in the Irish Times. It ended later on the Friday night, and

DERRY CITY LEAGUE RESULTS UNDER HEALY	
1994	
Galway United (a)	4-1
Dundalk (h)	2-0
Bohemians (a)	0-0
Monaghan United (h)	2-0
1995	
St Pats Athletic (a)	1-1
Cobh Ramblers (h)	3-1
Sligo Rovers (a)	0-1
Shamrock Rovers (h)	1-0
Cork City (a)	2-0
Galway United (h)	2-0
Dundalk (a)	0-2
Bohemians (h)	1-1
Monaghan United (a)	5-0
St Pats Athletic (h)	2-0
Cobh Ramblers (a)	1-1
Shelbourne (h)	2-0
Athlone Town (a)	1-1

Derry then had to fly to Cobh for a Sunday morning kick-off. "We showed great character given we had to play Cobh when we were really shattered. We were all over them but only came away with a draw, which meant we had to lift ourselves again to meet rivals

Shelbourne on the Tuesday night", recalls Healy. Roared on by a large home support, Derry rose to the occasion and won 2-0. The dream was alive again.

While Derry went to Athlone on the last day, Dundalk were at home to Galway and Shelbourne played St Pats. The first drama of the afternoon came direct from the kick-off in Athlone when Donal Golden dispossessed Paul McLaughlin and struck the ball (via a deflection off Gauld) past a stunned Dermot O'Neill. Liam Coyle equalised with a classic goal 15 minutes later, but Athlone's inspired goalkeeper Shane Curran would not be beaten again. Nine minutes into the second-half, he pushed Stuart Gauld's penalty kick onto a post and wide. It was only the third time in 45 penalties that the Scot had failed to score. Elsewhere, Shelbourne were losing 1-0 and Dundalk were scoreless, a state of affairs which would have been enough to give Derry the title, but the title race was about to take another twist.

Dundalk were the form team. They had won their last four games, including a 1-0 midweek defeat of Sligo with a superbly volleyed goal by Peter Withnell. "We'll be there or thereabouts, as we have been all season, and the pressure's off us", warned their manager Dermot Keely, though behind the scenes he admitted to his players that it would be a miracle if they won the league. Dundalk played poorly in the first-half against Galway, until Keely told them to "forget what is happening elsewhere, play your normal game and enjoy yourselves". His players responded with goals from Mick Doohan and Tom McNulty to win 2-0. "At the final whistle, we returned to our dressing-room as normal", recalls Peter Withnell. "Then we were told to come back out onto the pitch where we listened to commentary from Athlone". They heard how Derry finally managed to beat Shane Curran, only for a defender to hook the ball off the line. Four minutes into injury time, the signal came for the celebrations to begin at Oriel. Dundalk had caught everyone on the hop, squeezing past Derry and Shelbourne to land their ninth title. Their Scottish goal-scoring hero, Tom McNulty, was entitled to a side-swipe at the reporters who had written off their chances and failed to nominate any of his team-mates for the Player of the Year Award. "That's why they're pressmen and we're footballers."

BORD GAIS NATIONAL LEAGUE 1994-95

	P	W	D	L	F	A	Pts
Dundalk	33	17	8	8	41	25	59
Derry City	33	16	10	7	45	30	58
Shelbourne	33	16	9	8	45	32	57
Bohemians	33	14	11	8	48	30	53
St Patricks Ath	33	13	14	6	53	36	53
Shamrock Rovers	33	14	9	10	45	36	51
Cork City	33	15	4	14	55	42	49
Sligo Rovers	33	12	7	14	43	42	43
Galway Utd	33	10	9	14	39	53	39
Athlone Town	33	6	14	13	31	44	32
Cobh Ramblers	33	5	11	17	29	51	26
Monaghan Utd	33	5	4	24	22	75	19

Stuart Gauld holds his head in his hands after his penalty miss.

Stuart Gauld's uncharacterisitic penalty miss had effectively lost the league for Derry, not to mention the financial windfall that would have come with it. In ten years playing for City, since arriving from Edinburgh at the age of 21, Gauld had not known such disappointment. "He was as bad as I've ever seen in football. Shattered would be putting it mildly", recalls his manager. Liam Coyle helped him out, "We had to carry Stuart to the shower, he couldn't even get up, and he's such a confident person". On the journey home, Paul Curran tried to raise Gauld's spirits, "on the bus we said Stuart would score the second goal in the cup final!" Slowly, the Scotsman came to terms with the miss, "I couldn't keep on crucifying myself forever", and began to prepare himself for the final with Shelbourne. Some wondered whether he would have the nerve to take a penalty in the final, but he indicated that he would, after encouragement and support from all sides, "I even met an old lady who told me I had to miss one in Athlone to score one in the cup final".

There was no player more superstitious than goalkeeper Dermot O'Neill. The Dubliner had plenty of reason, after losing three finals (1982/83/94) and finishing runner-up in the league four times. The 33-year-old was still waiting for a winners' medal after fifteen years service. Paul Curran, who had lost two finals, remembers O'Neill's determination to get it right this time. "When we got to Lansdowne, Dermot made a dash for the away dressing-room, because Sligo had it when they beat us the year before. He still wasn't happy and made sure he was first out on the field so that we could warm-up at the same end as Sligo!" In contrast, 22-year-old Peter Hutton approached the game with confidence, to the extent that he waged a fiver on himself to score the first goal (at 9/1). Hutton had scored twice in the semi-final with Bohemians, including the extra-time winner, and true to form, he arrived in the box unmarked to side-foot McCourt's cross into the net. Two minutes later, Hutton aggravated an ankle injury and required a pain-killing injection at half-time to get him through the game.   With Paul Kinnaird tracking back on Brian Mooney, "Shelbourne's best player all year" according to Healy, Derry stood firm and were handed a chance to make it 2-nil going into the closing stages, when Liam Coyle was felled in the penalty area. All eyes turned, more than a little apprehensively, to the slim figure at the heart of the Derry defence, Stuart Gauld. They needn't have worried, as he stepped forward and sent the kick, with great authority, into the corner of the net.

"I really fancied it and knew exactly what I had to do. The early goal had given us that confidence, though I probably did think back to Athlone a bit. I cried like a child at St Mel's Park and it took me a while to get over it. People told me that losing the league was down to a combination of things, and eventually I decided that the Athlone keeper had saved well, but still, in the cold light of day, you tell yourself if the penalty had gone in then you would have won the league. Now, after scoring in the cup final, life is going to be easier for me".

Shelbourne pulled a goal back, from a Greg Costello penalty given for Paul Carlyle's hand-ball, but it merely served the purpose of making them the first losing finalists in eleven years to score. At the end, cheers rang around the ground for two men who were already together. "Dermot (O'Neill) was the first man I went to hug at the final whistle, even though he said he didn't watch my penalty!", recalls Stuart Gauld. The Irish Times noted the "sheer joy of O'Neill when he received the trophy and finally entered the kingdom". A winner at last. There were emotional scenes in the Derry dressing-room when Dermot met up with his brother, Alan. Dermot told Arthur Duffy of the Derry Journal why the cup win was so important to their family. "Our dad died four years ago and I know he was smiling down on me from Heaven after the final whistle sounded", said Dermot. "I made a point of visiting dad's grave on Thursday and said a few prayers to help me get through the game. That was a very important part of my preparation and now I know he will be very proud of me. "Alan has spent so much time comforting me in the past. When he came into the dressing-room, I almost collapsed. He had to be there. It was unbelievable for both of us". Dermot's young daughters, Cheryl (9) and Kelly (5), had watched the game from the West Stand, "I occasionally glanced over to make sure they were okay. Cheryl wasn't too keen on coming to the game as she's watched me lose so many times before!"

Felix Healy also had reason for great relief at the end of the game. He had been a cup final loser three times (twice at Coleraine, once at Derry), and a league runner-up three times. "You think it's never going to happen, but then I won the treble with Derry. Now, as manager, having lost the league, all those kinda thoughts come back - will I have to wait so long again? I'm not a guy for jumping up and down, but I felt that relief again when the ref blew the whistle". However, his favourite memories of the day came a short time later, "I'll never forget watching the players' faces as they came down with their medals, in marked contrast to Athlone, and the players asking me to take the cup up onto the balcony. Those are moments I'll cherish".

The manager could afford a wry smile as he reflected on his apprehension only five months before, when leaving a Coleraine job he had made a success of, to takeover the Derry hot seat. "It was the most difficult decision I've ever had to make. My young fella, Patrick (10), used to sit on the bench with me at Coleraine, and when I told him I was leaving, he cried. Also, my wife is still coming to terms with it. I was seven years a player there and we have great affection for Coleraine. I had had a love-hate relationship with Derry as a player and it's a very high-pressure job, so I asked myself why would I want to go to a place like that, from somewhere where I was very popular to a place where I had become very unpopular". His youngest son still wears his beloved Coleraine shirt, but accepted a Derry City one as well three weeks after his dad became boss. Healy's first move was to speak to the Derry squad for ninety minutes at a city hotel about his football philosophy. It centres on three things - moral courage, honesty and belief. Strangely, for such a talented player, ability was not mentioned. "I don't worry too much about ability. I never speak about it, you're born with it. A lot of the time it's more about moral courage. If you don't

At last! Derry captain Dermot O'Neill receives the FAI trophy from Louis Kilcoyne, President of the League of Ireland.

have it, you won't make it. Moral courage is where you have to be brave enough to do what you think is right, don't be hiding or playing to the crowd or fooling the manager". Healy said he had hardly missed a Derry game in ten years and told one defender that he watched him making bad tackles, for which he was fortunate not to have been sent off. Derry's disciplinary record and fitness has been transformed under Healy.

"Honesty and belief are important too, in fact they are all inter-linked and you need different amounts of the three qualities in each match. When the going gets tough, the people with all three are seen. I don't mind arrogance - you have to believe in your own ability and look after yourself during the week. A lot of players don't make the most of their ability, but others do, by having the desire and hunger to win. The game, more so today, is about fitness and organisation. There isn't much space to play, it's all compacted into midfield, so you have to have the will-to-win. The Northern Ireland team had it from 1980-84. They had tremendous resolve and character, though we carried a wee bit of luck too".

Healy has worked under a number of managers over twenty years as a player, but says the only one he learned from is Jim McLaughlin. "He's the spittin' image of Jim", reckons Paul Curran. "I have to keep pinching myself and look up to see if it's Felix or Jim talking". His team-talks can be profound, and rarely about football, though the message is always about how important every game is. Before the league showdown with Shelbourne, with a crowd of nearly ten thousand chanting outside, Healy talked about the troubles in Derry and how Belfast people think Derry people have a chip on their shoulders. "They don't", said Healy, "but if you read the history of Derry City FC, Chapter 4 is about how the league was lost, Chapter 5 is about how the cup was lost, and so on". Dermot O'Neill recalls another talk. "He told us about a woman who died in the place he used to work. Everybody's looking up at him, thinking 'has he gone loopy?' Then there was the St Pats game when he came in to the dressing-room and said, 'alright lads, sit down. Ah, don't bother doing any warm-ups. Do what you like. I'm going for a cup of tea'. Out he goes and we won 2-nil. I wouldn't say he's peculiar, but he's different".

Harry McCourt (£12,000), Paul Kinnaird, Paul Carlyle (£6,000) and Paul Doolin (£6,000) were all signed by Healy early in his reign. The new manager bought in experience after identifying an imbalance in the team: "Some very good players, some not so good". McCourt and Carlyle both scored on their debuts (against Galway and Cobh respectively), and proved themselves to be very good value for money, though the signing of Doolin arguably gave Healy most pleasure. "He was 32 but a bargain. I hear people say what he can't do but one thing he can do is win. Dooler has won more trophies and cups than anyone in Ireland in the last ten years. You can rely on him when the going gets tough". Healy also sorted out things at the back, conceding just nine goals in his 17 league games in charge. The goalkeeper and three defenders also played on the League of Ireland team.

The good times are back at the Brandywell, six years after the treble. Perhaps success came too quickly for the club, and they reached a low point six games into the 1993-94 season when they sat on the bottom of the league. Tony O'Doherty replaced Roy Coyle and performed minor miracles in taking the team to the cup final, while off the field the financial base is much-improved. Now, Felix Healy has a team filled with promise and there is confidence that they can become the top club in Ireland. 22-year-old Peter Hutton was made captain (Derry's youngest ever) after the surprising transfer of cup hero Dermot O'Neill to Glenavon. Hutton is a local man with the tradition of the club at heart and football in his blood (his father Peter won a cup medal with Finn Harps in 1974).

Another encouraging development is talk about a friendly with Linfield. 12,000 saw them play at the Brandywell in 1966, and it's possible those days could return, maybe in competitive football. There is a body of opinion in Irish League circles that Derry should be encouraged to return, Kenny Shiels (Coleraine) among them, and although their immediate future is pledged to the League of Ireland, there may come a day when the burden of travelling expenses becomes too heavy and when the political climate allows for such a move.

1994-95 Bord Gais League of Ireland Stars Team

Derry City's representatives are Dermot O'Neill (front, far left), Pascal Vaudequin (front, 2nd from left), and Paul Curran (front, far right).

113

Opel Personality of the Year

Liam Coyle

The premier individual award in the League of Ireland went to the premier individual on the Derry team, Liam Coyle. The football writers got it right, yet they did not see his best goal of the season, in a warm-up game against a local select a week before the cup final. Surrounded by four defenders, Coyle flicked the ball over his head, beat them all in the space of six yards and then deftly chipped the goalkeeper. "He does that kind of thing in training all the time", assures Felix Healy. "He's the best player in the country. Given what happened to him over the years concerning his fitness, not to mention serious doubts about his future career, his performances have been amazing". Coyle was born with a disease in his knee (not an injury) which came to light just as a glamorous career beckoned with a top Premiership club. The player has come to terms with the problem and has made a conscious decision to play on, though his father, the great Fay Coyle (an Irish Cup winner in 1964 and a goal-scoring record-breaker in his day) has regrets. "I am indeed a proud man, I really enjoy watching Liam because he is always a class above. His mind is brilliant, he sees so many things going on around him. From no age he could use both feet, though every time I see him doing something I could never have done, I think about that knee problem that robbed him from playing with the best.

Coyle is the third Derryman to win the Award, following Brendan Bradley (Finn Harps) in 1976 and Jim McLaughlin in 1989. The shortlist of nominees this year were Liam Coyle, Paul Curran, John Caulfield (Cork), Brian Mooney (Shelbourne), Colin Murphy (Shelbourne manager), and Jason Sherlock (UCD and Dublin gaelic footballer).

Roy of the Rovers

"The Manchester United Reserve team to play Tranmere tonight is as follows ... Gary Walsh, Gary Neville, Philip Neville, David May, Anthony Tohill, Nicky Butt, Simon Davis, Mark Hughes ...". The lady reading the team over the telephone kept going, but I had stopped listening at the mention of the big Swatragh man alongside such illustrious team-mates. Anthony couldn't quite believe it either, pulling on the famous red shirt he had supported since he was no age, and Mark Hughes crossing the same dressing-room to shake his hand and wish him good luck.

Truthfully, Tohill's comic-book trial at Old Trafford would not have happened had not it been for Eamonn Coleman, or rather the removal of the Derry manager in September, 1994. The All Star joined the boycott of the county team and kept fit by playing for Intermediate League side, Park. He had no intentions of pursuing a serious career in soccer, but his performances soon attracted the attention of Ipswich Town. When they offered Tohill a trial at Christmas, he was both flattered and amused. Manchester City came next, with another offer, and then United. "I was sitting in the house playing Nintendo with a friend when the call came that United were interested. It was unreal!" The Premiership giants asked for a list of Park's fixtures so that their Northern Ireland scout, Eddie Coulter, could watch the centre-half in action, though he wasn't the only interested spectator. Park's average gate rose from twenty to 300. Their manager, Jude Lynch, was pleased but not surprised, "he's played eight games for us and has been outstanding". Eddie Coulter watched Tohill play, and score, for Park in a 3-1 Intermediate Cup win at Donegal Celtic in

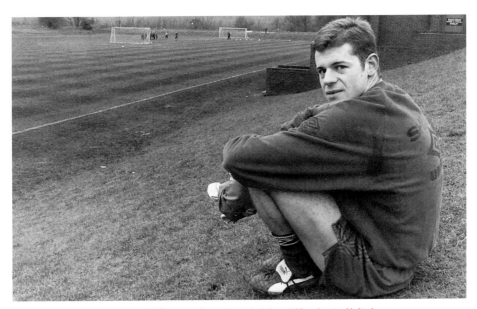

Anthony Tohill takes a break from training at Manchester United.

Belfast. "Anthony headed the third goal and put another one just over the bar. You could tell he was going to do something, because his height was causing problems for Celtic. I talked with him after the match and there is no doubt in my mind, he has a lot going for him. He's a good athlete, has good balance and is strong in the air, though in fairness he's a bit raw, which is of course to be expected". Coulter's report was glowing enough to earn Tohill a two-week cross-channel trial.

Kevin Moran moved successfully from gaelic football to full-time soccer, Niall Quinn was a hurler with Dublin minors, and young Pat McGibbon was already in the United Reserves after representing Armagh minors. "But they were all playing soccer before they went across the water", warned Coulter. "Even at reserve level, the pace over there is frightening". Tohill trained and mixed with the United players at The Cliff training ground, bumping into heroes such as Paul Ince, Roy Keane and Ryan Giggs. "They were okay, but Alex Ferguson was very friendly when he noticed me in the canteen. He came over and welcomed me. The Northern Ireland boys, Pat McGibbon and Colin Murdoch were great as well, especially considering I was supposed to be a threat to their positions". The Derry man didn't forget their generosity and returned a favour by fixing McGibbon with tickets for the Armagh-Derry Ulster SFC game in May.

Andrei Kanchelskis was on the same team for Tohill's first game, but apart from the five-million pound rated Ukranian, there was nothing glamorous about a midweek reserve game at Sunderland, in the snow. The conditions for his next match, an 'A' team game on the Saturday morning, were even worse. "It was a mud-bath and I was switched after twenty minutes to right-back, which was new to me. I was substituted before the end and I feel that game counted against me". Tohill's final chance to shine was for the reserves against Tranmere, before Alex Ferguson at Gigg Lane, Bury. Mark Hughes scored on his comeback from injury to give United the lead, and they eventually won 2-1. Tohill felt he did reasonably well, but he had to wait until the call came to go to the manager's office in the morning.

A statement was released for the media. "Anthony Tohill has done well but will be returning to Ireland. We will be monitoring his future career". Ferguson explained how age was against Tohill (23), how he hadn't played enough soccer and how United already had two 18-year-old centre-halves. But the United boss did advise Anthony to take up any other offers from English clubs, and he remained true to his word by ordering Eddie Coulter to "monitor his future career". That however, gave the scout a unique predicament, "How could I keep an eye on him when he wasn't playing soccer?!" Tohill returned home to find himself in the Derry team to play Down in the National League that Sunday, while three of the United back four that played with against Tranmere were named in the first-team to play Leeds. The Neville brothers and David May were promoted while Gary Pallister replaced Tohill! He had a few regrets, like not meeting Eric Cantona (in hiding) or Denis Irwin, and not getting a ticket for the derby game with Manchester City, but otherwise he remained philosophical and told himself he was lucky to have had such an experience.

The soccer "dream" died for a while after, as Tohill won his second NFL medal with Derry and concentrated on the Ulster SFC. However, the words of Pat McGibbon turned over in his mind: "I know all the coaches at Old Trafford respected Anthony's ability. Obviously, because he had taken soccer up at a later stage, some of the technical skills would have to be worked on, but they rated him very highly". When Tyrone ended Tohill's summer activity in June (apart from Swatragh), he was handed the ideal move to test his soccer skills once more. Derry City manager Felix Healy had shown interest before, inviting Tohill to play in a friendly against Lyngby when he came back from United (he didn't accept the invite), and watching the centre-half score a hat-trick against Churchill in Derry ("a header, a penalty, and a mis-kick!"). Healy heard about Derry's exit from the championship on his way home from holiday, and immediately arranged a meeting with Tohill, and representatives of Park and Derry City. The latter officials were a little taken aback when Anthony revealed that he had never been to the Brandywell, but an offer was put on the table. Tohill asked for a little time to consider the move, but knew in himself that he would "give it a go". Meantime, Healy phoned several times for any news. He knew Tohill's fitness was good and that he could help improve his control and touch. A day later, Derry City had a new player, though not before Tohill visited Mickey Moran to explain how gaelic football would still take priority.

At his first training session with Derry City, all the players gave the new man a warm welcome, though he was surprised when Frenchman Pascal Vaudequin greeted him with the question, "What happened to you against Tyrone?!" The Brandywell faithful soon noted the potential in the "gaelic man", not least for his kicking skills. Against St.Mirren in a pre-season friendly, Tohill landed goal-kicks well into the opposite half, and in Bulgaria he made his European debut as a stand-in goalkeeper when Tony O'Dowd was sent off against Lokomotiv Sofia. Late in that game, he came up for a corner, a la Peter Schmeichel, and got his head to the ball but failed to score. Adjusting to football in the fast lane will take time, especially with Derry's established back four, though Eddie Coulter is pleased to see Tohill on a soccer stage, so that he can now "keep an eye" on his progress. "It's a great move for the boy, and a necessary step to see how good he can become. I feel he could have been a superstar if he'd played soccer earlier, but even now, I think he could go on to play in the Premiership and maybe even for his country". The dream could yet become reality.

Anthony Tohill on his Derry City debut .

Always a great save!

"Not Bad For A Team With No Boots"

Crusaders - Irish League Champions 1994-95

Legendary Liverpool manager Bill Shankly said, "Football is not a matter of life and death. It's much more important than that". Crusaders manager Roy Walker is diametrically opposed to the famous Shankly statement, "Football is essentially a game, no more than that. The first and most important thing is faith and what we believe in, and for me, that's the Lord Jesus Christ. After that, it's family, work and friends, with football way down the list."

37-year-old Walker is articulate, confident, and successful, both in football and business. Manager of Crusaders since September 1989, he guided them to their first Irish League Championship in nineteen years. He's also a born-again Christian - saved at the age of 15, he rededicated himself in recent times. "I got down on my knees to God, acknowledged I was a sinner, and asked God into my life". During the championship run-in, Walker and four of his players, who are also born-again, attended gospel meetings where they talked openly about their football and their faith. Glenn Dunlop, Stephen Baxter, Glenn Hunter, and team captain Sid Burrows, spent the Friday night before Crusaders clinched the title, telling the audience that although football is important, their other beliefs are paramount.

Dunlop explained why he had turned down an offer from Partick Thistle, and others, to stay at Seaview. "I took a five-year break from the game, then played darts for Northern Ireland and drank the odd beer, but I became born again last January (1994) and my football career has literally taken off from there. I am hungrier, I feel fitter and have finally got a purpose to my life. At the start of the season I went to Alan Snoddy and apologised for any previous bad

Crusaders
Back, L-R: Roy McDonald (coach), Martin Murray, Glenn Hunter, Kevin McKeown, Gary Murray, Glenn Dunlop, Stephen Baxter, Aaron Callaghan, Stephen Bell (Management Committee), Stephen Stewart, Chris Morgan. Front: Jim Gardiner, Derek Carroll, Sid Burrows, Stephen Livingstone, Darren Moore.

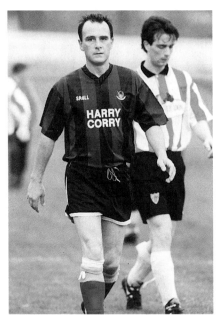

behaviour and told him I wanted to keep a clean slate. Money isn't important, I get enough kicks with Crusaders."

A few weeks later, the Gibson Cup, Walker, and the players, were special guests at The Cleft in Craigavon, one of Northern Ireland's top gospel meetings. Seven hundred people packed into the hall, with at least another fifty turned away. Roy Walker was asked how he reacted when the final whistle was blown at Ballymena. "When England won the World Cup in 1966, Alf Ramsey turned and walked down the tunnel. I did the same, and I went into the dressing-room and said a silent prayer of thanks. I said to God 'The glory goes to you'. That's my way of doing things, and it felt good".

Two Dublin Catholics were present at The Cleft, Martin Murray (above) and Liam Dunne, who also play for Crusaders. They were invited along for the purpose of recording a television feature, yet their presence was a reminder of another vital part of the success story at Seaview - the coming together of players from very different backgrounds. Who would have thought it would happen in Northern Ireland? Four born-again Christians and six Catholics on the one championship winning team! "We've done more for cross-border relationships than anyone. Our squad is the happiest and the friendliest in the league. We have Northern Protestants, Northern Catholics and Southern Catholics, and not a minute's bother between them. They get on great, they welcome new lads like Mick Deegan from Dublin into the fold, and they play together like they've known each other for life. It says a lot for the spirit in this team". Martin Murray, who pioneered the cross-border trend, agrees with Walker, "We accept one another's religions, that's the bottom line. We're all the same and we're just getting on with it. I see no barriers in football". There are more than fifty players from the Republic in the Irish League today. Ballyclare fielded as many as six in one game last season, and Linfield have abandoned their all-Protestant teams. One of their high-profile "Southern Stars" is Pat "Billy" Fenlon, "I was the first Dublin Catholic to play for the Blues in half a century. It wasn't easy at the start but when my wife and I travelled up to Lisburn to receive their Player of the Year Award, we were treated like royalty. It was magnificent".

Crusaders southern link is Tony O'Connell, who is also President of Bohemians. Four years ago, he began coming North to watch the Crues, at the invite of club sponsor Harry Corry, but he soon became more involved. "Harry Corry got the business side of the club sorted, and then sucked me in! They had no money and I knew who was available down here, and for the right price.

The men behind Crusaders, L-R: Tony O'Connell, Jim Semple (Chairman), Roy Walker, and Harry Corry (President).

Players were available cheaper than in Scotland or in the North. A player might have been valued at thirty-five grand up there, and only five thousand in the South". Martin Murray was an experienced campaigner who had left Dundalk, Peter Eccles came from Shamrock Rovers and Roddy Collins from Sligo Rovers, Robbie Lawlor had won the FAI Cup with UCD and was on his way back from two seasons out injured, Derek Carroll had been with Liverpool and Galway (O'Connell knew him since he was 12), Liam Dunne came North for eight weeks initially, after returning from St Johnstone, Aaron Callaghan had played 300 games in the England Second Division with the likes of Oldham and Huddersfield, but was released by Eoin Hand at Shelbourne, and Mick Deegan is a Dublin gaelic footballer! He hadn't played soccer seriously since winning the Junior Cup five years before with Tolka Rovers, but O'Connell knew his capabilites and when Crusaders were hit by suspensions in December, 30-year-old Deegan signed for a month. He scored at the Oval in his first game, and was offered a two-year contract within a month by Walker. "Mick came in as cover, but his box-to-box work-rate is amazing. He has a great engine".

Derek Carroll was voted Player of the Year by one of the Supporters Clubs; Dunne, Callaghan and Deegan hardly missed a game, and the manager singled out 36-year-old Martin Murray for special mention. "Kevin McKeown is my Player of the Year because he didn't have a bad game (he conceded 25 goals in 30 games and kept a record 14 clean sheets), but I describe Martin as the Rolls Royce of the team. He has brains, guile and vision, though they're all great players. To know them is to love them, they all have their own strengths and weaknesses, and there's none of them you wouldn't take home and put up for a weekend, that's for sure." "Everybody has just gelled so well", adds O'Connell, who taxies the Southern players along a well-worn path week-in, week-out. "They're all down-to-earth people playing for the enjoyment, while myself and Roy get on the best as well". Both men take turns at addressing the players before games, and their approach could not be different. "I like to do different things, such as asking for two minutes silence for the players to focus themselves, while Tony is all fire and full of racing parallels, like before the Ballymena game when he told them they had one more hurdle to jump!"

Walker pays tribute to the rest of his backroom team for the role they have played in the revival of a small, relatively poor club. "It's down to the coaches Billy Sinclair and Roy McDonald, to Bob McDonald who cleans the boots, Tom Gilmore, and even Madge who makes the tea. We've done it our way and that makes it even sweeter. I've signed players in the toilets at Seaview, because there isn't an office, but what we lack in finance, we make up for in spirit and determination. Besides, money in the game only breeds contempt. Other teams have higher wage bills than us, but what if a player on say 600 pounds a week has a bad game? Then, the others start saying that he isn't worth it. We won the league because of will-to-win, organisation, good players and because we have the best goalkeeper, not because of money. Other supporters tease us for being a poor club, but as I often say to the lads when we've done well, 'Not bad for a team with no boots'".

Crusaders went to the top of the league at the end of October, after beating Portadown 2-1. The critics said they didn't have the strength-in-depth to stay there, that they would have a bad January, that they would be hit with injuries and suspensions, and so on, but they were wrong. After losing to Ards on December 10, the Crues won eight games in-a-row and did not drop a point until March. They started by digging out four single-goal victories over Christmas and New Year, over Cliftonville, Ballyclare, Carrick and Coleraine. On January 14, they went sixteen points clear at the top after beating Newry 4-0 at Seaview, while Portadown and Glenavon both lost. Ronnie McFall and Nigel Best conceded the title, as Trevor Anderson had done a week earlier. In February and March, Crusaders protected their unbeaten away record by winning at Portadown, thanks to a 25-yarder from Martin Murray, and by drawing at Windsor Park 1-1, with a Liam Dunne goal. It was a record which would come under threat on the very last day of the season, at rivals Cliftonville. The Reds took a two-goal lead before Sid Burrows pulled one back coming up to half-time (with, incidentally, his 100th goal). "It was the only time all season that I lost my temper", recalls Walker. "I thumped the table and told them they were a disgrace, that they were league champions, and that not many teams have gone through a whole season without losing an

IRISH LEAGUE 1994-95	P	W	D	L	F	A	Pts
Crusaders	30	20	7	3	58	25	67
Glenavon	30	18	6	6	76	40	60
Portadown	30	15	5	10	59	41	50
Ards	30	15	5	10	55	42	50
Glentoran	30	14	8	8	53	41	50
Cliftonville	30	13	11	6	44	32	50
Coleraine	30	12	13	5	52	39	49
Linfield	30	11	11	8	48	34	44
Omagh	30	10	12	8	42	38	42
Distillery	30	12	6	12	45	47	42
Bangor	30	8	14	8	42	38	38
Ballymena	30	7	8	15	43	53	29
Carrick	30	7	7	16	46	75	28
Ballyclare	30	5	6	19	39	66	21
Newry	30	4	9	17	34	74	21
Larne	30	3	4	23	18	69	13

away game". Livingstone equalised just four minutes from time for a 2-2 draw.

On April Fools Day, Crusaders won 2-0 at Ballymena to win the league with four more games still to play. The goals came early in the game, from Stephen Baxter and Glenn Hunter (shown below), with the first leading to one of the manager's favourite moments of the whole season. "Big Stephen ran towards the dug-out after scoring and I held out my hand. He didn't slap it, he held it and said 'that one's for you'. He explained later that when I signed him from Distillery, I said I wanted 20 goals. That was his 21st".

The Crusaders team that day, only the third from the club to win the Irish League, was: McKeown, Carroll, McCartney, Dunlop, Callaghan, Murray, Deegan, Dunne, Baxter, G.Hunter, and Burrows. Subs: Livingstone and Stewart.

CRUSADERS GLORY SEASON

Month	Score	Venue	Opponent	Scorers
Sept	3-0	(h)	Ballyclare	G.Hunter 2, og
	6-2	(a)	Carrick	G.Hunter 2, K.Hunter 2, Lawlor, Dunne
Oct	3-3	(h)	Coleraine	Dunlop, G,Hunter, Lynch
	5-2	(a)	Newry	G.Hunter 2, Callaghan, Baxter, og
	2-1	(h)	Distillery	Dunne, G.Hunter
	1-1	(a)	Bangor	Dunne
	2-1	(h)	Portadown *	G.Hunter, Burrows
Nov	1-0	(h)	Linfield	McCartney
	1-0	(a)	Omagh	Baxter (& McKeown penalty save)
	3-1	(a)	Larne	Lawlor, Baxter, G.Hunter
	2-1	(h)	Ballymena	Baxter, Livingstone
Dec	0-0	(a)	Glenavon	
	1-2	(h)	Ards	G.Hunter
	2-0	(a)	Glentoran	Deegan, McCartney
	1-0	(h)	Cliftonville	Livingstone
	2-1	(a)	Ballyclare	Dunne, Burrows
Jan	1-0	(h)	Carrick	Baxter
	1-0	(a)	Coleraine	G.Hunter
	4-0	(h)	Newry	Livingstone 2, Baxter, G.Hunter
	3-0	(a)	Distillery	Livingstone, Baxter, G.Hunter
Feb	1-0	(a)	Portadown	Murray
Mar	1-1	(a)	Linfield	Dunne
	1-0	(h)	Bangor	Baxter
	1-1	(h)	Omagh	G.Hunter
Apr	2-0	(a)	Ballymena **	Baxter, G.Hunter
	0-0	(a)	Ards	
	1-3	(h)	Glenavon	Gardiner
	1-2	(h)	Glentoran	Murray
	2-2	(a)	Cliftonville	Burrows, Livingstone

* Crusaders went top of the league ** Crusaders won the league

Hat-Trick Man Glenn

At the start of the 1994-95 season, Glenn Ferguson achieved four hat-tricks in successive games, against Ballymena, Ballyclare, Crusaders, and Cliftonville. He grabbed another two hat-tricks in the first week of January, and finished the season on a total of 50 goals in 50 games. 27 came in the league, 22 in cups, and one for the Irish League against the League of Ireland. It was simply a magical year for the 25-year-old who arrived from Ards in 1990, though Stevie McBride pipped him for the Glenavon Player of the Year Award!

Ferguson became the first Glenavon player to reach 30 goals before the end of the year (he scored the winner against Portadown on Boxing Day), a feat even the great Jimmy Jones did not manage. Jones scored 74 goals in the 1956-57 season, including a post-war record of seven hat-tricks. He was the club's leading scorer from 1952-62, totalling 614 goals. At the end of the 1994-95 season, Ferguson had scored 154 goals in 236 outings.

TOP SCORERS

Glenn Ferguson	(Glenavon)	49
Garry Haylock	(Linfield)	39
Stephen McBride	(Glenavon)	31
Glenn Hunter	(Crusaders)	23
Stephen Baxter	(Crusaders)	22
Tom Cleland	(Distillery)	21
Justin McBride	(Glentoran)	21
Trevor Smith	(Glentoran)	21
Joey Cunningham	(Portadown)	19
Darren Erskine	(Ards)	19
Paul Cullen	(Ards)	18
Philip Mitchell	(Distillery)	16
Gary Peebles	(Linfield)	16
Ollie Ralph	(Newry Town)	16
Brian Robson	(Coleraine)	16
Tony Gorman	(Coleraine)	16
Sammy Johnston	(Glenavon)	15
Martin Russell	(Portadown)	15
Robert Casey	(Portadown)	14
Barry Patton	(Ballymena)	14
Pat Fenlon	(Linfield)	14
Dessie Gorman	(Linfield)	14
Iain Ferguson	(Portadown)	13
Ron Manley	(Cliftonville)	13
Barry McCreadie	(Omagh Town)	13
Sammy Shiels	(Carrick Rgrs)	13
Mickey Donnelly	(Cliftonville)	12
Peter Moran	(Ballyclare)	12

Glenn Ferguson.

Where the Trophies Went 1994-95

	Winners	Runners-up	Score in Final
Irish League	Crusaders	Glenavon	-
Irish Cup	Linfield	Carrick Rangers	3-1
Gold Cup	Glentoran	Crusaders	1-1, 3-0 on pens
Budweiser Cup	Portadown	Distillery	4-2
League Cup	Ards	Cliftonville	0-0, 2-0 on pens
Ulster Cup	Bangor	Linfield	2-1
Co. Antrim Shield	Linfield	Glenavon	4-0

"I don't know if I can field a team tonight", moaned Glentoran manager Tommy Cassidy before the Gold Cup Final against Crusaders, such were his injury and illness worries. Amazingly, Darren Parker came to the rescue. In the afternoon, he lay in hospital with suspected appendicitis, but when he realised it was a false alarm, he left his sick-bed and dashed to Windsor and won the Man of the Match Award! Scotsman Duncan Campbell scored on his debut and teenage goalkeeper Neil Armstrong saved two penalties in the shoot-out. It was the Glens first trophy in two years. Ronnie McFall was given a new five-year contract soon after Portadown won the Budweiser Cup. Distillery led 2-0 with only thirteen minutes to go, but the Ports scored four times in eight minutes, through Strain, Cunningham, Russell, and Doolin. It was their first trophy since the Budweiser in late 1992. Cliftonville missed all four of their penalties in the shoot-out with Ards for the League Cup. Paul Mooney and Darren Erskine were on target for Roy Coyle's team. In the Ulster Cup, Bangor beat Glenavon 3-2 after extra-time in the semi-finals, and Linfield by the same score in the final, thanks to two Mark Glendinning strikes and one from Marc Kenny on his return from serious injury. Linfield beat Glenavon 4-0 in the final of the County Antrim Shield with a hat-trick from Garry Haylock and one from Raymond Campbell. Cliftonville won the McEwans Lager Sixes at Dundonald Ice Bowl, beating Ballyclare 3-2 in the final.

Dermot O'Neill,
Guinness Player of the Month for August.

Trevor's Boyhood Dream Comes True

Irish Cup Final
Linfield 3   Carrick Rangers 1

Amid the post-match celebrations, Linfield supporters delighted in the style of their team's victory and in putting to rest the ghosts of 1976, but manager Trevor Anderson took great pleasure from leading the first Linfield side to retain the trophy since 1963. He's more aware than most of the tradition of the club, having been a supporter since the age of five. "My brother used to take me to games, and I saw most of the famous 1961 seven-trophy winning season. Although I was only eleven years of age, the quality of that team sticks with me, and that's what you constantly aim for. In 1979, when Linfield won four out of five trophies, the biggest disappointment was for the one we lost".

Anderson went on to maintain the club's high standards as a player on the 1980-86 championship winning team, before retiring becoming coach of the Youth Team. Then, in October 1992, his commitment to the Blues played a part in his promotion to manager of the first team. "You might say it was a surprise appointment, but they (the Board) had been watching me and obviously saw something. Linfield had been struggling for a few years, and they knew that I had played in a successful team here. At the time, I said I was happy to take over for four to six weeks, as long as I could improve things for the next manager coming along, and three years on, that's still the way I look at it. I enjoy the job, and when I do leave, there'll be no regrets. I'll still be up in the Stand cheering them on".

Gorilla's in the mist?!   Linfield fans celebrate the Irish Cup Win.

Trevor Anderson in the Linfield dug-out, flanked by Lindsay McKeown (left) and Terry Hayes.

Linfield's defeat of Carrick Rangers brought Anderson's trophy haul to seven, and his reward of bringing back the good times was a new two-year contract. One reason for his success is that he has spent wisely, on Dessie Gorman, Pat Fenlon, Garry Haylock, Raymond Campbell, and Gary Peebles. All are big names, though Anderson is quick to point out that most of them were not big names before they came to Linfield. The manager was also quick to bring Southern Catholics to a club infamous for it's scarcity of players from that religion, though he insists the move was not deliberate for that reason. "All I wanted was Linfield back at the top, and I needed quality players who were prepared to die on the pitch for this club". Gorman, formerly with Derry City, was an instant hit with the Windsor fans who dubbed him the "Dundalk Hawk", while the slight figure of Pat Fenlon soon became a valued member of the Linfield midfield. After scoring in the 1994 Irish Cup Final, his team-mates chanted, "There's only one Billy Fenlon!"

Anderson keeps the necessary managerial distance from his players, normally letting his assistant Lindsay McKeown do the "day-to-day" work at close-quarters, but that's not to say the boss is aloof. "I worked under Terry Neill, Billy Bingham, Tommy Docherty, Danny Blanchflower, and Roy Coyle, yet John Barnwell at Peterborough stands out because he was the first who used man-management. He taught me to care and talk to each individual, to make them feel good. You can talk as a team but each individual is important and has to know what you want from him. Success isn't for me, it's for the players, and they have different qualities, but you have to stick with your philosophy - work hard and enjoy".

The manager's favourite memory of the Irish Cup triumph came in their 5th Round defeat of Crusaders, who were already league champions-elect. The

Crues were hit by suspensions when the tie, like all sixteen in the Round, was historically washed out on the Saturday, but Linfield also had to name a makeshift team, with Noel Bailie in midfield. Garry Haylock scored both goals in the 2-0 win. Elsewhere, Alan Ewing's goal for Coleraine eliminated Glentoran, and David McCallan made a brief but brilliant 30-minute appearance for Bangor in their 5-1 rout of Distillery. Returning from injury, he scored three times before snapping a cruciate ligament and being ruled out of football for at least a year. The following evening, McCallan explained to television viewers that his career was in the balance as five thousand pounds was needed for a private operation. Fortunately, Barney Eastwood saw the interview and came to the rescue of his nearest team, which was managed by Steve Collins' brother Roddy.

Bangor had played in the last two finals and looked good for another cup run when Collins scored twice to beat Newry in the 6th Round. Niall Currie also saved a penalty in the 2-1 replay win, while Portadown took two games to overcome Coleraine, and Stevie McBride's double saw Glenavon through at Mourneview after they had drawn at Omagh. Dungannon led Linfield after 14 minutes, 2-1, but by half-time the Blues were 4-2 in front with superb long-distance strikes by Pat Fenlon and Stephen Beatty.

More Junior opposition awaited Linfield in the quarter-finals, in the form of Loughgall. "We didn't want them because we knew they would be well-organised, would defend in numbers, and would treat it as their cup final. That's exactly what happened, and they could have won either game". Gary Henderson stunned Windsor Park with his equaliser in the one-all draw, while the second game went to extra-time before Linfield scrambled a winner from a corner. Meanwhile, Carrick Rangers, 50/1 with the bookies at the start of the competition, surprised Bangor at Taylor's Avenue to reach the semi-finals for the first time in eleven years. Geoff Ferris and Dean Gordon scored while manager Colin Crawford watched from the Stand as he served a six-match touchline ban after

IRISH CUP RESULTS

5TH ROUND

Ards	3-1	Chimney Corner	
Ballyclare	2-3	Glenavon	
Omagh Town	0-0	Ballymena	(R:1-0)
Banbridge	7-0	Dunmurry Rec	
Carrick Rgrs	2-0	Ballinamallard	
Glentoran	1-1	Coleraine	(R:1-2)
Crewe Utd	0-2	Cliftonville	
Distillery	1-5	Bangor	
Dundela	3-1	Crumlin	
Dungannon	1-0	Cookstown Utd	
Limavady Utd	1-2	Dungiven	
Linfield	2-0	Crusaders	
Loughgall	2-1	Kilmore Rec	
Brantwood	2-2	Moyola Park	(R:3-2)
Newry Town	3-0	Larne	
Portadown	4-0	Donegal Celtic	

6TH ROUND

Ards	4-1	Brantwood	
Newry Town	1-1	Bangor	(R:1-2)
Carrick Rgrs	2-1	Dundela	
Cliftonville	4-0	Banbridge Town	
Portadown	0-0	Coleraine	(R:3-1)
Dungannon	3-5	Linfield	
Omagh Town	1-1	Glenavon	(R: 1-3)
Loughgall	2-1	Dungiven	

QUARTER-FINALS

Ards	3-2	Glenavon	
Portadown	1-1	Cliftonville	(R:1-0)
Carrick Rgrs	2-1	Bangor	
Linfield	1-1	Loughall	(R: 1-0)

SEMI-FINALS

Linfield	0-0	Ards	(R:2-1)
Carrick Rgrs	1-0	Portadown	

FINAL

Linfield	3-1	Carrick Rgrs

First page: **Wayne McCullough and Yasuei Yakushiji exchange punches during their WBC bantamweight title bout in Nagoya, Japan.**

Opposite page: **World Cup action**
Top: **Jonah Lomu looks for support as he is tackled by Eric Elwood in New Zealand's victory over Ireland;**
Bottom: **Malone's Denis McBride races through the Welsh defence to score a try for Ireland.**

Above: **Ballymena and Ireland's Davy Tweed gets a helping hand from Peter Clohessy (left) and Nick Popplewell to outjump Oliver Merle of France at Lansdowne Road.**

Above: **Action from Dungannon's victory over Instonians in the First Trust Senior Cup at Ravenhill.**

Below: **Pegasus celebrate Irish Senior Cup success. Back, L-R: Glynis Taylor (Coach), Erika Henry, Hilda Beamish, Michelle Rainey, Doreen Hood, Arlene Thompson, Donna Hawthorne, Heather McCullough, Joanne Campbell. Front: Kim Mills, Kathy Mitchell, Pamela Magill, Claire McMahon, Jeanette Turner (with cup), Nadine Long, Laura Brown, Claire Samways.**

Above: Brad Bevan prepares to climb Shipquay Street on his way to winning the Derry Triathlon.
Below: Ulsterman David Feherty is first to congratulate his friend and new Irish Open Champion Sam Torrance.

Above: Michael Hughes smothered by appreciative team-mates after his stunning free-kick goal for Northern Ireland in Portugal in the European Championhip.

Below: Action from the Bank of Ireland Schools Senior Cup Final at the Brandywell. Philip Deehan (St Peters) jumps above St Columbs attackers to clear his lines.

Above: Celebration time at Seaview. Crusaders captain Sid Burrows raises the Gibson Cup while team-mates Liam Dunne, Martin Murray, Robbie Lawlor, Glenn Hunter, Jim Gardiner, and Glenn Dunlop (both partially hidden) take the applause.

Below: Linfield's Irish Cup winners. Back, L-R: Ian McCoosh, Jake Gallagher, Paul McGee, Wes Lamont, Alan Dornan, Gary Eccles (Boot boy), Pat Fenlon (front), Stephen Beatty, John Easton, Terry Hayes (Physio), Raymond Campbell, Jeff Spiers, Andy Kerr (Team att), Philip Knell, Trevor Anderson. Front: Garry Haylock, Andy Caldwell, Noel Bailie, Davy Tibbs (Team att), Dessie Gorman, Gary Peebles, Kenny McKaigue (Trainer).

Following page: A profile of Wayne McCullough, by Irish News photographer Hugh Russell.

being sent off in the 5th Round. The same fate awaited Roy Coyle, banished from the dug-out for the rest of the season after being reported for kicking Glenavon's Ally Mauchlen in a clash towards the end of Ards 3-2 win. Two goals from Paul Cullen saw them through.

Cliftonville and Portadown were fined £1500 and warned by the IFA Senior Clubs Committee that their grounds could be closed down if there was a repeat of the crowd violence at both of their games. "Shamrock's Day of Shame" (Sunday Life), and "Game in the Gutter" (Irish News), were the headlines as Mickey Donnelly's last-minute equaliser was followed by fighting between supporters and the throwing of bricks. After the replay, there were reports of damage to property caused by so-called fans coming from Solitude. Former Rangers and Scotland striker Iain Ferguson scored the only goal for Portadown.

"A non-event", was how Trevor Anderson described Linfield's scoreless draw with Ards in their semi-final at the Oval. Paul Kee's penalty save from Garry Haylock provided the only excitement, though the Ards keeper was beaten by the modest Pat Fenlon in the replay, "If I'd hit it straight he'd probably have saved it!" Haylock added a second before Ray Morrison made for a jittery final twenty minutes for the Blues. Portadown were stunned by Carrick in the other semi, where Geoff Ferris converted a half-chance and Paul Miskelly, the smallest keeper in the league at 5'9, played the game of his life. Observers counted fourteen missed chances by the Reds.

Inevitably, much of the talk before the final centred on Carrick's famous cup defeat of Linfield in 1976, when they were still a Junior club, but Trevor Anderson urged his team before the game to ensure history would not repeat itself, "No way must it happen again". His players responded in style, as Gorman made a brilliant run down the right and sent a pin-point cross for Haylock to head into the corner of the net, though he confessed afterwards that the "Goal of the Season" was a mistake. "I was trying to place it, but not in the left corner where it ended up. I went for the right, but it spun off to the opposite side!" Carrick fought back and deserved their equaliser when Anthony Gilmore found the top corner from a free-kick. On 56 minutes, another free-kick led to Linfield's second goal. Noel Bailie, recalled after injury for the final, floated the ball towards Peebles who knocked down for Haylock to score his 39th of the season. "It was something we tried for two minutes in training on the Thursday before", revealed the manager. Substitute Ian McCoosh was sent in to sit in front of the back four, but he popped up in the Carrick box to score the insurance goal five minutes from time. Trevor Anderson leapt from the dug-out with fists clenched and a wide grin ... his beloved Blues were champions once more.

Teams in Final

LINFIELD: Lamont, Dornan(c), Easton, Peebles, Spiers, Beattie, Campbell, Gorman, Haylock, Fenlon, Bailie. Subs: Knell, McCoosh, Caldwell.

CARRICK: Miskelly, Wilson, Gilmore, Muldoon, Gordon, Coulter, Kirk, McDermott, Donaghy, Ferris, McAuley. Subs: Crawford, Doherty.

Note: Linfield started with the same team as in the 1994 final.

Garry Haylock, taking the applause of the Linfield fans (above) after scoring the first goal, and (below) receiving a pat on the back from Trevor Anderson after the match.

Goalscoring hero Garry Haylock got a pat on the back from Trevor Anderson but relations turned sour soon afterwards when the striker moved to Portadown ... for nothing. Owing to a contractual technicality, the Belfast club missed out on an estimated £70,000, and they were disappointed that the striker, who had contributed 76 goals in two seasons since arriving from Shelbourne, should have chosen to join a rival team. Anderson received news of the transfer in a brief telephone call from the player. "The conversation lasted 30 seconds and he did all the talking. It would not have mattered what we offered him. He was bound for Portadown and that's been obvious since last January". Linfield Chairman David Campbell commented, "I've never dealt with a more mercenary player - he wanted the sun, the moon and the stars", but Haylock hit back, saying his move was not just down to money, that he wanted a new challenge and that Portadown offered "certain conditions and clauses that Linfield weren't prepared to offer. Admittedly that helped make up my mind".

Joy and Dismay

European Championship Group Six

"When you measure the way we played in the home defeat by Latvia against how we performed against the top teams in Vienna, Dublin, and Oporto, it makes you wonder what goes on sometimes". Northern Ireland manager Bryan Hamilton was speaking after September's draw in Portugal, his emotions mixed somewhere between joy at the superb result and dismay at what might have been. "We were one up against Latvia at Windsor Park and should've won. We would then have been really well-placed to go through, and with taking a point in Portugal, we would have been level with the Republic and just behind Austria with two games to go. And, we have Austria to come at home!"

Put simply, Northern Ireland have been very good or very bad in Group Six, with little in between. Considering the team is young and inexperienced, it's away record has been outstanding, but at home their limitations have been cruelly exposed. Early in the campaign, the impressive Portugese should have won by more than 2-1 when they came to Belfast, when their super skills and speed going forward showing up a lack of pace in the centre of Hamilton's defence. Yet, in their next game in Vienna, Keith Gillespie volleyed a wonder goal and Philip Gray added another in a 2-1 victory. Ards goalkeeper Paul Kee made several fine saves while Alan McDonald played a captain's part. He had missed the Portugal game and would now, crucially, miss the clash with the Republic of Ireland after being booked against Austria.

"Lambs to the Slaughter", exclaimed the Newsletter after a four-goal drubbing in Belfast. Aldridge, Keane, Sheridan, and Townsend helped themselves as Jack Charlton's boys won for the first time at Windsor Park and looked bound for the finals in England. They had won their first three games by a distance, 3-

International Player of the Year Iain Dowie with Bryan Hamilton (left) and Michael Ryan, Guinness NI.

0, 4-0, and 4-0, but the first chink in their armour was revealed by the team they had just steam-rolled ... Northern Ireland. At Lansdowne Road in March, Niall Quinn settled the Republic with a goal early in the second-half, but when Paul McGrath played a sloppy ball out of defence, Keith Gillespie darted down the right and delivered a perfect cross for Man of the Match Iain Dowie to power a header past Alan Kelly. Once again, McDonald had bolstered the rearguard, helped by the presence in front of the back four of Colin Hill.

Morrow, Magilton, Taggart, and Michael O'Neill, all withdrew from the trip to Latvia, but the door opened for Neil Lennon, George O'Boyle, Barry Hunter, and Kevin Horlock. The latter two made their debuts in a 1-0 win before a crowd of one thousand, the goal coming from a Dowie penalty. Two defeats on a Summer tour, by Canada (2-1) and Chile (2-0), were followed by the Latvia disaster. Pat McGibbon and Gerard McMahon were selected after impressing in Canada, with Gillespie left on the bench, but the manager's criticism was directed at his defence. McDonald, winning his 50th cap, could not prevent his country's third successive home defeat.

GROUP SIX RESULTS

1994

N.Ireland	4-1	Liechtenstein
Latvia	0-3	Rep. of Ireland
N.Ireland	1-2	Portugal
Liechtenstein	0-4	Austria
Latvia	1-3	Portugal
Austria	1-2	N.Ireland
Rep. of Ireland	4-0	Liechtenstein
Portugal	1-0	Austria
Liechtenstein	0-1	Latvia
N.Ireland	0-4	Rep. of Ireland
Portugal	8-0	Liechtenstein

1995

Rep. of Ireland	1-1	N.Ireland
Austria	5-0	Latvia
Latvia	0-1	N.Ireland
Rep. of Ireland	1-0	Portugal
Austria	7-0	Liechtenstein
Portugal	3-2	Latvia
Liechtenstein	0-0	Rep. of Ireland
N.Ireland	1-2	Latvia
Rep. of Ireland	1-3	Austria
Liechtenstein	0-7	Portugal
Latvia	3-2	Austria
Portugal	1-1	N.Ireland
Austria	3-1	Rep. of Ireland
Latvia	3-2	Liechtenstein
Liechtenstein	0-4	N.Ireland
Rep. of Ireland	2-1	Latvia
Austria	1-1	Portugal
N.Ireland	Nov 15	Austria
Portugal	"	Rep. of Ireland

A makeshift team went to Portugal in September to face the group leaders, and a partisan fifty thousand people were poised to celebrate qualification for the finals. McDonald and Taggart were absent, goalkeeper Alan Fettis had only played two minutes in the Hull City first team because of a contract dispute, Pat McGibbon and Steve Morrow had not featured for their respective first teams, and Hill, Hunter, Lennon, and Dowie were all playing in the lower divisions. Domingos broke the Northern Ireland resistance just after half-time, but a screaming (though deflected) free-kick from Michael Hughes sailed into the net after 66 minutes. Some assured net-minding by Fettis kept out Domingos and Rui Costa, to postpone the party.

Northern Ireland began the year in 45th place in the FIFA ratings and dropped to 52nd by May, the lowest of the home countries, but there have been encouraging signs over the past twelve months. Bryan Hamilton has been forced to introduce players before he may have liked, but their displays have heartened the manager who can look to build his team around other young, established players like Taggart, Morrow, Gillespie, Hughes, Magilton, and

Lomas. Perhaps a few under-21 internationals would help the process along, as suggested by Hamilton and supported by Gerry Taggart. "All the other countries in our group compete at under-21 level and I feel it definitely helps players coming out of youth teams. As it is, the likes of Gillespie, McMahon and Lomas, have been drafted in to win full caps without any real international experience". Northern Ireland did however play a B international this year against Scotland, in which Gerard McMahon stood out. Bryan Hamilton is also willing to strengthen his squad with players who qualify under international rules, such as goalkeeper Trevor Wood. Walsall boss Chris Nicholl discovered that the Channel Islander could declare for any of the home countries and Wood was called up for the game in Dublin in March, despite having no Ulster connections whatsover. He made his debut as a substitute in the 4-0 win in Liechtenstein.

19-year-old Keith Gillespie joined the million-pound club when he signed for Newcastle United on January 9th as part of the exchange which took Andy Cole to Manchester United. Kevin Keegan and Alex Ferguson agreed Cole was worth seven million and Gillespie one million, hence Manchester handed over six million, yet the Northern Ireland's performances have increased his market value substantially. His first Tyneside goals were scored against Manchester City in the FA Cup, on the day after his 20th birthday, and his contract runs until the end of the 1997-98 season.

Keith Gillespie,
Newcastle United and Northern Ireland.

1995 Moves by Northern Ireland Players

	From	To	Fee	Date
Keith Gillespie	Man.Utd	Newcastle	£1,000,000	Jan, 95
Iain Dowie	Southampton	C.Palace	£500,000	Jan, 95
Kingsley Black	Notts.Forest	Sheff.Utd	Loan	Mar, 95
Anton Rogan	Oxford Utd	Millwall	Free	July,95
Neil Lennon	Crewe Alex.	Reading	£350,000	July, 95
Gerry Taggart	Barnsley	Bolton	£1,500,000	Aug, 95
Darren Patterson	C.Palace	Luton	£230,000	Aug, 95
Iain Dowie	C.Palace	West Ham	£475,000	Sep, 95
Michael Hughes	Strasbourg	West Ham	Loan	Oct, 95
Kingsley Black	Notts. Forest	Millwall	Loan	Oct, 95

Support Northern Ireland

An Open Letter from Jim Boyce,
new President of the Irish Football Association

"Bryan Hamilton visited Cliftonville Football Club in March, before the European Championship game with the Republic in Dublin. He met some kids and was busily signing autographs when one youngster exclaimed, 'I hope Jack's boys beat you'. Bryan asked the lad where he was from, and when he pointed to the Oldpark Road, the international manager explained that as he had been born in Northern Ireland, then surely he should be supporting his home team. The boy looked at him and replied, "I never thought of it like that".

This is not an isolated case, for I realise and understand why many Ulster people choose to go to Lansdowne Road rather than Windsor Park. I cannot condone the jeering by a minority of so-called Northern Ireland supporters of some players in the past, or the antagonistic feelings evident in some sections of our support at the World Cup game with the Republic in November, 1993. However, my earnest wish is to for the many people, who for whatever reason have stayed away, to come along and support the country of their birthright, and for Windsor Park to be completely filled once again for international matches. Politics should have no place in sport and no-one is more sickened by sectarianism at football games than I am. Northern Ireland teams have always been very mixed, at all levels, and every player wearing the shirt of the country in which they were born gives their all, irrespective of class or creed.

Northern Ireland soccer, especially at local level, has survived 25 years of trauma, albeit with incidents of a sectarian nature bringing clubs and the game into disrepute on occasions. We must encourage all supporters to turn away from sectarianism, and to go along and support their local teams in a proper manner, and above all, to support the many hard-working officials who try to ensure their teams are successful by signing players because of their ability, not their religion.

Everyone in life has a dream. My dream is that during my term as President of the IFA, that sectarianism will become a thing of the past, especially where sport is concerned, and that Windsor Park will be bursting at the seams, hopefully to see Northern Ireland qualify for the finals of the World Cup in France in 1998.

The Best I've Played With …

by Trevor Anderson, Felix Healy, and Roy Walker

Pat Jennings
(N.Ireland)

Bertie Vogts	**Alan Hansen**	**Bobby Moore**	**Terry Cooper**
(W.Germany)	(Liverpool/Scotland)	(West Ham/England)	(Leeds/England)
Colin Bell	**Bobby Charlton**	**Johann Cruyff**	**George Best**
(Man.City/England)	(Man.Utd/England)	(Holland)	(Man. Utd/N.Ireland)
	Kenny Dalglish	**Denis Law**	
	(Celtic/Scotland)	(Man. Utd/Scotland)	

"The three best players ever are Pele, Johan Cruyff and George Best. Therefore, I feel fortunate enough to have played against the Dutch master and with Bestie in the same game. Northern Ireland drew 2-2 with Holland and our manager, Danny Blanchflower, made me Man of the Match, but I wasn't a tenth of their class. Cruyff was European Player of the Year and did it in the World Cup, while George and I were at Manchester United together for a couple of years. He was my idol before I arrived and was suspended soon afterwards, but I recall him putting on an exhibition in a gym, nutmegging and scoring goals with ease. Even on international nights, George could beat five players on one of his runs. Why should he pass to lesser players when he could go it himself? I was amazed one night in Portugal when he went past five men and passed to me. I didn't know what he was going to do next, and neither did defenders.

"All the players I have picked were special, but they were/are also nice people. I roomed with Bestie and he is a lovely guy, despite all the bad press. Bobby Moore was a gentleman and always had time if he met you off the field, while Denis Law could make you laugh at the worst moments. On my United debut, as a substitute in a friendly in Dublin, I moved towards the near post to meet a cross from Willie Morgan, only for the "Law man" to push me out of the way and sidefoot the ball into the net! He was grease lightning. In goals, Big Pat was just awesome, in every way. He welcomed me on my N. Ireland debut in 1972 and was always a tower of strength, a big character and a superb goalkeeper.

"Alan Hansen looked elegant in his sweeper role, quick and good at using the ball, but believe me, he could tackle as well. In a youth game against Scotland, he went through me with his first tackle, he was as hard as nails! Bertie Vogts was also hard and physical, but could play a bit. He was inspirational for West Germany when they beat us 5-0 in '77, and is now their manager. Terry Cooper was a fine attacking left-back, though I'll never forget the night at Elland Road when I scored the winner to relegate Leeds.

"In midfield, Colin Bell had everything - a terrific engine, he could hit 40-yard passes and could score goals. Bobby Charlton, a man with great presence, retired at the end of my first year at United, but Kenny Dalglish was definitely a contemporary of mine as he was born the day after me! He had good feet, could hold onto a ball and play it through, or he could race onto through-balls. My five substitutes are Peter Shilton, Eusebio, Alan Ball, Paul Madeley for his versatility, and Johnny Giles, a great passer of the ball".

FELIX HEALY'S INTERNATIONAL SELECT

		Pat Jennings	
		(N.Ireland)	
Danny McGrain	**Paul McGrath**	**David O'Leary**	**Mal Donaghy**
(Celtic/Scotland)	(Aston Villa)	(Arsenal)	(N.Ireland)
Herbert Prohaska	**Ricky Villa**	**Norman Whiteside**	**John Robertson**
(Austria)	(Spurs)	(N.Ireland)	(Scotland)
	Kenny Dalglish	**Ian Rush**	
	(Celtic/Scotland)	(Wales)	

"What can you say about Pat Jennings? He was simply the best goalkeeper in the world. My full-backs are similar in that they rarely played a bad match. Mal Donaghy was Mr. Consistent, a very good athlete, though players who played with Mal felt he should have gone to Manchester United earlier. At centre-half, I have arguably the best two centre-halves around in the last number of years. I played against O'Leary when Arsenal came to the Brandywell and against McGrath when he was at Shelbourne.

"On one of my international appearances, Prohaska (now the Austrian coach) tore us apart in Vienna in a European Championship qualifier after the World Cup in 1982. He was quite young at the time and went on to take over the mantle of Hans Krankl. Ricky Villa was possibly the most impressive of all my opponents down the years. Coleraine played Spurs in Europe and in the second game, at White Hart Lane, his all-round game was brilliant. People said he was lazy, but that was nonsense. He had everything. He actually nutmegged me, and later I did the same to him! We afforded one another a smile. Norman Whiteside was a brilliant finisher. I've never seen anyone hit the corner of the net like him, like the famous FA Cup winner for United against Everton in 1985, and a volley against Arsenal in the semi-final the same year. Both times, the ball went into the corner of the net. At the age of 21, Norman moved back from centre-forward to midfield, and did well there too. He wanted to compete and win, and he never gave the ball away. I played against John Robertson in a Scotland-N.Ireland game, when he was at his peak. For those 2/3 years he was as good as there was, he could really play and crossed some great balls, like the cross for the winner by Trevor Francis in the European Cup final.

"I first came across Kenny Dalglish a long time ago, when I was at Sligo and Celtic beat us 6-1. Bobby Lennox scored four times and I got our goal by chipping Peter Latchford, brother of Bob (Everton and England). Dalglish played midfield that night and went on the become as complete a player as you get. He had everything and played with his brain, not his legs. Ian Rush was lightning and a brilliant finisher, though in my opinion, he was never the same player after Dalglish left".

George Dunlop
(Linfield)

Alan Fraser	Peter Rafferty	Lindsay McKeown	Noel Bailie
(Linfield)	(Linfield)	(Linfield)	(Linfield)
Johnny Jameson	Ivan Murray	Jim Cleary	Warren Feeney
(Glentoran)	(Coleraine)	(Glentoran)	(Linfield)
	Felix Healy	Martin McGaughey	
	(Coleraine)	(Linfield)	

"I make no excuses for picking seven Linfield men! They were the best team when I returned at the start of the eighties, and won nine out of ten league championships between 1978-87, while Alan Fraser and Noel Bailie were/are excellent players from different eras. I remember noting Noel's unbelievable potential when I saw him with the Swifts and I think he should be in the Northern Ireland team. They could do with his pace in the centre of the defence, as sweeper, though I have him at left-back.

"Peter Rafferty was the character of the Irish League, known as the 'Bald Eagle' or 'The Dome', and also a solid defender with loads of skill. He scored an awful lot of goals and some say Linfield have never replaced him. Another bubbly character and my current assistant is Lindsay McKeown. He doesn't mind me saying he lacked pace, because it's true, but he could read the game and pass the ball well when he moved upfield. I remember Alan Fraser excelling in a game against Manchester City in the late sixties; he was unlucky not to go across the water.

"Johnny Jameson moved from the Blues to the Oval where he scored goals and made them, such was his speed and crossing ability. Also in midfield, Jim Cleary had one of the sweetest left feet the Irish League has ever seen. He was always dangerous, and was still a great player when he retired at the age of 33. I never blame players for quitting early, they know themselves and it's important in this game never to cheat anyone. Ivan Murray would have been a good partner for Cleary, skilful and a hard man who knew how to tackle, while Warren Feeney consistently and accurately crossed balls onto the Bald Eagle's forehead. He too had a sweet left foot.

"Felix Healy was a terror for Linfield, and more dangerous up front than in midfield, in my opinion. He could beat people, score goals, and play as a target man. Martin "Buckets" McGaughey would have been the perfect foil for Healy, known for his outstanding goal-scoring, but also a tremendous worker outside the box".

Note: Trevor Anderson played for Portadown, Manchester United, Swindon, Peterborough, Linfield, and Northern Ireland. In his 22 international appearances, between 1973-79, he scored four times, including two against Cyprus at Craven Cottage, one against Scotland in a 2-1 victory at Hampden, and one in a 2-1 defeat of Denmark in Belfast. He has won league and cup medals with Linfield, as player and manager.

Kevin McKeown
(Crusaders)

Billy McKeag	**Peter Rafferty**	**Glenn Dunlop**	**Nigel Worthington**
(Glentoran)	(Linfield)	(Crusaders)	(Ballymena)
Sid Burrows	**Billy Humphries**	**Felix Healy**	**Robbie Dennison**
(Crusaders)	(Ards)	(Coleraine)	(Glenavon)
	Billy Hamilton	**Jimmy Martin**	
	(Linfield)	(Linfield)	

"When Scotland manager Craig Brown enquired about Kevin McKeown, I told him that Kevin's record is the best in the league, that he is a consummate professional, and that he should come and have a look for himself. I've not worked with a goalkeeper who trains harder than Kevin, and he's a joker, great in the dressing-room but even better out on the pitch. He fully deserved his Scotland B call-up in October.

"Another character is Peter Rafferty. I played sweeper behind him for a season at Ards and got about two kicks of the ball in every game, such was the big man's heading ability and will-to-win. John Flanagan and Eric Bowyer were also fine defenders, but my current centre-half, Glenn Dunlop, has it all. He's got pace, good control, and is naturally left-sided, which helps the balance. My full-backs are from different eras - tough-tackling Billy McKeag who got up and down the line very well, and Nigel Worthington who won an Irish Cup medal with Ballymena, and stood out as as tenacious left-back with plenty of energy and good distribution.

"Billy Humphries must be in his late fifties now, but is still lean and mean, as he was in his playing career. He was real dynamo, working from box to box, scoring goals and as stylish a player as you're likely to see. He played for his country 17 times, though I feel he got better as he got older and played some of his best football as player-manager of Ards. One of the very best I've played with, he used to tell me where he wanted the ball. I had some battles with Felix Healy in my time - he was strong, had two good feet, a ferocious shot, and could score goals from midfield. I always strive to pick a team with balance, so I have two wide-men in Sid Burrows and Robbie Dennison. Sid is a great professional, good from set-pieces and with boundless energy, while Dennison gave Glenavon width. He spent so much time out on the line that he could end a match with a white chalk mark down his back! A bit like Ginola at Newcastle, he likes to make space on the left and cut inside before having a crack with his right foot.

"Up front, the 'Little and Large Show' with Jimmy Martin and Billy Hamilton, would fetch 80 goals a season. Jimmy wasn't tall but a natural finisher, never booked, and good in the air, just like big Billy who was terribly hard to play against. He could take a ball down and lay it off without you even seeing it. All in all, a team of natural athletes, good talkers, organisers, matchwinners, and internationals, bar Jimmy Martin".

Jim Platt
(Coleraine)

Pascal Vaudequin	Mick Neville	David Pugh	Kevin Brady
(Derry City)	(Derry City)	(Sligo)	(Derry City)
Pat Mullan	Kevin McCool	Paul Doolin	Kevin Mahon
(Coleraine)	(Sligo)	(Derry City)	(Derry/Coleraine)
	Des Dickson	Liam Coyle	
	(Coleraine)	(Derry City)	

"Jim Platt was unfortunate to be around at the same time as Pat Jennings, as he was as good a goalkeeper as I played with in Ireland, though I would also mention Tim Dalton. Pascal Vaudequin has been the best full-back, in the attacking sense, in Irish football for some time. Teams actually plan before games how to stop him attacking. Kevin Brady is the best defensive full-back for some time - nobody goes past him. A super athlete and a great professional.

"Mick Neville was like Mal Donaghy in that he never had a bad game, and was known as a sweeper but could play other positions. David Pugh was the Mick Neville of his time, in the 60s/70s with Sligo - a tower of a man from whom team-mates drew strength. I was pleased to meet him at the cup final this year. Unlike me, he didn't give managers any problems! At midfield, Pat Mullan always did the simple thing and never stopped running. I remember one night at the Oval when Jim Cleary became sick looking at him. Kevin McCool was a Derryman who had a spell with Celtic when he was about 19, but came home to Sligo. Soon afterwards, Celtic came over to play Sligo and after the game Kenny Dalglish told Kevin, "You shouldn't be here, you should be with us", but he stayed at home and went on to play for Finn Harps - a terrible waste of talent. Paul Doolin is just a "dog", as christened by Jim McLaughlin. If you want to win, you get Dooler. If you need an important goal, get Dooler. Whatever it takes, when you're in the trenches, he's the man. I played with Kevin "Badger" Mahon when we were kids at Long Tower Boys Club and it's probably fair to say that neither of us made the best of what we had. He was the "George Best", you gave him the ball and he was away. Great ball control. He had offers to go professional, but like me, he waited too long and never took the game seriously enough. Perhaps we suffered from there being no Derry City. Up front, Des Dickson had a frightening change of pace over 5-10 yards. He wasn't very tall but had two good feet and if there's a better finisher, I haven't seen him. Liam Coyle is one of the few players I felt on the same wavelength with, a unique talent today because he plays with his brain, not his legs, like Dalglish did. He and Dickson would have been like Dalglish and Rush. Liam has touch, awareness and vision, aligned with anticipation. I don't think we've seen the best of him yet, but we will. He's working harder, will become more consistent and will have more control over games. On my subs bench, I'd like to have Tony Fegan, Ricky Wade, Ray McCoy and Roy McCreadie".

Note: Felix Healy won four Northern Ireland caps, all in 1982, against Scotland, Wales, Honduras, and Austria. He played for Sligo Rovers, Distillery, Finn Harps, Port Vale, Coleraine (twice), and Derry City.

139

WILKINSON SWORD

THE NAME ON THE WORLD'S FINEST BLADES

Sponsors of:

• The League Cup •

• The Irish League 'B' Division •

• The George Wilson Cup •

WILKINSON SWORD

THE NAME IN IRISH LEAGUE FOOTBALL

Mid-Ulster Has The Edge

Wilkinson Sword B Division

A crowd of 700 thought they had seen the destination of the Windsor Cup decided at Stangmore Park on the second last Saturday of the season. John Montgomery's 40-yard free-kick goal had won the game for Dungannon and leap-frogged the Tyrone side over their beaten rivals, Loughgall, at the top of the Section One table. The Swifts were expected to clinch the title with a home win over the Welders the following Thursday, with Loughgall's final game on the Saturday, against RUC, being academic.

After Dungannon's 1-0 win, the rival chairmen exchanged pleasantries in the Board Room, with Loughgall congratulating their neighbours and taking some solace from the fact that the title would be coming to Mid-Ulster for the first time. Dungannon chairman Gordon Lee also believed it was all over bar the shouting, and no wonder, given the manner of the winning goal. "He could score from here", whispered Lee as John Montgomery stepped back to take the free-kick forty yards from goal and close to the touchline, "I've seen him do it before". Loughgall goalkeeper Brian Hanley expected to deal with a flighted cross into the box, but as he came out to meet it, the ball floated over him and into the top corner of the net. Later in the game, Loughgall's Gary Henderson crashed the ball against the crossbar after a goalmouth scramble and, with Stephen Vance in inspired form, the equaliser that would have been enough to win the title, just wouldn't come. But, the following Thursday evening, Dungannon also had one of those days. Manager Joe McAree and his team will never know how they only managed a one-all draw against the Welders. The point put them two points clear at the top, but Loughgall had been handed a lifeline they would not refuse at Lakeview Park two days later. Former Larne striker Stephen Barnes scored his 37th goal of the season to settle the nerves, and when Tommy Leeman converted a penalty three minutes from time, Loughgall were champions. "Last year we lost out narrowly to Dundela, and this time we thought we had lost it to Dungannon, so it's a tremendous relief to finally win the title", exclaimed manager Alfie Wylie. He was completing nine years in charge, though only the last four had been in the B Division. Their story is truly one of rags to riches, from joining the Mid-Ulster League in 1973 to the Intermediate League in 1987 and then the B Division. Success had come along the way, with George Willis and Sam Robinson guiding Loughgall to a run of Mid-Ulster titles, and Wylie winning the Intermediate League and Cup double in 1988-89. "We can go forward from here too", promised Wylie, "possibly into the Irish League". Linfield know all about them, after being taken to two games in the Irish Cup. The Blues also had to come from behind to win 5-3 at Dungannon. Both Mid-Ulster clubs have improved their facilities and could form part of the next shake-up in the Irish League.

B DIVISION SECTION ONE
FINAL TABLE - TOP TWO

	Pd	Pts
Loughall	30	70
Dungannon Swfts	30	69

Smirnoff Cup Final

Dundela 1   Loughall 0 (aet)

Mervyn Bell is Mr.Dundela. He joined the club as a player in 1966, became player-manager in 1973, and marked his 22nd season in charge with the Smirnoff Cup, his 21st trophy. The extra-time winner, from a Laurence Fyfe 30-yard free-kick, sparked the almost annual celebrations, but all the success paled into insigificance when 38-year-old team captain Michael Goddard tragically died during a game at Stangmore Park at the start of the 1995-96 season. After blocking an attempted cross, Goddard stumbled and fell to the ground. "In all my thirty seasons with Dundela, this is without doubt the most difficult moment I've experienced. Everyone at the club is devastated", said Bell.

Intermediate Cup Winners

Ballinamallard United

Ballinamallard - Bob Carroll, Seamus Bonnar, Gary Armstrong, Jim Harley, John McClean, Paul Bogle, Paul McMullan, Damien Ming, Anthony Benson, Sean McCallion, Nigel Keys, Gary McGettigan, Marty Kelly, Derek Ballard, Seamus Finnegan. Manager, Greg Turley.

Ballinamallard defeated Park 3-1 in the Intermediate Cup Final at Stangmore Park, Dungannon, with two goals from Seamus Bonnar and one from Nigel Keys. Bonnar made his name at Omagh Town, as did McMullan, Ming, and Ballard.

4

Rugby World Cup

Moments to Remember, by Mark Robson

Ireland 19   New Zealand 43 - May 27, Johannesburg

Jonah Lomu. That was all the neutrals wanted to talk about, write about, shout about after Ireland's opening game. The fact that Richard Wallace was marking him and not Simon Geoghegan, whose hunger for the tackle seemed insatiable, may have made a little difference but probably not a lot. The black rhino announced his arrival on the World stage by smashing and writhing and powering past flailing Irish arms. Mere flesh and blood wasn't enough to stop him - Ireland would have needed drugged darts or, as Denis McBride said later, a baseball bat. Nigel Carr made, as usual, an accurate summation, "A freight train with the speed of a Ferrari". Still, this was Ireland at their irresistable, if losing best, and their start was as awesome as Lomu would be later. Kingston's leadership was excellent and Ireland, way below New Zealand in terms of pace, athleticism and overall class, competed as well as anyone dreamed they would. Was that shattering and embarrassing defeat by Italy (22-12 in Treviso on May

Get out of my way! Nick Popplewell hands off Walter Little.

Simon Geoghegan looks for support from Jonathan Bell.

6) an hallucination? Unforced errors and missed kicks blow-torched the sheen from a performance that took Ireland close to the limit of their potential. Possession in the line-out was won, on our own ball, and while the scrummaging was less than convincing the Irish were galvanised by the suspicion that later opposition would not be as strong in the tight. In the loose, Ireland did well, screaming around like hyperventilating children. A wrecking crew in green, but with significant control. The difference - New Zealand's superior rucking technique, the very obvious fact that they have better players, and the presence of Glen Osborne, a full back who appeared to ghost past tacklers, and Lomu who simply crushed them.

		Ire	NZ
8 mins	Halpin	5	
	Elwood	7	
10 mins	Mehrtens (P)		3
13 mins	Mehrtens (P)		6
30 mins	Lomu		11
	Mehrtens		13
32 mins	Bunce		18
	Mehrtens		20
39 mins	McBride	12	
HALF-TIME			
42 mins	Lomu		25
48 mins	Mehrtens (P)		28
69 mins	Kronfield		33
	Mehrtens		35
70 mins	Mehrtens (P)		38
75 mins	Corkery	17	
	Elwood	19	
78 mins	Osborne		43
FULL-TIME			

Ireland: J.Staples, R.Wallace, B.Mullin, J.Bell, S.Geoghegan, E.Elwood, M.Bradley, N.Popplewell, T. Kingston (c), G.Halpin, G.Fulcher, N.Francis, D. Corkery, D. McBride, P.Johns. Replacements: Maurice Field for Bell (12 mins - temp), Field for Staples (37). **New Zealand:** G.Osborne, J.Wilson, F.Bunce, W.Little, J.Lomu, A.Mehrtens, G.Bachop, C.Dowd, S.Fitzpatrick, O.Brown, I. Jones, B.Larsen, J.Joseph, M.Brewer, J.Kronfield.

144

Ireland 50 Japan 28 - May 31, Pretoria

Free-scoring at the Free States Stadium, but Ireland's victory was as uncomfortable as the performance against New Zealand was encouraging. Ireland made a good and productive start, leading 19-0 after 26 minutes. We could all relax and make jokes about the Japanese approach to the game being as raw as the fish they eat. But we hadn't bargained for the sharp teeth and frenzied vigour of the piranhas in the red and white striped shirts. Rising panic greeted a revival by the men from the land of the Rising Sun. Japan taught lessons in how to keep the ball alive, showed imagination and adventure. They ran elusively and passed skilfully. All that and pace as well. Ireland were panting in the warm sunshine. Twice Japan came to within five points of the Irish, refusing to be bolted down despite Ireland's second surge in the second half. It took a late assertion of forward power in the closing stages to see Japan off. Thank heavens for Ireland's sixteenth player, a Mr.P.Try, who scored twice. In the loose, the opposition were energetic and ran from all points, and they varied the line-outs intelligently to win an alarming amount of ball. Ireland did score fifty points though, and it was probably a loss of concentration that allowed Japan the opportunity to fight back. The most disappointing aspect, by comparison, was Japan's quicker, smoother, more penetrative back line. We have no excuse in that department, while the tackling, so committed against the All Blacks, was often poor.

Ireland: C.O'Shea, R.Wallace, B.Mullin, M.Field, S.Geoghegan, P.Burke, N.Hogan, N.Popplewell, K.Wood, P.Wallace, D.Tweed, N.Francis, D.Corkery, P.Johns, E.Halvey. T.Kingston for Wood (9), A.Foley for Tweed (75) Scorers: Corkery, Francis, Geoghegan, Halvey, Hogan (tries), two penalty tries, Burke (6 cons, 1 pen).

Ireland 24 Wales 23 - June 4, Johannesburg

In keeping with their performances so far, Ireland made an electrifying start and hammered Wales onto the back foot so hard and so early that they never really regained their balance. Seven points clear after six minutes, and 14 points clear by the 14th minute. If it was green, it had the ball, and tries by Popplewell and McBride gave Ireland the explosive beginning they craved. McBride, criticised by many before the tournament as lightweight and paceless, had a fabulous game. Courageous and consistently first to the breakdown, he tore at Welsh hearts. By the time Wales had settled into any semblance of rhythym, the match was almost over. Ireland were helped by a Welsh team lacking confidence and direction, and with ten minutes left they led 21-9. Order the stout. Not so fast. There followed a final period of excruciating anxiety.

		Ire	Wales
6 mins	Popplewell	5	
	Elwood	7	
14 mins	McBride	12	
	Elwood	14	
28 mins	Jenkins (P)		3
40 mins	A.Davies (DG)		6
HALF-TIME			
53 mins	Jenkins (P)		9
70 mins	Halvey	19	
	Elwood	21	
73 mins	Humphreys		14
	Jenkins		16
78 mins	Elwood (P)	24	
85 mins	Taylor		21
	Jenkins		23
FULL-TIME			

Ireland: C.O'Shea, R.Wallace, B.Mullin, J.Bell, S.Geoghegan, E.Elwood, N.Hogan, N.Popplewell, T.Kingston, G.Halpin, G.Fulcher, N.Francis, D.Corkery, P.Johns, D.McBride.

Johnathan Humphreys scored a try and Neil Jenkins converted. Surely not. Eric Elwood kicked a penalty with two minutes to go for an eight-point cushion. Order the stout. Not so fast. Injury time was hectic, even frenzied, and Wales scored a try in the fifth minute of time added on, Hemi Taylor the villain. Would the referee ever press the whistle to his lips for that final shrill. When it came, Ireland's players leaped high in jubilation. Victory was fashioned by hard graft, not high quality, but it was well-deserved nevertheless.

Ireland 12 France 36 - June 10, Durban

Where had it all gone wrong. The fire, the passion. Yes, the match was close for a long time, but Ireland never, not once, looked like a side capable of making the French work any harder than hardly at all, for victory. Ireland lost almost every battle within the battle. While it would be unfair to use phrases that include white feathers or flags, it is fair to say that Ireland confirmed that they are on the second tier in World terms. France were superior in the line-outs, and particularly disappointing was the sight of French forwards pouring through on Niall Hogan. Perhaps fortunately for Ireland, France insisted on driving around the fringes, especially whilst the game was still close, instead of releasing their potentially mesmerising backline. Also thankfully, their out half Delaud proved that he is possibly the worst French number ten of all time. He certainly couldn't have coped with the pressure Eric Elwood felt from the French pack almost every time he touched the ball. Hogan was also on the retreat, although on a positive note David Corkery again played well. But overall, mis-placed were the great hopes that the perennial underdogs would produce the sort of isolated greatness that has punctuated Irish rugby history. All we are left with is the emptiness that follows such a jaded performance. Missing was the vibrancy of the marvellous first half hour against the All Blacks. Gone was the forward unity that carried Ireland through against Japan. Mislaid was the intensity of desire so crucial in the emotional win over the Welsh, but then those are the moments we should remember when we look back at Rugby World Cup '95. After all, Ireland did achieve their goal of a quarter-final place.

		Ire	France
3 mins	Elwood (P)	3	
6 mins	Lacroix (P)		3
14 mins	Ellwood (P)	6	
18 mins	Lacroix (P)		6
20 mins	Elwood (P)	9	
30 mins	Lacroix (P)		9
37 mins	Elwood (P)	12	
40 mins	Lacroix (P)		12
HALF-TIME			
49 mins	Lacroix (P)		15
50 mins	Lacroix (P)		18
70 mins	Lacroix (P)		21
73 mins	Lacroix (P)		24
80 mins	Saint-Andre		29
	Lacroix		31
85 mins	N'Tamack		36
FULL-TIME			

Ireland: C.O'Shea, D.O'Mahony, B.Mullin, J.Bell, S.Geoghegan, E.Elwood, N.Hogan, N.Popplewell, T.Kingston, G.Halpin, G.Fulcher, N.Francis, D.Corkery, P.Johns, D.McBride. E.Halvey for Fulcher(60).

New Zealand captain Glen Osborne charges up the wing.

POOL C RESULTS

New Zealand	43 - 19	Ireland
Wales	57 - 10	Japan
Ireland	50 - 28	Japan
New Zealand	34 - 9	Wales
Ireland	24 - 23	Wales
New Zealand	145 - 17	Japan

FINAL STAGES

Quarter-finals

England	25 - 22	Australia
Ireland	12 - 36	France
New Zealand	48 - 30	Scotland
South Africa	42 - 14	Western Samoa

Semi-finals

England	29 - 45	New Zealand
South Africa	19 - 15	France

Final

South Africa	15 - 12	New Zealand

POOL C

	P	W	D	L	F	A	Pts
New Zealand	3	3	0	0	222	45	9
Ireland	3	2	0	1	93	94	7
Wales	3	1	0	2	89	68	5
Japan	3	0	0	3	55	252	3

A Personal Perspective on South Africa - Mark's Diary

The cage. Flaky paint on rusting iron bars, encased in crumbling brickwork. And there is was, brightly-coloured, obviously crafted with care, but chilling nevertheless. The Shambok. Inside the cage, around twenty black men. Arms stretching, faces pressing, pleading for release to any passer-by. There were many mornings when I walked past these poor impounded souls. Why should I, an inquisitive journalist, be allowed to stroll anywhere near such a place during the World Cup? Especially as a sensitive and protective South African government saw the tournament as a showcase for the 'new' South Africa. But I was nowhere near any prisons - this was a Golf Club in Johannesburg. The black men were caddies.

David, a young, bright Sowetan, carried my clubs. As my temporary employee, he was well looked after financially and physically - we became close friends, but I'll never forget the first day he caddied for me. David gave me a dodgy yardage for a shot, and my ball plummetted into the water. I looked at him and he was cowering behind the bag, waiting for the back of my hand. It was such a sad sight. In terms of apartheid, South Africa definitely has improved, but by how much? Differentiating between truth and propaganda is difficult. It would be naive to expect the overnight evaporation of bigoted colonialism, but there is still a strong Afrikanner commitment to what they see as the Good Old Days. I met an old friend while I was there. A South African. I hadn't seen him for 25 years. We went out, and within 20 minutes we were having an animated row. "What do you think of the current changes here", I posed, as an icebreaker. "Well", he said, "these days I try to treat the blacks as if they were human beings, but I still wouldn't have them in my house". You can imagine the ensuing mayhem.

And then there was the rugby. A fabulous tournament crammed with incident, passion, flair, and controversy. Gary Halpin's try against New Zealand was the highlight for me. That shaven head of grey stubble and the attached mass of heaving white muscle and flesh crashing through a barrier of black to score. And then, there was the exultant, if ill-advised, two-fingered salute that followed. The Irish made an impact, and showed that sheer commitment has its role at International level. Sadly, the days when it will be enough on its own to forge victory are almost over. The birth, or rather the public birth, of professionalism, during the tournament, confirmed that South Africa '95 would indeed be a platform for a massive watershed. I was at that historic press conference at Ellis Park. The arrogant and bombastic Louis Luyt took an almost sadistic pleasure in announcing the Rupert Murdoch deal, adding that the Southern Hemisphere, already a lap or two clear, would now pull away from the North at warp factor speed. The Home Unions representatives were in shock. They knew in their hearts that they would spend eternity playing catch up. I recall the answer one hack got when he asked an England committee man how

Paddy Johns, Gary Halpin, and Gabriel Fulcher sing the Irish anthem.

important a moment like this was in the history of rugby union. The reply - "About as significant as the day when William Webb Ellis picked the bloody ball up in the first place!"

Jonah Lomu was sensation of the World Cup. I'll never forget my one and only encounter with him, before the Ireland game. The All Blacks were training at Ellis Park and there was Lomu catching, kicking, and running. He looked impressive, he looked big, but not ferocious. Then training finished. Lomu left the pitch and walked towards me, removing his shirt as he moved. The sky darkened, my eyes widened, the sweat trickled as a huge slab of breathing muscle bore down on a trembling, cowering former wing forward called Mark Robson. He looked at me and I froze. It was part fear, part awe, and I remember thinking, "God, I hope he's not hungry." Lomu, the exceptional athlete, the rugby warrior.

The final moment, the vision amongst the World Cup recollections, was South Africa united at last, as one people, overwhelmed with delirium as Francois Pienaar lifted the William Webb Ellis Trophy. The official version. Meanwhile, David endures endless empty nights in a Sowetan shanty town. By day, a bag on his shoulder brings relief from the shadow of the Shambok, and a few hours of freedom from the cage.

Note: Mark Robson commentated for ITV Sport at Rugby World Cup '95.

"A Cracking Day Out"

The romantic sports story of the year was surely the debut of 35-year-old Davy Tweed for Ireland against France at Lansdowne Road in the Five Nations Championship. A Railway Engineer from Ballymoney, he became the oldest player ever to win his first international cap when called up at the last minute. Tweed did not let the occasion pass him by, "I had such a cracking day out, it was an electric occasion. I just didn't imagine that it could be such fun!"

Tweed could not have played better, from catching the very first ball to other brilliant two-handed takes in the line-out (see colour section), a department in which Ireland was supposed to struggle. In fact, they won the line-outs 23-17 and lost the match 25-7. The new boy had only one nasty moment. "I had heard about some of the tricks the French get up to, so when Olivier Merle caught me, I grabbed him by the throat and we stared at each other momentarily. He got the message that I was not going to be intimidated by anyone. I'm old enough now to know that if you get a smack, you'll meet up again somewhere along the track".

His jersey was promised to the Ballymoney Junior club where be began his career, "it's only fitting I re-pay them in some way". Tweed played for them until aged 28, refusing offers from nearby seniors Ballymena, because "he didn't want to be seen as deserting the juniors for a bigger town club", recalls then Ballymena Coach Maurice Crabbe. At 18 stone and 6"5, he soon became a loyal servant to a successful Ulster team and won eight caps for Ireland A. Early

this year, Tweed scored three tries for his club in a league game, and then played for Ireland at an age older than that of Willie John McBride when he won the last of his 63 caps. He felt honoured "to have played at Lansdowne Road just once", and maintained there were better players around, but he kept his place for defeat of Wales in Cardiff (16-12), and made a fairytale appearance in the World Cup in South Africa.

Note - Ireland came third in the Five Nations Championship, losing 20-8 at home to England, and 26-13 at Murrayfield, despite a try from Jonathan Bell.

Lansdowne Road next stop.
Davy Tweed with the Clerical Medical Man of the Match Award for scoring three tries for Ballymena.

Willie's Cup Specialists
Club Rugby

Willie Anderson's Dungannon didn't lose a single cup match all season, yet lost their precious place in Division One of the Insurance Corporation All Ireland League. "Winning the Smithwicks Boston Cup, the All Ireland Cup, and the First Trust Senior Cup, proves we're not a bad team, as does the fact that we lost five league games by only a few points". Dungannon ended the season with a better points difference (minus 27) than any of the bottom six clubs, but were relegated after finishing their match with St Marys agonisingly short of the line three minutes into injury-time (see page 153). The Tyrone side beat Instonians in the Boston Cup Final in January, 10-3, and went on beat Old Wesley in the national decider. Collegians crumbled before the cup specialists in the First Round of the Senior Cup, conceding four tries to both Stanley McDowell and Peter Sandford, to lose 80-7. The same try-scorers went over the line in the 18-11 Quarter-final defeat of Ballymena, and Ashley Blair's accuracy saw Dungannon overcome Malone in the last four. Trailing 11-3 at the interval, Blair kicked two second-half penalties and a brilliant conversion, after McDowell had scored a try in the corner. Blair contributed another eleven points against Instonians in the final, as his team came from behind once more. Johnny Boyd's try secured a 21-16 victory and Dungannon's third Senior Cup in-a-row.

Mr.D.Harvey, Managing Director, First Trust, Jeremy Hastings, Mr.R.Reilly, IRFU President, Mrs.Reilly.

ALL IRELAND LEAGUE DIVISION ONE BOTTOM FIVE 1995		
	Pd	Pts
Lansdowne	10	7
Young Munster	10	6
Instonians	10	6
Sunday's Well	10	5
Dungannon	10	4

FIRST TRUST SENIOR CUP WINNERS IN THE 90s	
1990	Ballymena
1991	Ballymena
1992	Malone
1993	Dungannon
1994	Dungannon
1995	Dungannon

FIRST
ON ALL
SCORES

FIRST TRUST
Bank

Dungannon Despair

Dungannon Delight

Top: Dungannon's relegation battle is lost, just short of the St Marys line. Bottom: Mud-covered trio Gary Leslie, Hugh McCaughey and Brian Morrow celebrate winning the Smithwicks All Ireland Floodlit Cup.

First Trust Senior Cup Final Teams

Dungannon: Stanley Mc Dowell, Ronnie Carey, Richard Stevens, Alistair Redpath, Peter Sandford, Ashley Blair, Richard Weir, Jeremy Hastings (c), Johnny Boyd, Johnny Hastings, Jeremy Davidson, K.Walker, John Gamble, Hugh McCaughey, Gary Leslie. Replacements: W.Nelson, B.Smith, W.Dunne, B.Steenson.

Instonians: Graeme McCausland, Innes Gray, Andrew Hewitt, Keith Crossan, Graeme McCluskey, Stuart Laing, Keith O'Donnell, Roger Wilson, Kevin McKee, Bruce Cornelius, Colin Hamilton, Jeremy Cruiks, Gary Bell (c), Andrew Adair, Brian Barrett. Replacements: N.Robson, V.Kirk, D.Sufferin, G.Collins.

Referee: Stephen Hilditch   Touch Judges: B.Stirling, N.Hamilton.

5

Wayne Better Than Barry?

Professional Boxing

Wayne McCullough's achievement in winning the WBC bantamweight title in Japan on July 30th surpassed that of Barry McGuigan when he beat Eusebio Pedroza in 1985 to become world champion, according to former double British champion Hugh Russell. However, he also has a warning for Northern Ireland's new boxing hero, "People say Barry was a better challenger than he was a champion, Wayne has to watch the same doesn't happen to him. They have the same punishing styles, and there are only so many of those kind of fights in you".

So far, the 1992 Olympic silver medallist's professional career has gone exactly to plan, under American manager Matt Tinley. Based in Las Vegas, McCullough stopped the Mexican, Geronimo Cardo, in March for his 16th consecutive win, and to set-up a shot at Yasuei Yakushiji's world title in Nagoya, Japan. Making his fifth defence, the champion was rated the number one bantamweight by the highly-regarded Ring magazine, with a record of 24 wins out of 27 fights, with sixteen knock-outs and one draw. "Hand on heart, I didn't think Wayne could go there and win", confesses Russell. "Before fights, they can give you faulty scales or poor hotel service, but Wayne showed a lot of guts in probably the biggest achievement ever by an Irish boxer. No offence to McGuigan, but you have to consider that Pedroza was in the twilight of his career and the fight was in London, whereas Yakusiji was at his peak, and in his own back yard".

American judges Tom Kaczmarerk and Barbara Perez awarded the contest to the Ulsterman by 116-113 and 118-110, while South Korean judge Kim Jaebong made Yakushiji the winner, by 116-115. Although surprised, McCullough didn't really complain, "I was often forced into corners and sustained a couple of minor cuts, which gave a bad impression, but I wasn't really hurt. I took the fight to him and dominated. Even when he tried to come back in the 10th, I gained another gear for the closing rounds". The champion's all-action style has been honed to perfection by legendary trainer Eddie Futch, but it's also a demanding style which can take it's toll on the body. "Wayne knows only one way to fight", explains Russell. "It's exciting to watch, but he has to spar the same way, and after a while it shows. You might think the time will never come, until you wake up one morning and you know you've had enough. The guy that beats him could be no better than the one he has just beaten". Russell retired young, a month before his 25th birthday, after a professional career spanning only four years. As an amateur, he won a Commonwealth bronze medal and five Ulster Senior titles. In the Pro. game, he became Bantamweight champion before

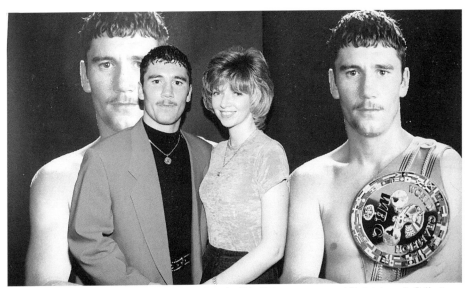

Wayne McCullough and wife Cheryl at the launch of his Guinness-sponsored first defence in Belfast.

moving down to Flyweight to repeat the feat, the only British fighter ever to do so. "My last opponent was Charlie Brown. He had a poor record, but he took me twelve rounds and I had 32 stitches after the fight. I felt I only had so many fights in me".

Russell became the first Ulsterman to win a Lonsdale Belt (for three British title fight victories) since Freddie Gilroy, and he was delighted to welcome Sam Storey into the elite club this year, when he regained the Super-middleweight crown he lost in 1989. After being stopped by Chris Eubank in 1994, the 31-year-old looked to have reached the end of the line, but an impressive performance against Colin Manners on March 18 at Mill Street on the undercard of Collins-Eubank won Storey a last chance. Six weeks later, the Holy Family boxer out-pointed Ali Forbes (118-117) at Bethnal Green. "There were 1300 blacks and only about forty whites in the place, so when I looked round after the decision was announced, only my brother and dad were cheering!" Gerry Storey Senior takes much of the credit for his son's return to the top, from witholding Harry Mullan's pre-fight prediction in Boxing News of a Forbes win, to restraining Sam's tactics during the fights. "Sam came back to corner saying he wanted to take Forbes out, but Gerry said 'You knock him out and I'll knock YOU out!' He knew Forbes was still strong and didn't want Sam to take any chances", recalls Harry McGavock of Matchroom. Storey Snr has coached numerous Commonwealth medallists, including Edmonton 1978 when Barry McGuigan and Gerry Hamill won gold, Kenny Beattie took silver (he lost to Mike McCallum), and Hugh Russell won bronze. "Gerry was ahead of his time. I remember him giving the boxers a tennis ball to bounce from hand-to-hand as they walked around the gym, to help co-ordination. Ten years later, a Cuban came here to tell us the same thing".

Noel Magee mirrored Storey's success when he captured the Commonwealth

Keeping it in the family. Gerry Storey (centre) with Lonsdale Belt holders Sam Storey and Hugh Russell, pictured at the Holy Family Club in Belfast.

Light-heavyweight crown in Basildon on May 9th, his first professional title in five attempts (he lost to Storey in a British title fight in 1988). Unbeaten champion Gary Delaney failed to come out for the 8th Round because of a damaged hand, but the Belfast boxer, based in Newcastle, had fought a composed fight. Despite suffering a cut eye, the ten to one shot avoided Delaney's big punches by working in close-quarters. "I wore him down and although he quit on the stool, he was wilting and I would have stopped him. At the end, I was choked and just went nuts because I had waited ten years for this". Like Storey, Magee's career had been petering out, nobody would have noticed if either man had lost and retired. They had nothing to lose and came away with some reward for all the work they have put in, though Magee lost his first defence when he was stopped in nine rounds by Nicky Piper.

Eamonn Loughran has already had considerable success at a young age, yet he has not caught the imagination of the paying public. Since wining the WBO Welterweight title in 1993 (he beat Lorenzo Smith) , the Ballymena man has made successful but often unsatisfactory defences against Alessandro Duran (Points win), Manning Galloway (Retired in 3rd Round), Angel Beltre (No contest declared after Beltre sustained a cut), and Tony Gannerelli (Stopped in 6th Round). "Eamonn's surrounded by disaster", views Hugh Russell, "He trains hard, seven days a week, but too many of his fights have been postponed or ended badly, and they can't sell him. What's more, they don't try to sell him. Barney Eastwood wouldn't sleep until tickets for his promotions are sold, but a lot of the others fulfil television contracts and treat tickets sales as extra". Still, Loughran made no mistakes in a re-match with Beltre, taking a landslide points decision and can go on to greater things.

Ray Close and John Lowey had their world title dreams dashed in 1995, the former by a defect shown up on a brain scan, and the latter by Kennedy McKinney when they met in Chicago in August. Close was forced to withdraw from a third fight with Chris Eubank in February, yet experts in Utah later studied scans dating back to 1989 and saw no reason for him not box. He has been granted an Irish licence, but not a British one. John Lowey has also been refused permission to fight in Britain, due to an irregular brain scan in 1991. However, after three years out of the ring, he re-started his career in Chicago and won the IBO World Super-bantamweight title in April, stopping Juan Cardone in the 5th Round. Lowey surrendered his title and missed out on the new WBU version, when he was stopped by McKinney in the 8th Round. He blamed his first defeat on pre-fight diarrhoea which sapped his energy, "My mind was clear but my legs were gone".

The past twelve months has seen an unprecedented clear-out of the amateur ranks with no fewer than eight Ulster boxers turning professional. Neil Sinclair, Paul Ireland, Darren Corbett, Eamonn Brolly, and Frankie Slane have signed up with Barry Hearn's Matchroom stable, while Jim Webb, Danny Ryan, and Mark Winters are with Frank Warren. South of the border, Kevin McBride, Michael Carruth and Paul Griffen have made the same move in recent times, and Bernard McComiskey from Banbridge is with Owen McMahon. The reason is that there are more options for young fighters than there was ten years ago. Barney Eastwood now faces competition from Warren and Hearn, who have both set up stables in the province. However, Pat McCrory, President of the Ulster Council of the Irish Amateur Boxing Association, is dismayed at the exodus; "Some of our lads have a lot more to give to the amateur sport, more to learn and with the potential to gain honours for themselves and their country". Hugh Russell argues that the trend is a sign of the times and that the amateur game has to move with it, "the professional and amateur games here are poles apart, but why can't we have Pro-ams like they have in America, and why doesn't the amateur game in Ireland do more to keep their fighters, like every other country does?" McCrory acknowledges the latter point, especially in the case of Neil Sinclair, arguably the biggest loss to the amateurs. The explosive 21-year-old, a gold medallist at the '94 Commonwealth Games, seemed set to stay until Atlanta, but with grant aid slow to come through, the unemployed boxer turned Pro. Barry McGuigan singled out Sinclair on his debut as a "real prospect", though his inexperience told in losing the second fight because of a gash he had received in training.

Mark Winters is also learning fast. The Antrim man was put on the floor within ten seconds of his second fight in Manchester, but recovered to beat Mark Magowan. Hugh Russell tips Donegal's Danny Ryan to do well, "given the right handling", but has this advice for the new boys. "You may have the best trainers and the best corner-men, but when the bell goes, they all step down from the

Neil Sinclair - on the ropes but looking to go all the way to the top.

ring. You're on your own, it's not a team sport, but if you get something out of it, then you owe nobody. You will know if you have put it in or not, and, if you haven't reached your goals within say eighteen months, you have to be honest with yourself and ask if you are prepared to be an undercard fighter". Damien Denny had even more forthright advice after Paul Jones ended his eight-year professional career in April. "I regret the day I turned pro. I saw the world, met a lot of friends and got tremendous enjoyment from boxing, but you also meet a lot of nasty people determined to exploit you. It can be a rotten, filthy game".

Smithwicks Ulster Seniors

Amateur Boxing

Bantamweight Tommy Waite (above) accepted the Hanna Cup from Michael McCann of Smithwicks after the best bout of the finals, against Oliver Duddy from Coleraine. Waite also won the Best Boxer Award and Duddy was voted Most Improved Boxer. At the Irish Seniors, Waite fell victim to the computer-scoring system in losing to Donal Hosford from Cork. The 21-19 score was the average taken from five judges, but coach Mickey Hawkins, protested, "One judge had it 71-30, which totally wrecks the overall average. It's not the computer, it's the people using it. That guy must have been playing the piano! We must appoint top officials for these contests and make the master scorecard available so the judges can be scrutinised". Light-heavyweight Stephen Kirk (below) beat Hugh McNally to receive the McAlinden Cup from Terry Loughins of Smithwicks, and went on to become Irish champion, as did Damien Kelly, Adrian Patterson, Glen McLarnon, Neil Sinclair, Brian Magee, and Paul Douglas.

6
From Belvoir Park to Oak Hill
Irish Golf, by Tony McGee

The Smurfit Irish PGA Championship at Belvoir Park in May proved to be the launch-pad for Europe's matchwinning hero at the Ryder Cup at Oak Hill, Rochester in September, even though Philip Walton insisted after his victory in Belfast that he was dead-set against the competition. "I'm not interested in making the team. I was ready last time and didn't get in. Also, the Ryder Cup can destroy players". But, when other successes at the Catalan and English Opens lifted the Malahide man into 7th place on the points table, he changed his tune, and the rest is history. Walton's best-ever season began with four missed cuts and little apparent hope of a first tour victory since 1990. Yet, by high summer, he was contesting his first US PGA Championship in Los Angeles. A closing round 68 left him a very creditable 13 shots behind Colin Montgomerie and Steve Elkington (who won the play-off). Walton was at a loss to explain his dramatic change in form, and quipped after winning the English Open, "I've had near pneumonia and a sore eye this week, and I win - it's a gas, isn't it? I'll probably get healthy and start missing cuts again!"

Philip Walton receives his prize at Belvoir Park from Michael Smurfit.

In September, the Irishman teamed up with Ian Woosnam on day two of the Ryder Cup. He didn't want to play with Seve Ballesteros, because "his very presence is intimidating and I might be distracted. I don't think he's the type of guy I could grab by the shoulder and say 'Come on. Let's get up and at them'".

Walton and Woosnam lost their match, but the former was destined to reclaim the Cup for Europe on the final green of the penultimate singles game, holding his nerve to beat Jay Haas by one hole."I never felt pressure like it. It was unreal, but I said to myself 'just calm down, you've got two putts to make it, why not use them'. It was an unbelievable moment". Team captain Bernard Gallacher was first to run onto the green to embrace the 33-year-old, who had completed a remarkable European recovery from 9-7 down to a one-point victory.

Bunkered. Smurfit Irish PGA Runner-up Paul McGinley.

Smurfit Irish PGA Championship

The successful return of this tournament to Northern Ireland, for the first time in 23 years, owes as much to the smooth handling of the event by the Belvoir Park authorities, as it does to the superb setting and condition of one of the best parkland courses in Britain. The weather and quality of play were also first-class, with a new course record set at the pro-am, and then equalled five times. Billy Todd's 65 was followed within 24 hours by Gordon Fairweather, the Knock professional whose grandfather Syd won the championship in 1926 and 1935. Walton was next to match the record, then Raymond Burns (with a rolling forty feet putt at the eighteenth), Kevin Morris, and Brendan McGovern. The championship came down to a head-to-head between Walton and Paul McGinley, with large galleries following their fascinating duel over the last two days. After nine holes

TOP 20 AT SMURFIT IRISH PGA CHAMPIONSHIP

273	Philip Walton (Unattached)	72, 65, 66, 70
274	Paul McGinley (Luttrelstown)	70, 67, 66, 72
275	Des Smyth (Unattached)	66, 72, 70, 67
277	Brendan McGovern (Headfort)	71, 71, 70, 65
278	Raymond Burns (K Club)	73, 70, 65, 70
281	Karl O'Donnell (Newlands)	70, 70, 67, 74
282	Eamonn Darcy (Delgany)	71, 70, 69, 72
283	Martin Sludds (Hesketh)	77, 69, 69, 68
	John Murray (Sidcup)	71, 71, 67, 74
284	David Jones (Knockbracken)	73, 70, 69, 72
	Christy O'Connor Jnr (Galway Bay)	72, 73, 67, 72
	Stephen Hamill (Ballyclare)	72, 73, 66, 73
	Damian Mooney (Laganview)	73, 67, 69, 75
	Roger Giles (Killarney)	73, 67, 68, 76
285	Jimmy Heggarty (Rathmore)	75, 72, 67, 71
286	Darren Clarke (Mere)	73, 74, 71, 68
	Michael Bannon (Holywood)	70, 76, 67, 73
	Kevin Morris (Fota Island)	74, 71, 65, 76
287	Gordon Fairweather (Knock)	65, 75, 75, 72
	John Coone (Courtown)	67, 72, 73, 75

of the final round, McGinley led by one, but the 15th and 16th holes were to decide the destination of the £15,000 first prize. Walton birdied 15 after a miraculous second shot to within a few feet of the green. McGinley, whose drive had been forty yards better, held par, but then bogeyed 16. "My plan was to upset Paul and the way things worked out, I believe it gave me the edge", revealed Walton afterwards. The Smurfit Irish PGA Championship, the richest in Europe in 1995 for a 'Close' event, goes to the K Club next year, but will return North in 1997.

British Seniors Open

The future has never looked rosier for the province's premier golfing venues, with organisers rushing to bring tournaments here. 1995 will go down in history as one of the greatest ever from a spectating point of view, with Royal Portrush being the main mecca for world-class action. The Dunluce course was home to the British Ladies Championship, the Carlsberg North of Ireland, the British Seniors' Open, and the men's Senior Home Internationals. The most significant of all was the Seniors' Open, which came to Royal Portrush in July and was Northern Ireland's richest-ever tournament at £350,000. It also had a fairytale ending, with Brian Barnes collecting the title on the course where his father-in-law Max Faulkner won the British Open in 1951. Max, who celebrated his 79th birthday during the Seniors' Open, delighted the gathered media by re-playing and re-living every stroke he carded 44 years ago, during an interview. His son-in-law clinched the title with a fabulous eagle putt from close to twenty yards at the third play-off hole, to defeat Bob Murphy. One of the local highlights was the performance of amateur Kenny Stevenson from Warrenpoint (and Banbridge). Had he been a professional, Kenny would have taken home £4,000 for joint 21st place, but he had the consolation of a bronze medal.

Golfing legends Arnold Palmer and Gary Player helped set a new attendance record for the event, with 18,272 paying customers, up 2,066 on the previous year at Royal Lytham & St Annes. The Seniors will return to the Causeway Coast in 1996/97, and it is being freely suggested that this year's staging was a trial run towards Royal Portrush being allocated the 2001 British Open. Gary Player gave his wholehearted support to the motion, "I feel the Royal & Ancient have almost an obligation to bring the Open here, for the sake of your beautiful country, and to encourage the peace process".

	BRITISH SENIORS' OPEN		
1.	Brian Barnes	67,67,77,70	281
2.	Bob Murphy	68,69,73,71	281
3.	John Morgan	71,68,75,68	282
	Bob Charles	70,73,73,66	282
5.	Tommy Horton	78,68,67,70	283
	John Fourie	70,71,73,69	283
15.	Neil Coles	72,75,74,71	292
	Mick Murphy (Ire)	68,74,78,72	292
17.	Paul Leonard (Ire)	74,71,72,76	293
21.	Liam Higgins (Ire)	71,73,77,73	294
	Kenny Stevenson (Am)	77,70,75,72	294
24.	Gary Player	77,69,75,75	296
32.	Arnold Palmer	71,78,76,73	298
39.	Christy O'Connor	74,78,75,73	300

Carslberg North of Ireland Championship

A field of 300-plus came down to two southern players in the final for the first time, with Keith Nolan snatching the title from Padraig Harrington at the first extra tie-hole. In the semi-finals, Nolan had beaten young West of Ireland champion Eamonn Brady, a nephew of former Arsenal and Republic of Ireland soccer star Liam Brady, while Harrington defeated two-time former North winner David Long from Shandon Park. Five-time winner Garth McGimpsey (1978/84/91/92/93) crashed out in the quarter-finals, by 5 & 4 to Brady. Harrington made up for his disappointment by winning the leading amateur event on the Irish scene, the Bank of Ireland Close Championship, played at Lahinch. The tall, 23-year-old Dubliner set a new course record 66 in qualifying and beat USA-based student from Birr, Richard Coughlan, by one hole in the final. Harrington also won the revived Irish Open Strokeplay Championship at Fota Island, four strokes clear of Garth McGimpsey, and lost the final of the South of Ireland to Jody Fanagan. Both men were part of Great Britain & Ireland's Walker Cup success at Porthcawl in September, and Harrington later turned professional. The East of Ireland Championship was won by Declan Brannigan (beating Eddie Power in a play-off), and the Mullingar Scratch Cup, reckoned as the Sixth Irish Championship, went to Kilkenny's Gary Murphy. Munster relieved Ulster of the Senior Interprovincial title at Royal Portrush.

Peter O'Hara, Chairman, Ulster Branch, Golfing Union of Ireland, presents the cup to Keith Nolan.
From Left: Frank Keenan, Carlsberg Manager, N. Ireland; Jean Francois Jamet, Sales & Marketing Director, Guinness N. Ireland; Frank Trufelli, Captain, Royal Portrush.

LAST 16			
David Long (Shandon Park)	bt	Mark Kilgore (Portstewart)	2 and 1
Colin McElderry (Royal Portrush)	bt	Davy Jackson (Clandyboye)	2 and 1
David Cameron (Royal Portrush)	bt	Richard Coughlan (Birr)	23rd
Padraig Harrington (Stackstown)	bt	Ciaran Fitzsimmons (Ardglass)	6 and 5
Garth McGimpsey (Bangor)	bt	Colin Murphy (Clandyboye)	2 and 1
Eamonn Brady (Royal Dublin)	bt	Colin Glasgow (Clandyboye)	1 hole
Gordon Forbes (Newtownstewart)	bt	Brian Omelia (Newlands)	6 and 4
Keith Nolan (Bray)	bt	Declan Moran (Elm Park)	2 and 1
QUARTER-FINALS			
Padraig Harrington	bt	David Cameron	2 and 1
Keith Nolan	bt	Gordon Forbes	2 and 1
David Long	bt	Colin McElderry	1 hole
Eamon Brady	bt	Garth McGimpsey	5 and 4
SEMI-FINALS			
Paidraig Harrington	bt	David Long	3 and 2
Keith Nolan	bt	Eamon Brady	3 and 2
FINAL			
Keith Nolan	bt	Padraig Harrington	19th

European Tour

Couples, Montgomery, Price, Norman and Els - not bad company to be in at the end of your very first event on the European PGA Tour. Banbridge lad Raymond Burns joined the giants of modern golf in the top ten of the Dubai Desert Classic after a superb debut which earned him more than ten thousand pounds. It could have been even better, for the new boy was just four shots behind Couples going into the last round, and closed with a 69 as opposed to the Americans' 66. Still, Burns had begun the senior tour in the same stylish way that he had secured his card in 1994, and was all the wiser for the experience of failing to win his card in 1993. "Failure is a major ingredient of success", he explained. "I am a much-improved player now. My rhythm is better, my course management has improved, and above all, I have learned to be patient". Burns, who is attached to the K Club, also gave credit to his faithful caddie Scottie Gilmore, who he met in America. A week after Dubai, he came down to earth with a dull thud when he missed the cut at the Johnnie Walker Classic in Manila and finished 137th (last place), but bounced back to come joint 16th at the Turespana Open two weeks later. In September, Burns carded a superb first round 65 (six under par) at the Ulster Professional Championship at Blackwood, and eventually took the title after a six-hole play-off with Paul Russell.

Inconsistency has been Darren Clarke's main problem, with early season promise unfulfilled and a Ryder Cup place narrowly missed. The burly Dungannon man was 9th in Manila, 5th at the Turespana Open, led the Malaysian Open after two rounds, and

DUBAI TOP TEN	
268	Fred Couples
271	Colin Montgomery
272	Michael Campbell
	Nick Price
	Wayne Riley
273	Greg Norman
274	Ernie Els
275	RAYMOND BURNS
	Wayne Westner
	Retief Goosen

lost the Portugese Open in April after a play-off with Scotland's Adam Hunter. At Wentworth, Clarke lost his way with a third round 82 at the Volvo PGA Championship, but after a soul-searching chat with his manager, Andrew Chandler, he fired a last round 67 and had top ten finishes at the Dutch and Czech Opens. On the eve of the Ryder Cup, Clark set a new course record 62 at the British Masters. Meanwhile, Ronan Rafferty came close to winning three tournaments. A last round 73 left him third behind Sam Torrance at the Italian Open in May; he came second in Austria behind Alexander Cejka (who had a first round 61), and stumbled on the homeward nine when leading the Czech

Darren Clarke at Belvoir Park.

Open. He was the top Ulster finisher at the Irish Open at Mount Juliet in July, just behind Des Smyth (24th). Darren Clarke was joint 50th and Stephen Hamill 67th, while Raymond Burns and David Feherty both missed the cut. Sam Torrance survived a play-off with Howard Clark and young Stuart Cage to take the first prize of £111,107. At the second extra hole, Clark made a birdie, but Torrance struck a three wood of world class quality and then holed a nine-foot eagle putt. First onto the green to congratulate his old buddy was David Feherty (see colour section), though the Bangor man had had a traumatic year on and off the golf course. In May, he returned from America to announce that his marriage was over, and to perform poorly in two tournaments, though he didn't lose his famous sense of humour and told the assembled press at the English Open that he had lost weight "because I'm running more than Forrest Gump".

Ladies Golf

English ladies Laura Davies and Julie Hall took the top prizes in Irish golf in 1995, by winning the WPGA Irish Open and the British Womens Amateur Championship, respectively. Davies, the world number one, created a number of world records in winning the professional title, with a 25-under par 267 and a sixteen-shot winning margin. Her only bogey came at the last hole in the last round, and she covered the five par-fives in 16-under. The only Irish qualifiers for the event, Maureen Madill and Aideen Rogers, came joint 38th, while Paula Gorman from Malone was the leading amateur. At Royal Portrush, Julie Hall from Felixstowe beat Kristel Mourgue D'Algue in the amateur final, by 3 & 2. Hazel Kavanagh (Grange) lost to the French girl in the semi-finals. Elsewhere, Laura Webb from Cairndhu won the Ulster Ladies Championship at Portstewart, at the 20th hole from Alison Coffey (Warrenpoint); Eileen Rose Power won the Lancome Irish Ladies Championship at Little Island; Dympna Keenan of Belvoir Park won the Ita Wallace Trophy (Plate competition), and Naoimh Quigg from City of Derry stunned the big names to win the Irish Strokeplay Championship at Grange.

IRISH OPEN

277	Sam Torrance	68,68,70,71
	Stuart Cage	70,69,69,69
	Howard Clark	71,68,68,70
	(Torrance won play-off)	
278	Craig Stadler	69,73,70,66
	Robert Allenby	67,72,70,69
	Derrick Cooper	74,69,66,69
	Sven Struver	65,70,73,70
	Peter Baker	72,69,67,70
	David Gilford	70,69,67,72
	Colin Montgomerie	68,68,69,73
279	Greg Norman	70,71,65,73
280	Ian Woosnam	73,67,71,69
	Roger Wessels	70,68,71,71
	Michael Campbell	68,69,70,73
	Wayne Riley	68,71,68,73
281	Wayne Westner	70,67,73,71
	Jean Van de Velde	71,73,66,71
	Domingo Hospital	68,71,70,72
	Miguel Jiminez	68,73,67,73
282	John Mellor	74,69,71,68
	Bernhard Langer	72,72,69,69
	Gary Orr	70,68,73,71
	Sandy Lyle	68,71,72,71

Irish Scores

283	Des Smyth	71,71,72,69
284	Eamonn Darcy	71,68,73,72
	Ronan Rafferty	71,71,70,72
	Paul McGinley	73,66,71,74
285	Philip Walton	69,69,71,76
288	Darren Clarke	73,71,76,68
	John McHenry	73,71,71,73
292	Stephen Hamill	73,70,75,74

7

Nomads Find Their Goal

Womens' Hockey - Pegasus win Irish Senior Cup

P-E-G-A-S-U-S stands for Physical Education Girls And Students from the Ulster College and Stranmillis. The club was founded in 1961 and confined to current and former students from Jordanstown and Stranmillis until 1986, but they have no home. Games are played at Olympia or Jordanstown and meetings are held in neutral venues. "We've always been quite nomadic", says one of the founding members, Joan McCloy. "However, we are closely-knit because of the original idea, and there's no better team spirit than that among students".

Pegasus won their first Ulster Senior League in 1968, and the All Ireland Senior Cup in 1974, and have contributed a line of players for Ireland and Great Britain. Sandra Millar, Jenny Redpath, Hilary Brady, Eilish Macken

SHARWOODS ALL IRELAND SENIOR CUP

FIRST ROUND

Belvedere	bt (R)	Greenfields
Cork Harl	1-0	Catholic Inst
Hermes	bt	UCC (R)
Old Alexandra	4-0	North Down
Pegasus	4-0	Collegians
Pembroke	2-1	Clontarf
Portadown	3-1	Ards
Randalstown	0-2	Muckross

QUARTER-FINALS

Portadown	0-2	Pegasus
Muckross	4-1	Pembroke
Cork Harl	bt (R)	Old Alex
Hermes	1-0	Belvedere

SEMI-FINALS

Cork Harl	0-1	Muckross
Pegasus	2-0	Hermes

FINAL

Pegasus	2-0	Muckross

and Glynis Taylor have brought distinction to their club, while 49-times capped Taylor coached the current team to this year's Irish Senior Cup success. Now a teacher at BRA, she saw her game-plan work to perfection in the 2-0 defeat of Muckross at Belfield: "It was one of the best performances I've ever seen in an All Ireland Final, and I've played in four. It went like a dream but then again, we worked very hard and I've had them on quite a harsh training programme". Claire Samways scored both goals, beating world number one goalkeeper Sandra O'Gorman with inch-perfect strikes, while Ireland captain Sarah Kelleher was well-contained. Arlene Thompson organised the defence and Heather McCullough made some fine stops as Pegasus made up for coming second in the league and for losing the 1994 final. They can now look ahead to the European Cup Winners Cup at Easter.

Above: Jubilant Pegasus captain Jeanette Turner holds aloft the Irish Senior Cup.

Below: Instonians, 1995. Back, L-R: Haydyn Taylor (Manager), Gavin Clarke, Tim Taylor, Tim Hogg, Nigel Skillen, Kenny Rutherford, John Atkins, Denis Guiler (Coach). Front: Paddy Browne, Paul Cooke, Paul Hollway (c), Mark Wainwright, Mark McCullough, Neil Cooke.

Lisnagarvey Reign Over

Instonians Win Mens Irish Senior Cup

Lisnagarvey won the Harp Kirk Cup and walked away with the Renault Senior League, in which they are unbeaten in two seasons, yet 1995 will be remembered as the year 'Garvey lost in the Irish Senior Cup. It hadn't happened since 1987, so most of the reporters and cameras went to the Banbridge-Holywood Second Round tie at Olympia on January 7th rather than Lisnagarvey against Cookstown. There wasn't even time to scurry across to Blaris, as the winning goal came a minute from time. Coach Philip Anderson tried to explain the fall of the kings of Irish hockey, "We lost experienced men in Packenham Pim, Bruce Agnew and Ivan Morris, and replaced them with schoolboys. We're building a good structure at the club and I think we're still the best in Ulster, though maybe not quite the team that won the Irish Cup seven times in-a-row".

Another reason for the media staying at Olympia on 2nd Round day was extra-time, forced by Norman McGladdery's equaliser 24 seconds from time, for Banbridge against Holywood. Lee Tumelty scored twice to secure a 5-3 victory and leave Kenny Morris on the losing side, despite his hat-trick. Banbridge nearly pulled off a similar escape in their quarter-final with Instonians, coming back from 2-0 to 2-2. Rory Madeley and David McAnulty cancelled out earlier strikes by Mark Irwin and John Atkins, but Paul Cooke scored an extra-time winner for Instonians, the newly-installed cup favourites. They would play Stephen Martin's Newry in an all-Ulster semi-final, with the County Down side defeating Cookstown to reach the last four for the first time, thanks mainly to three goals from the Lutton brothers, Errol and Ivor. Neil Cooke and Chris Burns exchanged first-half scores, before Neil and Paul Cooke booked their place in the final in Cork.

It may have been a 200-mile trip to play on Cork Harlequins home pitch, but Instonians travelled well and were not flattered by their 2-1 success. "Our best performance in three years", glowed coach Dennis Guiler. "Only for their goalkeeper, Ivan Bateman, we would have won by much more". Mervyn Cooke and John Atkins set up Neil Cooke for the opener on twelve minutes, and Mark Irwin made it 2-0 before Graham Todd scored a late consolation. Fittingly, Irish Hockey Union President Brian Hanna presented the trophy to Instonians captain Paul Hollway, as Hanna was involved with the club in its foundation

IRISH SENIOR CUP		
SECOND ROUND		
Corinthians	1-0	Portrane
Dublin YMCA	1-4	Newry
Holywood	3-5	Banbridge (aet)
Instonians	4-1	Glenanne
Lisnagarvey	1-2	Cookstown
Mossley	4-0	Portrush
Pembroke	0-1	Cork Harl
Three Rock Rvrs	3-1	Avoca
QUARTER-FINALS		
Cookstown	1-3	Newry
Corinthians	0-2	Cork Harl
Instonians	3-2	Banbridge (aet)
Mossley	1-2	Three Rock Rvrs
SEMI-FINALS		
Instonians	3-1	Newry
Cork Harl	1-1	Three Rock Rvrs
(R: 2-2, Cork won 4-3 on pen strokes)		
FINAL		
Instonians	2-1	Cork Harlequins

years. The success also meant the Senior Cup stays in Ulster for the sixteenth successive year.

South Antrim captain Iain Watson and Man of the Match Dean Beckett receive their trophies after the Harp Intermediate Cup final, from Sam Jones, Ulster Branch President (left), and John Kelly, Guinness NI.

European Nations Cup

Ireland's national mens hockey coach, Cees Koppelaar, had more reason than most to delight in the 2-1 defeat of his home country, the Netherlands, at Belfield in July. It was Ireland's first victory over the world number two side in 22 attempts, and it came in Koppelaar's 100th game in charge (since 1987). Robbie Taylor's first-half strikes also gave the Irish team the perfect boost ahead of August's Nissan European Nations Cup, at the same venue. The coach set a pre-tournament target of 5th place, and again he was a happy man, as a thrilling 4-3 defeat of Poland achieved Ireland's highest-ever finish. Two more goals from Taylor, and a double from Liam Canning, earned the victory. Earlier in the tournament, Ireland beat Belarus (2-1), Spain (3-1), drew with England (1-1), and, weakened by the loss of Jimmy Kirkwood in midfield, surprisingly lost 2-1 to Switzerland. Team captain Marty Sloan reached a personal milestone in July when he overtook Billy McConnell's record of 135 international appearances. He now sits on 149 caps. Ireland's ladies beat France, Italy and Belgium at their European Nations Cup in Amsterdam in June, before losing on penalty strokes to France, 4-3 after a 1-1 draw.

8

Joey Still King of the Road

writes Dermot James

Amid rumours of retirement Joey Dunlop's 25th season in the saddle has been something special. At 43 years of age, he ought to be past his prime ... but like good wine, Dunlop is still maturing! Yes, life in the fast lane of motorcycle road racing has been good to the unassuming North Antrim ace, and in return, biking's best ambassador has bridged all sorts of barriers, from Tandragee to Tallin in Estonia, where he managed to squeeze in a first-time trip between his record-breaking Isle of Man TT and Ulster Grand Prix success stories. The greatest TT rider of all time is still the fans favourite.

"I just can't resist going for another lap", he says. "I love the TT like I love motorbikes and racing on roads. I can't even say it's in my blood. My brother Robert and me are the only motorcycle racers in the family". But, with a record of 19 TT victories under his belt - five more than the legendary Mike Hailwood - the question on everyone's lips concerns Dunlop's future. Will he go on for another year, or will he finally hang up his leathers for good? He has a stock answer. "No, I'm not ready to disappear just yet. I still enjoy racing, especially the great feeling when you cross the finishing line in first place. If I gave up, I wouldn't know what to do at weekends. Honda keeps offering me bikes to race, so I can't turn them down! However, I will be cutting back on my schedule and I might just concentrate on the

125 and 250 classes. In 1995, I took in too many races during the first half of the season, and I just had to admit that I'd had enough".

The first thing people noticed about the young Joey Dunlop when he came on the scene a quarter of a century ago, apart from his racing ability, was his scruffiness! His long hair soon became his trademark, there's no show about him and he doesn't worry too much about things like appearance, but nobody takes more care on a motorbike than him. Joey's motto is to "go out and finish. To win is a bonus". Dunlop made his TT debut in 1976 and hasn't looked back. In June this year, he did the double in the 250cc Lightweight and Senior races. Following a family holiday in Portugal, Dunlop returned refreshed for the Ulster Grand Prix at Dundrod, where the track action was on a parallel with the freak weather conditions - hot! For the 66th 'Prix', Dunlop submitted six race entries, started in five, won three and had a fourth place and a seventh place. He admitted the Senior race was "tough going", and, due to sheer exhaustion, he didn't contest what should have been the main Superbike race. Still, he was able to steal a march on the men of the future with two 250 wins and a Superbike success that brings his tally of international victories at Dundrod up to 22. And, just for good measure, Dunlop submitted a last-minute entry for the final Ulster road race of the season, the Carrowdore 100, where he finished first, second, and third.

When Dunlop does decide to bow out, do we have any riders waiting in the wings to take his place? Not according to Joey's personal manager, Davy Wood, who says, "There will never be another Joey Dunlop. He was, and still is, something unique. However, I do feel that we have a few lads like James

Courtney, Denis McCullough and Chris Richardson, who're beginning to carve out a niche for real road racing. One of the launching pads for this brand of racing is the Manx Grand Prix, and in that contest we produced two excellent winners this year in Ricky Mitchell and Norman Gordon". Unlike the days of Robert Dunlop and Stephen Cull, few of the current crop of racers can successfully combine road and track racing. However, for Dungannon's Phelim Owens (pictured left), these two specialised speed branches are inseparable - he can win at the North West and at Dundrod, while still more or less holding his own on the English tracks. Talking about tracks, Jim Falls is beginning to make a big impression on the man-made circuits, just as Eugene McManus did in 1994. McManus, from Randalstown and with Padgett-Yamaha, is nearing the end of his first full 500cc Grand Prix season, and has every reason to feel proud of his learning curve which, by the end of August, had earned him four precious World Championship points. Glengormley's Jeremy McWilliams had high hopes of improving on his twelfth place in the 1994 World Championship, but early in the season he crashed in Australia and was fourteenth in Malaysia. It's been a frustrating time for Jeremy, with a string of niggling problems, though he did have the satisfaction of a personal best seventh place at Le Mans.

But, when all is said and done, and the roar of machines fade into the distance, the punters will still be talking about William Joseph Dunlop MBE ... he's still King of the Road!

North West 200

Phillip McCallen was a double winner, crossing the line first in the 250 and Regal 600 races. Phelim Owens won the battle of the 125s, Ian Newton took the Junior 250/400 title, Ian Simpson won the Mobil 1 Superbike contest, and Robert Holden was successful in both the Superbikes and Supermono.

Ulster Grand Prix

Joey Dunlop won both 250 races and the opening Superbike class. Robert Holden took the second Superbike race, Iain Duffus won the Regal 600 title, Rob Fisher won the sidecar race and James Courtney was first in the 125 class.

Bowls

Northern Ireland's Eileen Bell made her 150th international appearance at the British Isles Championships at Ballymoney, to become the most-capped woman player in the world. The tournament returned to the province for the first time since 1969. On the club scene, Carrickfergus beat Ballymena to take the top team prize in Irish Bowls, the CIS Senior Cup, and Noel Graham won the Irish Singles Championship.

Snooker

Julian Logue (Coleraine) defeated Colin Bingham (Antrim) 10-6 to win the N.Ireland Championships at the Coach Club, Hillsborough. The semi-final losers were Barry McNamee and Joe Meara, while 17-year-old Mark Easdale made a record break on 125, bettering Joe Swail's previous best (118). On the club scene, Parkside from Lurgan became All Ireland champions for the third year in-a-row. Joe Swail beat Nigel Gilbert 10-8 at the World Championships in Sheffield, and led John Parrott 10-7 in the 2nd Round, but lost the match 13-11.

Bertie Achieves his Goal

Persistence paid off for Bertie Fisher when he won the AA Circuit of Ireland Rally for the first time in his two-decade career. The Ballinamallard driver had won almost everything except Ireland's premier event, and had been on the verge of calling a halt to his career, so even when he spun twice on the fourth and final day, he was not going to be denied. Partnered by Letterkenny's Rory Kennedy, Fisher brought his Toughmac Subaru Impreza home safely, ahead of Stephen Finlay. He had led from the first stage in Castle Park, Bangor, on Good Friday. Frank Meagher was third, Ian Greer 4th, and David Greer 5th. A revitalised Fisher went on win the Shell International Donegal Rally and the Stena Sealink Ulster Rally. In the former, he had just 15 seconds to spare over Donegal's James Cullen, after a titanic struggle right to the end of the last stage on Malin Head. At one point, the gap closed to just five seconds, and Fisher admitted after winning the rally for a record-equalling fourth time, "Neither of us deserved to lose". The Fermanagh driver completed his hat-trick in the Ulster Rally at the expense of Finlay. He led from start to finish, and knew he was on his way when he beat the Ballygawley man over his home stage. Liam O'Callaghan was third, Alistair McRae 4th, Gwyndaf Evans 5th, and Andrew Nesbitt 6th.

Eddie Irvine Pays for Success in Canada

Conlig's Formula One Motor Racing driver Eddie Irvine appeared on the winner's podium at a Grand Prix for the first time in Montreal, but at a cost. "I promised all the mechanics Breitling watches if I finished in the top three. After coming third, the bill came to ten thousand pounds, but it was worth it". Irvine's previous best was 4th in Jerez in 1994. Considering winter testing went very well (only Shumacher was quicker), 1995 was disappointing. He was 5th in Spain, 7th at Silverstone, 8th in France, 10th in Portugal, and failed to finish eight races, but Irvine has much to look forward to after his "dream move" to Ferrari. In 1996, he will partner Michael Shumacher and aims to emulate the World Champion, now that he is part of a top-four team. "Every driver dreams of Ferrari. This is an opportunity which I would not want to miss".

9

No More Tea and Buns

International and Local Cricket

"The tea and buns version of the game is over. We have got to find out which players really want to play for Ireland". Ireland captain Alan Lewis was in angry mood after the unsuccessful experiment of taking part in the early season new-look Benson and Hedges Cup, in which Ireland suffered four one-day defeats. They were dismissed for just 80 runs by Surrey at the Oval, they lost to Sussex at Hove by 63 runs, then to Kent by ten wickets at Comber, and by 233 runs to Somerset at Eglinton, our heaviest-ever one-day loss. The last five batsmen failed to score (see score-card). There were bright spots, like Michael Rea's innings of 73 in his 50th international at Hove, Lewis's 67 against Kent, and the introduction of some new blood, but the 31-year-old captain would like to be involved in major changes.

"Let's face it, Irish cricket is fraught with parochialism. We need to pull together and get organised as a national team. Before the first B & H game with Surrey, we didn't have a single outdoor practice session. Indoor facilities are a priority for the winters, and I feel we need a system where a body of selectors pick a group of 20-25 players and then leave it to a supremo to choose the 11 in consultation with the captain of the day" (there are currently seven selectors). However, it's not all gloom. Indoor facilities have since been secured at Queens University, Garfield Harrison has been active in taking cricket into the schools, in his role as Development Officer, and in February, the Irish Cricket Union appointed former England fast bowler Mike Hendrick as their first full-time coach, on an initial six-month contract. He was disappointed but not surprised by the B & H displays, "there is a massive gap between amateurs and county professionals, but we want to close that gap, and at least, the players now know how tough you have to be to perform consistently against county sides". Hendrick's brief was also to work with the Ireland Youth Team and to help structure the game throughout Ireland.

Young players given their chance in the senior team in 1995 include Peter Gillespie (Strabane), Jason Molins (Carlisle), Ryan Eagleson (Carrickfergus), Mark Patterson (Cliftonville), Owen Butler and Stephen Ogilby (Bready), most of whom featured in a short tour of England in June. Ireland beat the Duchess of Norfolk XI and drew with the MCC,

IRELAND V SOMERSET	
S.Warke lbw Rose	19
A.Dunlop lbw Rose	1
S.Smyth c Trescothick b Rose	11
A.Lewis b Trump	23
J.Benson c Trescothick b Rose	4
G.Harrison c T'coth b Hayhurst	18
D.Curry b Trump	0
U.Graham lbw Hayhurst	0
M.Patterson c Turner b H'hurst	0
S Ogilby c T'coth b Trump	0
O Butler not out	0
Extras (lb 4, w 3)	7
Total (39.2 overs)	83

WEST INDIES	
S.Williams c Smyth b Doak	34
S.Chanderpaul st Ogilby b Harrison	101
B.Lara c & b Doak	9
K.Arthurton not out	94
R.Richardson c Doak b Eagleson	57
C.Hooper not out	1
Extras	10
Total (4 wkts declared)	306

IRELAND	
S.Warke c Bishop b Gibson	0
J. Molins b Gibson	0
S. Smyth not out	98
A.Lewis c Williams b Drakes	8
J.Benson not out	74
Extras	7
Total (3 wkts)	187
MATCH DRAWN	

thanks to innings of 72 and 74 by Alan Lewis, and 66 from Stephen Smyth. In July, Eagleson took the wicket of West Indies captain Richie Richardson at Clontarf while Neil Doak, who made his rugby debut for Ulster against Northern Transvaal earlier in the year, claimed the prize scalp of Brian Lara. There was further encouragement when Justin Benson and Stephen Smyth, (who is also known for his rugby talents), put on an unbeaten 161 for a record one-day partnership for the fourth wicket, even though the tourists had taken their foot of the pedal after scoring a scintillating 306 for 4 in only 52.3 overs. Richardson hit Garfield Harrison for three sixes in one over, while Chanderpaul reached his century in less than two hours.

Stephen Smyth batting for Ireland against Somerset at Eglinton.

Last-Ball Drama for North Down
Royal Liver Assurance Irish Senior Cup

The McCrum brothers played central roles in taking North Down to the decider. Paul scored 74 not out in the quarter-final defeat of Railway Union, and 98 in their semi-final with Downpatrick. Charlie totalled 125 in the latter, so making a record partnership of 239-0 for a ten-wicket win. Bready beat Eglinton (Mark Olphert 72 not out), and Woodvale on the way to the final where Charlie McCrum took their last wicket off the last ball when they were two runs short of victory.

QUARTER-FINALS			
Downpatrick	bt	Brigade	by 5 wkts
North Down	bt	Railway Union	by 8 wkts
Woodvale	bt	Limavady	by 57 runs
Bready	bt	Eglinton	by 4 wkts
SEMI-FINALS			
North Down	bt	Downpatrick	by 10 wkts
Bready	bt	Woodvale	by 8 wkts
FINAL			
North Down	bt	Bready	by 1 run

Ivan is 51 Not Out
Waringstown win the Touche Ross Senior Cup

QUARTER-FINALS			
North Down	bt	Laurelvale	by 9 wkts
Lisburn	bt	North	by 6 runs
Waringstown	bt	Instonians	by 86 runs
Lurgan	bt	Downpatrick	by 5 wkts
SEMI-FINALS			
Waringstown	bt	Lisburn	by 43 runs
Lurgan	bt	North Down	by 4 wkts
FINAL			
Waringstown	bt	Lurgan	by 8 wkts

Strangford Road, Downpatrick, has to be Waringstown's favourite second home, for they have won all of their thirteen finals since the decider moved there in 1973. 51-year-old Ivan Anderson also maintained his winning sequence in those finals in the defeat of Lurgan, as it brought him his fifteenth winners medal (beating Roy Harrison's record). And, he took the important Lurgan wicket of Ross McCollum. Alan Nelson became the twentieth Waringstown captain to receive the trophy (North Down lead the Roll of Honour with 24 wins). On their way to the final, Waringstown beat Derriaghy by 104 runs (Garfield Harrison 4/17), Instonians by 86 runs (Neil Carson 90), and Lisburn by 43 runs (Shane Harrison 50) in their semi-final. Meanwhile, Lurgan's Ross McCollum amassed a total of 185 in their defeat of Collegians, while Craig Irwin (64 and two wickets) was Man of the Match in the tense quarter-final defeat of Downpatrick. Lurgan passed their victory target of 248 with just five balls to spare. In the semi-finals, opener Graeme Hunter's 97 not out contributed to the defeat of North Down. Elsewhere, Lisburn and North had a rare old battle in their quarter-final, with North's Davy Johnston dismissed in his attempt to win the match with a six off the last ball. Lisburn captain Uel Graham scored 83.

No Mercy From Hendy
Eglinton win the North West Northern Bank Senior Cup

Eglinton captain Henderson Wallace promised "no favours" to cup final newcomers Crindle at Beechgrove, and he didn't give any as his team cruised to victory by a record margin of 259 runs. Eglinton made 285 in their first innings before skittling Crindle for just 107 (top scorer 16), and choosing to bat again rather than force the follow-on. Wallace and Stephen Smyth added centuries (144 and 100) in a fourth-wicket partnership of 217, taking their team out of reach. Crindle were left to chase an impossible target of 496. Nigel McElwee made a gallant 99, but the losers were badly handicapped from early in the match by the loss of their professional, Shantu Sugwekar, with a hand injury.

Eglinton players applaud as their captain Henderson Wallace raises the Senior Cup. Wallace also won the Man of the Match Award for innings of 45 and 144, and for taking six wickets.

Cliftonville Win Ulster Bank Senior League Title

Cliftonville claimed the league title for the first time since 1938 when they defeated rivals Lisburn by two wickets at Wallace Park. 21-year-old Irish international Mark Patterson hit the winning runs while New Zealander Simon Winter top-scored with 47. Limavady clinched the North West Lion Sports Section One title with a superb 109 from Dessie "Decker" Curry against Sion Mills.

Ulster Harp Derby

'Munif', ridden by Mike Kinane and from the Dermot Weld stable, was first home in the Northern Ireland Ulster Harp Derby at the Maze in July. Ireland's richest premier handicap was worth £50,000 overall, and 32,500 to the winner. Jean Francois Jamet presented the Ulster Harp Trophy to David Caffery.

Driven by Guinness!

Guinness Northern Ireland Sales Representative Ken Welby and his son Simon, Group M9 winners at the Circuit of Ireland International Rally, pictured with Guinness NI Managing Director Brian Duffy.

Carlsberg Ulster Tennis

Ireland Davis Cup player Owen Casey won the Carlsberg Ulster Tennis Mens Championship
at the Belfast Boat Club, beating Paul Robinson in the final, 6-0 6-4.
Dublin's Karen Nugent defeated Claire Curran from Belfast in the ladies singles, 3-6 7-6 6-4.

Smithwicks Darts

Smithwicks N.Ireland Open champion John Magowan (Donaghadee) receives his trophy from
Danny O'Brien, Guinness NI. L-R: Michael Bunting, Secretary; Sam Kirkpatrick; Brian Elder, beaten finalist;
Trevor Ditty, Comp.Sec.; Norman McCutcheon, Treasurer; Raymond Wilson, Chairman.

10

Netball

Northern Ireland Plays 'Catch-Up'

Northern Ireland finished the World Championships in Birmingham in July in 17th place, well out of the running for honours and years behind winners Australia in terms of skill, technique, and athleticism. "It's no wonder", explains Linda Brien, "Australia have 750,000 netball players, we have 300. They are fully supported by the Australian Institute of Sport and even had physchiatrists and physchologists with them. They've also had an advanced coaching development scheme in place for years, and until we start something similar, we'll always be playing catch-up". Ironically, N.Ireland has improved since the 1991 World Cup, under English coach Anne Anderson, but other countries have improved even more. The Aussies have spread the word in the Southern Hemisphere, to the likes of Singapore, while interest in New Zealand in the Championships was such that all their games were televised live at 4am. South Africa almost made a glorious return to the competition, losing 68-48 to Australia in the final, but they helped boost the number of entries from 21 to 28. N.Ireland dropped from 12th in the world to 17th, but rose in status on these shores with convincing victories over the Republic (66-49) and Scotland (60-37). Singapore, Bermuda, and Namibia were also accounted for in a demanding schedule, but defeat by Wales in their last game cost N.Ireland an automatic place next time round.

Action from a warm-up match for the World Championships, between Northern Ireland and Trinidad & Tobago in Belfast. Pictured are Lynn Sheldon (shooting), Helen McCambridge, and captain Jenny Bradley.

11

Mairin The Star of County Down

Mairin McAleenan has undoubtedly been the "Star of the County Down" in 1995, with scoring exploits to rival and better Peter Canavan. The team captain (pictured right) accounted for 3-6 of Down's 3-8 in their Intermediate Championship semi-final defeat by Tipperary, and she contributed 1-2 to the Ulster Senior Championship Final victory over Antrim at Corrigan Park in October (2-13 to 1-8). Mairin also powered her club, Leitrim Fontenoys, to the Ulster Club title with a personal tally of 1-10 in the final. Elsewhere, Armagh were victims of their own success, as the step-up to National Senior level proved to be a sobering experience. They had gained promotion by virtue of winning two Junior League titles, and became the first county from the province to contest the Senior equivalent, but were heavily defeated in the final by Cork. Still, Tom Monaghan's team has made good progress in the nineties, as has the game of Camogie in Ulster. The Ashbourne Cup (Higher Education) came here for the first time in 1991 and stayed until last year, while the number of clubs has risen to 152. Lavey (Derry) and Lacken (Cavan) emerged in 1995 to win their first county championships, while new champions in Antrim and Armagh were Cushendall and Ballymacnab. The Ulster Junior title was claimed by Antrim for the first time time since 1981, as they defeated Derry in the final. Goalkeeper Karen Coyles links the Antrim success of fourteen years ago with today. At under-age level, Derry is recognised as the camogie power-base for the future. St Marys, Magherafelt, and St Pats, Maghera, accounted for all five provincial trophies this year.

"Surely" the best! Down '95. Back, L-R: Maeve O'Neill, Pauline Green, Tracey Donnan, Cathy Mulholland, Edele Mason, Nuala Magee, Sinead McGovern, Nicky McGee, Monica McCartan, Ciara McGovern, Carol Gilmore, Ann Ward, Valerie Hynds, Jennifer Braniff. Front: Kathleen Smith, Veronica McGreevey, Bridgeen Sands, Deirdre Savage, Donna Greeran, Dolores Smyth, Laura Smyth, Mairin McAleenan, Colleen Hynds, Claire McGovern, Wendy Trimble.

SURE

✓

"IT WON'T LET YOU DOWN"
IRELAND'S NO. 1 DEODORANT

OFFICIAL SPONSORS
OF THE
DOWN COUNTY CAMOGIE TEAM
1995 / 1996

12

Crocodile Derry!

World Cup Triathlon, by Edward Smith

Sometimes events occur which transcend the ordinary, and silence the unbelievers. When this occurs, they are entitled to be known as happenings. The sport of triathlon seemed an implausible candidate to be added to the list of happenings, as it was surely a minority consideration practised by "nutters".

Three men had met in a bar in Hawaii seventeen years before. One was a swimmer, one a cyclist, and one a runner. They got drunk and started to argue over who was the fitter. No accommodation could be found, so they decided to have a race. It was to be over the classic distance for each sport - a 2.4 mile swim, a 112 mile cycle, and a 26.2 mile run. The race became known as the Hawaii Ironman. Today, it enjoys global recognition, though in the ways of Darwin, severe tinkering has been necessary to pander to the masses, to television, and to gain Olympic status (Triathlon is in the Sydney 2000 programme). And so, the World Cup race came to Derry on June 17, and would be raced over a 1.5k swim in the Foyle estuary, a 40k cycle, and a 10k run. How Derry came to be in a series that read like the Times Atlas: San Sebastian, Gamagori, Ilheus-Bahai, Auckland, etc, was uncomplicated. Various government agencies had stomped up over £100,000 for the privilege, wooed by television exposure around the world that would show Derry in favourable light, post ceasefire. Sport was in the frontline for spreading the gospel of peace. Irish-American Garrett McCarthy provided a focal point for the home crowd, though his mind appeared to be on a new Irish pub he'd opened back home in Colorado, and he was disgruntled by the World Cup management who had scrapped the drafting rule in the interest of a more exciting race, allowing triathletes to shelter behind each other on the bike section. The race began modestly enough, but as they hurtled over the Craigavon and Foyle bridges, the reigning world champions, Brad Bevan and Emma Carney, both Australian, showed first. Bevan is known as "The Croc" because he used to race the long-tailed amphibious tropical saurian across the creek near his home, to improve his swimming. Carney had been rocketed virtually overnight from Commonwealth 10,000 metre runner to world champion triathlete, and although she lacked Bevan's charisma, there was a steely resolve behind the shyness. When asked what her chances of winning were, she replied: "I didn't sit in a 747 for 28 hours to come second". By the time the leaders reached the last stage of their respective races, all vantage points were taken on Derry's historic walls, and on Shipquay Street which the athletes had to climb five times. It would probably have been easier to climb a gable wall. The Diamond and the confines of the city burned with appreciation as Bevan completed the trip in a shade over one hour, 50 minutes, and as Carney won the womens race in 2.01.22. Bevan, perhaps the world's fittest man, said the reception had been better than at the World Championships. It had been a happening. It would happen again.

Above & Below: The Derry public turned out in force to support the triathletes.

Mens race: 1. Brad Bevan (Australia), 2. Hamish Carter (New Zealand), 3. Philippe Fattori (France),
4. Richard Allen (GB), 5. Remy Rampteau (France).
Womens race: 1. Emma Carney (Australia), 2. Isabelle Mouthon-Michellys (France),
3. Jenny Rose (New Zealand), 4. Sophie Delemer (France), 5. Kristie Otto (Canada).

OUR OBJECTIVES

To increase committed participation in sport and physical recreation amongst the population with particular emphasis on young people.

To raise standards of performance amongst participants and to enable those with the potential to excel to do so.

To promote the good reputation and efficient administration of sport in Northern Ireland.

For further information please contact:

The Sports Council for Northern Ireland
House of Sport, Upper Malone Road, Belfast BT9 5LA
Telephone: (01232) 381222

13
Masterful Maghera

Bank of Ireland MacRory Cup/Hogan Cup

Sean Lockhart made history on becoming the first player to be named on both the Colleges All Stars football and hurling teams. He also captained St Pats, Maghera, to an emphatic MacRory Cup triumph, and played the final with a broken finger! "The ball hit my finger in training a few days before, but I thought it was just staved. I strapped it up for the final and found out the next day that it was broken".

Sean was already out of the Hogan Cup semi-final, because of the age ruling, but his successor as captain, Conleth Murphy, did not let Lockhart's heroics go unnoticed. "It's a measure of the man that he played in a MacRory final with a broken finger. If it had been me, I would have been out for ages. Sean has been the rock of our defence all year". He's a centre-half-back in the mould of Henry Downey, who just happens to be Sean's favourite player. And, just like Henry, Lockhart got forward to register a point for Maghera in the final at Clones, while also successfully managing to keep an eye on the St Colmans

Sean Lockhart plays through the pain barrier in the Bank of Ireland MacRory Cup final.

	Maghera	Colmans
Daly (F)		0-1
Gribben (F)	0-1	
Gribben	0-2	
McErlain	0-3	
Martin	0-4	
Diamond	0-5	
Gribben	0-6	
McErlain	0-7	
Diamond	0-8	
Lockhart	0-9	
Tohill	0-10	
HALF-TIME		
McErlain	0-11	
McErlain (F)	0-12	
Cushnahan	0-13	
Gribben (P)	1-13	
Quinn (F)		0-2
Daly (F)		0-3
McErlain (F)	1-14	
Allen		0-4
Morgan		0-5
FULL-TIME		

attack. The Newry team did take the lead early on, but amazingly, they did not hit the target again until the second-half when they trailed by 1-13 to 0-1. The eventual winning margin, 12 points, was the widest in a final since 1968.

Adrian McGuckin Junior did not make the scoresheet, yet he won the Man of the Match Award for his involvement in the build-up to most of Maghera's best moves. Playing full-forward, he set up Michael Gribben and Damien McErlean for scores, and was fouled for point number seven. Gary Cushnahan was another beneficiary of McGuckin's clever play in the second-half, just before Gribben thumped a penalty left-footed, a la Ross Carr, to the Newry net. Maghera's trademark of crossfield passing and support play was once again in evidence, as they swamped and demoralised the challengers. For this, Adrian McGuckin Senior gets the credit, though he was assisted by a familiar face, as Dermot McNicholl returned to the school where he made his name as a four-time MacRory winner and the youngest-ever All Star. "There's a slight difference in training since my days, in that we ease up a bit before the final, but otherwise, Adrian still prepares thoroughly. He does his homework on every potential outcome and caters for every move".

Maghera finished top of their qualifying group and wrapped up their quarter-final, against Monaghan at Moortown, within ten minutes. Goals from Gribben and David O'Neill killed the contest. A stiffer test supposedly lay ahead, in the form of the fancied Abbey team, but again, the Derry side won convincingly at Armagh. Playing with the breeze, they led 7-0 at the break. When Maghera re-appeared for the second-half, they faced a snow blizzard, yet upped their game. Mark Diamond and Cushnahan pointed, and Fintan Martin set up Diamond for a glorious goal. Abbey coach Val Kane, who finally saw his team score in the 38th minute, paid tribute to the winners after the game. "Your work off the ball and closing down was brilliant".

Maghera's dominance of the competition (they have appeared in 17 of the last twenty finals, winning ten) may be a little concerning for the organisers. In recent times, Dungannon, Enniskillen and St Colmans have taken the title, but Maghera, with more than 1300 pupils, looks capable of leaving the smaller CBS and

TOP SCORERS

Michael Gribben (Maghera)	2-10
Rory Gallagher (E'killen)	0-14
Damien McErlain (Maghera)	0-11
Paul Holmes (Armagh)	0-10
Conor Daly (St Colmans)	1-7
Mark Diamond (Maghera)	1-4
Gavin Treanor (Abbey)	1-2
Brendan McKenna (E'killen)	1-2
Aidan Quinn (St Colmans)	0-5
Aidan O'Rourke (Abbey)	1-1
Adrian Doran (Abbey)	1-1
David O'Neill (Maghera)	1-1

competition these days from a neighbouring school. St Marys, Magherafelt, made an encouraging debut in the MacRory Cup when they ran St Colmans close in their quarter-final at Armagh, losing 8-7. Coached by Henry Downey and captained by Johnny McBride (Derry minor captain), they led 4-3 at half-time

and really should have won. "I suppose our superior experience at this level told in the end. When it was needed, we got the scores but they should take great heart from their performance", explained Peter McGrath after Conor Daly and substitute Ronan Allen had won the game with late scores for St Colmans. The Magherafelt team, which was without the injured Joe Cassidy and Cathal Diamond, was: Michael Scullion, Cormac McIvor, Ronan Shields, Seamus McGuckin, Paul McFlynn, Adrian McCallin, Brian Lavery, Johnny McBride (c), Michael Muldoon, Thomas Martin, Noel Doyle, Kevin Madden, Gavin Scullion, Ben Henry, and Gerard Cassidy. Fourteen-man St Colmans produced another storming second-half to win their semi-final with Enniskillen. After full-back Paul Shields had been sent off, Conor Daly scored the clinching goal following a 40-yard soccer style run. The Fermanagh boys had come through a two-game tussle with Armagh at Aughadrumsee. Rory Gallagher equalised for Enniskillen from a free-kick at the end of the first contest, and the home side again came from behind the next day, to force extra-time. Substitute Michael Quinn struck the decisive goal in the second period. In the last quarter-final, the Abbey led Dungannon by 1-8 to 1-1 at half-time, with a goal from Aidan O'Rourke, and two more from Gavin Treanor and Adrian Doran won the game.

Bank of Ireland 1995 Ulster Colleges Football All Stars.

St Colmans, losing MacRory Cup finalists: Back, L-R: Alan O'Neill, Diarmuid Reid, Kevin Franklin, Shane Collins, Stephen Neeson, Aidan Quinn, Thomas Morgan, Eamonn Farrell. Front: Conor Daly, Ronan Allen, Brian McKeown, Kevin O'Reilly (c), Sean McCusker, Padraig Matthews.

St Pats Maghera
MacRory and Hogan Cup Winners, 1995

St Pats, Maghera, 1995 Back, L-R: John Heaney, Damien McErlain, Dominic Lynn, Brian Tohill, Gary Doyle, Sean McPeake, Michael Kelly, Gary Cushnahan. Middle: Ryan Lynch, Padhraic McCloskey, Paul Wilson, Michael McMullan, Niall Farren, Danny McGrellis, Tomas Scullion, Paul Diamond, Eoighinn Farren. Front: Adrian McGuckin (coach), Aengus Murphy, Conleth Murphy, Adrian McGuckin, Sean Lockhart, Sean McElwee (Principal), Mark Diamond, David O'Neill, Michael Gribbin, Stephen McGeehan, Dermot McNicholl (assistant coach). Missing from picture: Fintan Martin.

Hogan Cup

Semi-Final - St Pats, Maghera 1-10   Tuam 0-9
Final - St Pats, Maghera 2-11   Good Counsel, New Ross 1-6

Mrs Tohill went through a mixture of emotions on the first day of May. There was pride and joy with Anthony starring for Derry in their National League semi-final defeat of Tyrone in Croke Park, and with younger son Brian winning a Hogan Cup final. She was also nostalgic with Brian being the last of her sons to play for Maghera, and she was concerned to hear that he had suffered a dislocated shoulder in the final. Brian recovered quickly enough, especially as he had a Hogan medal to bring home. MacRory winners may be easy to find around South Derry, but only three Maghera teams have gone on to win the All Ireland. Part of the reason is the loss of players though the age ruling, but this year they overcame the obstacle. Only a week after the MacRory final, Maghera beat Tuam at Ballyshannon, and then a goal from Damien McErlean saw his team lead New Ross by six points at half-time in the Hogan final. The excellent Aengus Murphy added a second goal.

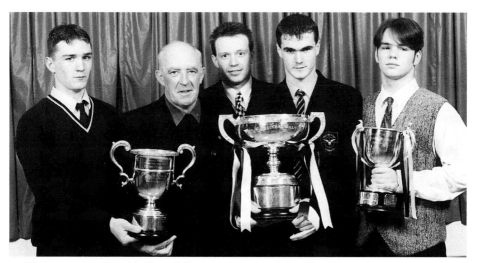

Winning captains. From left: Kieran Kelly, Cross & Passion, Ballycastle (Mageean Cup); Brother Ennis;
Harry Baxter, Bank of Ireland; Sean Lockhart, St Pats Maghera (MacRory Cup),
Martin Catney, St Michaels, Lurgan (MacLarnon Cup).

MAGHERA (HOGAN FINAL)
Danny McGrellis, Ronan Lynch, Niall Farren, Michael Kelly, Conleth Murphy (c), John Heaney,
Paul Diamond, Brian Tohill, Gary Doyle, Michael Gribben 0-4, Damien McErlean 1-2, Paul Wilson 0-1,
Gary Cushnahan 0-4, Adrian McGuckin, Aengus Murphy.

BANK OF IRELAND ULSTER COLLEGES ALL STAR FOOTBALLERS (see page 191)
Michael Scullion (Magherafelt), Malachy Murray (Abbey), Aidan O'Rourke (Abbey), John Heaney,
Conleth Murphy (Maghera), Tony McEntee (Abbey), Sean Lockhart (Maghera), John McCoy (Monaghan),
Sean O'Hare (Armagh), Justin Murray, Eamonn O'Neill (Dungannon), Rory Gallagher (Enniskillen),
Gavin Treanor (Abbey), Brian McGuckin (Dungannon), Darren Swift (Monaghan).

St Michaels win MacLarnon

St Michaels, Lurgan 0-14   De la Salle, Ballyshannon 2-7

St Michaels, Lurgan, learned from their mistakes to survive a late charge from Ballyshannon and go on to lift their fifth MacLarnon Cup at Clones. In 1994, they conceded an injury-time goal to Magherafelt in the final, but when the Donegal side repeated the act, the Lurgan boys had done enough to squeeze home. Martin Lavery and Neal Shanks had earlier scored vital points. However, St Michaels could not save their All Ireland semi-final, losing to a late goal. Lurgan's first MacLarnon success came in 1984. Past-pupils include Jim McCorry, Barry O'Hagan, Damien Horisk, Neil Lennon, and Pat McGibbon (N. Ireland international footballers).

SEMI-FINALS			
St Michaels, Lurgan	2-5	St Eunans, L'kenny	0-7
De la Salle, B'shannon	1-3	St Columbs, Derry	0-5 (R: 1-12 2-9, aet)
FINAL			
St Michaels, Lurgan	0-14	De la Salle	2-7
ALL IRELAND SEMI-FINAL			
St Michaels, Lurgan	1-10	Banada Abbey, Sligo	3-6

ST MICHAELS, LURGAN (SEE PHOTO)

Brian Fitzsimmons, Martin Toal, Shane Scullion, Adrian Campbell, Andrew Hamill, Kieran McVeigh, Gary Murphy, John Catney, Neal Shanks, Paul McStay. Front:: Michael Lavery, Jim McKeveney, Stephen Boyd, Neil McStravick, Philip Oldham (c), Anthony Gallagher, Michael Lavery, Martin Catney, Brendan O'Hara.

DE LA SALLE

Sean McGee, Damien Carr, Sean Maguire, James Phelan, Brendan Boyle, Patrick McGrath, Bobby Reynolds, Kenneth McGurrin, Paul Daly (c), Raymond Daly, Stephen Ward, Shane O'Donnell, Patrick O'Donnell, Barry Travers, Keith Mannion. Subs: Jason Regan, Matt Hughes. Squad: James Connolly, Brendan McHugh, Barry McEniff, Ciaran Connolly, Martin McCarron, Gerard Ferguson, David Hoey.

Hurling

All Ireland B semi-final
St Pats Maghera 1-14   St Jarlaths Tuam 1-7
All Ireland Final
St Pats, Maghera 0-5   Doon CBS 5-11

An exhibition of score-taking by Maghera's versatile captain Danny McGrellis saw his team through to the final at Navan. Fresh from helping the school's footballers in the Hogan Cup (he was the goalkeeper), McGrellis fired over eleven points against Tuam, with nine from frees, including a sideline cut. In the final, James Butler emerged the hero for Doon, with four goals to his name. The Maghera team was:

Joe McEldowney, Ryan Lynch, Gregory Brunton, Paul Kelly, Richard O'Kane, M. Kelly, Joseph McCloskey, Eoghan Farren, Padhraic McCloskey, Raymond O'Hagan, Danny McGrellis (c), Paul Murphy, Kieran Hinphey, Niall Farren, Gary Bradley. Subs: R. Kennedy, G. Bradley, M. Quigg.

Bank of Ireland 1995 Ulster Colleges All Star Hurlers

Conor McCarry (Ballycastle), Gregory Brunton (Maghera), Joseph Quinn (B'castle), David Cherry (La Salle), Kieran Kelly (B'castle), Sean Lockhart (Maghera), Stephen Grego (St Marys, B'fast), Kieran Killyleagh (La Salle), Ciaran McCaughan (B'castle), Sean Harvey (Garron Tower), Danny McGrellis (Maghera), Kevin Ward (St Marys), Eoin Farren (Maghera), Declan Toland (La Salle), Liam McMullan (B'castle).

Donegal Win All Ireland Vocationals

ULSTER FINAL
Donegal 1-18 Derry 0-7
ALL IRELAND SEMI-FINAL
Donegal 5-7 Kerry 2-10
ALL IRELAND FINAL
Donegal 1-12 Leitrim 0-7

"Surely a promising career lies ahead for many of these lads, like the Monaghan boys, Don and Barry. You will also hear the name of Reddan from Inishowen again. The captain, Brian McLaughlin, stands at over 6 feet tall, is a promising forward with obvious physical advantages, and James Boyle, brother of Tony, is quick with good talent to take a score" - Donegal Senior team manager, PJ McGowan. This year's Donegal Vocational Schools team was the first from the county to take the title in ten years. They beat North West neighbours Leitrim in the final, with Brian McLaughlin playing a captain's part with 1-6 of the winning total. Brian totalled 5-18 in the competition, with a remarkable four goals in the semi-final defeat of Kerry, which left Donegal manager John Joe O'Shea, with a few mixed feelings … he's a Kerry man. James Boyle contributed 1-20 to Donegal's cause, which began with Ulster victories over Tyrone, Cavan, and Derry. Barry Monaghan, son of Donegal All Star of the seventies, Donal, was outstanding at midfield.

DONEGAL (V LEITRIM)
David Greene, Gary Hilferty, Martin McMenamin, Don Monaghan, Rory Sweeney, Eamon Reddan, Gerard Cannon, Barry Monaghan, Dermot McColgan, David Carroll, Raymond Sweeney 0-1, Aodh Brennan, James Boyle 0-4, Brian McLaughlin (c) 1-6, Conal Doherty 0-1. Subs: Ciaran Browne for Carroll, Vincent Kennedy for McMenamin, Adrian McColgan for Brennan. Squad members: Shane McArt, Conal McFadden, Peter McHugh, Charles Boyle, Shane Griffin, Shaun McHugh, Martin Robinson, Bernard McGeehan, Paul Stevenson.

Vocational Schools Final

St Marks Warrenpoint retained the All Ireland Junior Vocational Schools title by beating Tullow Community School, 5-5 to 3-4 at Navan.

Their goalscorers were Lorcan Mussen, Shane Ward, Glenn McMahon, Shane Magill, and Paul Gannon. Ward, a Down minor, also scored two goals in the Ulster final at Dungannon. The team that day was: Ciaran Sloan, Paul Gannon, Paul McConville, Damien Campbell, Padraig Bradley, Declan Rooney, Brendan O'Hanlon, Louis O'Hare, Sean Farrell, Lorcan Mussen, Joe Rooney, Shane Magill, Glenn McMahon, Eddie Murtagh, Shane Ward.

Under-18	St Malachys, Castlewellan	bt	Abbey Vocational School, Donegal	
Under-16	St Marks, Warrenpoint	3-9	St Ciarans, Ballygawley	1-5
Under-14	St Malachys, Castlewellan	3-4	Dean McGurk School Carrickmore	0-11

St Marks, Warrenpoint celebrate their victory at Dungannon.

Jordanstown Win Sigerson Derby

Jordanstown beat Queens before a 1,000 crowd at the Dub in the quarter-finals, by 2-9 to 1-9, with goals from Ciaran McCabe and Ciaran McBride. But, in the semi-finals, they caved in to eventual winners UUC, by1-17 to 2-5, after early goals from Des Mackin and Mark Gallagher. UUJ turned the tables in the Ryan Cup final, winning by 2-11 to 1-7. The team that beat Queens was: Johnathan Kelly, Brian Grant, Brian Burns, Sean McGuckin, McGrady, Dermot Dougan, Jody Gormley, Rory Sharvin, Ger Colgan, Mark Gallagher (c), Mattie McGleenan, Gareth Bailie, Shane King, Des Mackin, Ciaran McBride, Ciaran McCabe.

Inst Re-Live Former Glories

Ulster Bank Schools Cup

Andrew Hirst was a member of the 1995 Schools Cup winning squad at the Royal Belfast Academical Institution. His Great Uncle Sidney was a member of the 1919 Cup winning squad at the same school, and his great uncle Wesley played in the team that won the Cup in 1912. Andrew's mother, Margaret, received a letter from Sidney, before this year's final. He wrote, "I'm glad to know the boys, Andrew and David, are keeping up the family tradition on the rugby field".

"Tradition" is the key word at RBAI. Many past-pupils maintain their links by joining the Instonians hockey and rugby club, by sending their sons to the school, and by supporting their teams. Eight of Instonians' 1995 Irish Senior Cup winning hockey team had been to the school, and much more of the older generations got behind the Inst teams which won the Schools Cup and Burney Cup on St Patricks Day. "There's a tremendous willingness among the old Instonians to see the school do well. We went to Shane Park (home of the Instonians club) on the night of the cup win with the hockey lads, and you could see how fanatical the people were", recalls current rugby coach Brian McLaughlin. The fact that Inst had bridged a gap of 25 years in lifting the Schools Cup was a further reason for elation among the old hands, especially given the standards set throughout the 20th century. In 1919, a report on the Cup final in the Schools News concluded, "this was the first time in the history of the school the the Cup had been won for two years in succession. We now stand second on the list of

Gareth McCullough (RBAI) makes a determined run in the Ulster Bank Schools Cup Final at Ravenhill.

schools, but second place is not good enough for Inst ... we hope it won't be long before we stand at the top of the list".

Brian McLaughlin was not a pupil at Inst, but is steeped in the tradition of the competition he regards as special. "The Schools Cup is very important, for Inst, Methody, and the others. I captained Ards to a Senior Cup Final but it's not the same, maybe because the Schools Cup has been

			RBAI	Bangor
6 mins	C.Shields (P)			3
9 mins	Stewart		5	
	Tate		7	
14 mins	C.Shields (P)			6
37 mins	C.Shields (P)			9
HALF-TIME				
44 mins	Arnold (DG)		10	
49 mins	McCullough (P)		13	
67 mins	P.Shields		18	
FULL-TIME				

going so long, or the fact that the players are well looked after and some of them probably play the best rugby of their career at school". McLaughlin played for Regent House in 1977, and coached Wallace to three semi-finals and a final, all without success. "That's why I'll never forget looking up at Arnie (RBAI captain Paul Arnold) holding up the cup at Ravenhill. He was nearly getting blown away but there was no chance of him letting go!"

There was also little chance of the coach being lifted off the ground by the gale-force winds, as his feet were firmly planted in the pitch beneath him. "I've never seen the conditions as bad. People in the Stand thought the roof was going to blow off, and I kept wondering if mud was going to come up over my wellies as I walked up the sideline. It was like a bog, particularly in the second-half". Given the conditions, Bangor captain Chris Shiels kicked superbly, but two Inst tries from Ashley Stewart and Paul Shields, proved decisive. Paul Arnold, who also played cricket for Ulster and Irish Schools this year, added a drop goal, while Jonathan Tate converted Stewart's try, and Gareth McCullough kicked a penalty.

"They're all good lads", reflects McLaughlin. "Arnie is a fine leader, Ashley is one of the hardest, aggressive and powerful players I've known, and Gareth is cocky - he knows how good he is and it shows in his play. He isn't scared to try things because he knows he can do it, which isn't always a bad thing". McCullough's willingness to accept responsibility was a key factor in their Second Round victory on another windy, wet day, at Portadown. Inst had led 8-0 at half-time with a try from wing forward Mark McAnally and a conversion by Tate, but when Neal Kennedy lifted Portadown with a try, McCullough took control of the game. He scored one of two late tries, the other from Richard Wayne-Barrett, as Inst ran out winners, 18-5. The 12-6 defeat of Coleraine took on a similar pattern. Tate scored a try in the opening five minutes, and Stephen Gray got another in the last five minutes, but in between Coleraine led 6-5. "That was our least convincing win", reckons Brian McLaughlin. "We were on the way out, despite dominating for 25 minutes, until a great break led to the late try. But, that day told me that we really had something. Before then, we had been beaten in several friendlies late on. Now, the tide had turned, and we never looked back". Inst confidently accounted for Belfast rivals BRA and Methody on their run to the final, giving particular satisfaction. "There's a lot at stake in derby games, you're playing against boys you socialise with and it's very keen. We

TEAMS IN FINAL			
BANGOR		**RBAI**	
Stuart Farmer	15	Kieron Holmes	
Glenn Devine	14	Ross Nicholl	
Kris McAuley	13	Gareth McCullough	
Ian Martindale	12	Stephen Gray	
Jeffrey Wright	11	Jonathan Tate	
Bryn Cunningham	10	Paul Arnold (c)	
Chris Shiels (c)	9	Michael Agnew	
Gavin Whyte	8	Ashley Stewart	
Neal Johnston	7	Patrick Heffron	
David McGinty	6	Mark McAnally	
Peter Maitland	5	Paul Mulholland	
Welsey Linton	4	Jonathan Keatings	
Richard Nelson	3	Paul Shields	
Richard Coghlin	2	Richard Wayne-Barrett	
Craig Blair	1	Ross Caldwell	
REPLACEMENTS			
Jonathan Bradford	16	James Oliphant	
Steven Garrett	17	Christopher McCandless	
Glen Corbridge	18	Andrew Roy	
Gavin Whan	19	Richard Latimer	
Mark English	20	Jonathan Whiteside	
Philip Barr	21	John Minnis	
John Coyle	22	Andrew Hirst	

were excellent in the second-half against BRA, pinning them in with the wind behind us, and our defence was brilliant against Methody. They weren't just tackling, they were knocking their men back".

Ross Nicholl scored the only try of the semi-final, while Tate and Gray kicked penalties, and McCullough landed a drop goal. Against BRA, Tate contributed 13 points and No.8 Ashley Stewart went over twice in a second-half try blitz.

Cup finalists Bangor defeated Antrim Grammar, Dalriada, Omagh Academy, and the holders, Regent House, on their way to the Ravenhill decider. The winning margin narrowed with each game, until their 10-9 semi-final success. Against Dalriada, two tries from Glen Devine cancelled out similar efforts from the losers by Stephen Lennox and Wesley Henry, while Bangor broke Omagh hearts with a last-minute try in their clash. The teams had been tied at 5-5, with Bryn Cunningham and Eric Smith exchanging tries. When Bangor pulled off a similar escape act in the semi-final defeat of their neighbours, Regent, hopes were high of the cup coming to the school for the first time since 1988. Ian Martindale scored a try at the start of the game, and another at the very end. In between, Andrew Laird kicked three penalties for Regent, but the same player was off-target when presented with a difficult chance from the last kick of the game.

As the delighted Bangor supporters spilled onto the pitch, I couldn't help but feel that the gaelic football equivalent of the Schools Cup, the MacRory Cup, might be enhanced by taking a few ideas from rugby. There was a superb atmosphere at the match, partly because Bangor and Regent are rival schools, and partly because the game was at 3 O'Clock on a school-day afternoon at Ravenhill. Hundreds of pupils arrived in Ulsterbuses and cheered their team from a packed Stand. The second semi-final was also played at Ravenhill on a school-day, whereas the MacRory semi-finals were played at Armagh and Knockbridge in County Louth on Saturday mornings. The organisers of that competition had enormous headaches with finding pitches, such were the poor conditions, but there does seem to something to be said for making the games more accessible and for making an occasion of the semi-finals.

RBAI – Back: Richard Latimer, Michael Kimber, Patrick Heffron, Andrew Roy, Richard Wayne-Barrett, Jonathan Whiteside, Jonathan Keatings, Chris McCandless, Mark McAnally, James Oliphant, Paul Mulholland, Stephen Gray, John Minnis, Paul Shields, Andrew Hirst, Ross Caldwell. Front: Kieron Holmes, Ross Nichol, Jonathan Tate, Paul Arnold (c), Ashley Stewart, Michael Agnew, Gareth McCullough.

Elsewhere, Portora from Fermanagh knocked out Foyle & L'derry with ten points from Ulster Schools out-half Timothy Thompson, and tries from Graham Lyttle and Andrew Carruthers. They then ran into Regent who scored all three tries in the match, by Michael Anderson, Neil Patton, and John Anderson. Dungannon began the competition as favourites, but fell to BRA after three meetings, with Sheldon Coulter finally sealing the tie for the Belfast side. Sullivan reached the quarter-finals thanks to two tries from Patrick Gregg against Lurgan, but were eliminated by Methody (Peter Gourley two tries, Peter Armstrong one). Omagh came from behind to beat Banbridge with two penalties from Daryl Simpson and a try from Adrian Hamilton. Simpson also came to the rescue in the 8-6 defeat of Rainey.

LAST TEN	
SCHOOLS CUP WINNERS	
1986	Bangor GS
1987	Methody
1988	Bangor GS
1989	Methody
1990	Methody
1991	Methody
1992	Coleraine AI
1993	Campbell College
1994	Regent House
1995	RBAI

TOP SCORERS, 1995	
Andrew Laird (Regent)	37
Jonathan Tate (RBAI)	28
Chris Shiels (Bangor)	19
Michael Anderson (Regent)	15
Kyle Johnson (Methody)	15
Ashley Stewart (RBAI)	15
Patrick Gregg (Sullivan)	15
Timothy Thompson (Portora)	10
James Beattie (Omagh)	10
Glen Devine (Bangor)	10
Bryn Cunningham (Bangor)	10
Ian Martindale (Bangor)	10

SCHOOLS CUP RESULTS, 1995

FIRST ROUND			
Antrim Grammar	0-17	Bangor Grammar	
Belfast High	7-15	Rainey Endowed	
BRA	11-3	RS Dungannon	(Rs)
Campbell College	57-11	Down High	
CAI	6-12	RBAI	
Grosvenor Grammar	7-11	RS Armagh	(R)
Larne Grammar	8-10	Foyle & L'derry	
Limavady Grammar	22-8	Friends	
Omagh Academy	16-5	Banbridge Academy	
Portora RS	13-8	Ballyclare High	
Regent House	19-18	Ballymena Academy	
Wallace High	6-10	Sullivan Upper	

SECOND ROUND		
Bangor Grammar	18-12	Dalriada
Campbell College	13-22	Methody
Foyle & L'derry	3-20	Portora RS
Limavady Grammar	10-28	BRA
Omagh Academy	8-6	Rainey Endowed
Portadown College	5-18	RBAI
RS Armagh	0-13	Regent House
Sullivan Upper	20-8	Lurgan College
QUARTER-FINALS		
Omagh Academy	5-10	Bangor Grammar
BRA	5-23	RBAI
Regent House	21-0	Portora RS
Sullivan Upper	7-26	Methody
SEMI-FINALS		
Methody	7-14	RBAI
Bangor Grammar	10-9	Regent House
FINAl		
RBAI	18-9	Bangor Grammar

Opposite page: Top: Jamie Hamilton (Omagh Academy) makes a spectacular pass.
Bottom: (from front) Omagh's John McCracken, Timothy Mairs, and Alan Knox wait for a line-out.

This page: Bangor, beaten finalists in the 1995 Ulster Bank Schools Cup.

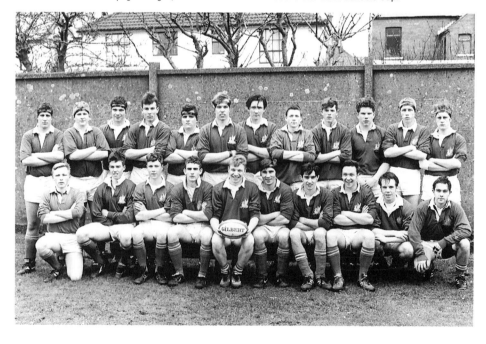

Regent House, Semi-finalists. Back, L-R: John Anderson, John McBride, Darren Hetherington, Michael Anderson, Andrew Laird, Stephen Kennedy, Richard Patton, Stephen Gardiner. Front: Paul Dempsey, Lee Waddell, Richard McCallum, Chris Caughey (c), Stephen Hollinger, Tom Trainor, Peter Sharpe.

Methody, Semi-finalists. Back, L-R: John Gray, Kyle Rowley, Neil Murphy, Fergus Magill, John Reynolds, Stephen Setterfield, Keith Haughey, David Munion, Kelly Crawford, Phil Murphy, Jonathan Todd, Peter Gourley, Stephen Kane, David Irwin, Andrew Penney. Front: Stephen Powell, Michael Finlay, Kyle Johnson, Stephen Boyd (c), Michael Irwin, Peter Armstrong, Steven Gilmore.

Ireland's Best Rugby School!

Dromore High School in County Down can lay claim to being the best rugby school in Ireland, by virtue of having the "School of the Year" Award bestowed on them by the IRFU. Under Headmaster Rex Russell, and coaches Charlie McAleese, Sandy Todd, and Andrew McClelland, they won several cups and were represented on the Ulster Youth Squad by Jonathan Wilson, Nigel Johnston, Mark Crothers, Mark Maguire and Jeffrey Aiken. At senior level, Richard Markey became the first past-pupil to play for Ulster, winning two caps.

Back, L-R: Charlie McAleese, Craig McCracken, Colin Kerr, Rex Russell. Front: Shane Sloan, David Cantley, Philip Morrow.

Inchmarlo Win Northern Bank Mini-Rugby

Inchmarlo Preparatory School beat Armstrong Memorial Primary, Armagh, at Ravenhill in June to become Mini-Rugby champions for the fourth year in-a-row.20 schools participated on finals day.Back, L-R: Richard Lowden (Northern Bank), Johnathan McMurray, Ryan Donaghy, Mark Wilson, Stephen Allen (Coach), Gavin Rainey, Des O'Donnell (Coach), Brian Halliday, Russell Coey (IRFU Ulster Branch). Front: David Kay, Simon McCabe, Richard Rainey, Patrick Simm (c), Simon Wells, Steven Rainey, Angus McCaffrey, David Brangam.

Clean Sweep for Inst

Northern Bank Burney Cup

FIRST ROUND		
Banbridge Academy	1-2	Sullivan Upper (R)
Friends, Lisburn	4-2	Grosvenor
Kilkeel High School	4-0	BRA
Portadown College	2-7	Cookstown High
Royal & Prior	0-2	RBAI (holders)
Wellington College	3-1	Newry High School
QUARTER-FINALS		
Bangor Grammar	0-2	Sullivan Upper (R)
Methody	0-2	Friends
RBAI	3-2	Cookstown High
Wellington	3-1	Kilkeel HS (R)
SEMI-FINALS		
RBAI	2-0	Wellington College
Sullivan Upper	1-2	Friends (aet)
FINAL		
Friends	1-2	RBAI

On the same day as their rugby colleagues lifted the Schools Cup, the Inst boys hockey team added the Burney Cup to their own impressive trophy cupboard. Captain Julian Lewis had already received the McCullough Cup and the Irish Schools Championship (beating Cookstown High in both deciders), though the atrocious conditions on St Patricks Day ensured the treble celebrations and Burney Cup presentation were held indoors. Inst have now won the cup nine times (and shared it three times), with four of those titles coming in the last eight years. Friends' last triumph was in 1978. Inst second eleven made it four trophies for their school by winning the Dowdall Cup, 2-0 against Banbridge Academy in the final. It wasn't a good year for Banbridge as their senior team surprisingly lost in the First Round of the Burney Cup, 2-1 to Sullivan Upper in a replay.

Safe and dry! Richard Lowden of the Northern Bank presents the Burney Cup to Julian Lewis.

FRIENDS: Patrick Bingham, Simon Crowe, Joceran Gichuke, Richard McNeill, Craig Lyness, Kevin Lunn, Brian Waring (c), David Carlisle, Neal McKnight, Niall Graham, Geoffrey McCullough.

INST: Johnathan Burns, Clark Kennedy, Mark Frawley, Jonathan Cowie, Patrick Towe, Mark Hill, Julian Lewis (c), Stephen Traub, Andrew Cousins, Mark Irwin, Jonathan Gibson. Manager - Colin Gault

Coaches - Simon Bell, David Scott

Dungannon Girls Make History

Irish Schools cap Claire Redpath became the first girl from Royal School Dungannon to lift the Senior Cup, after a nail-biting penalty shoot-out with holders and favourites, Ballymena Academy, in the final at Blaris . Coached by Instonians Cup winner John Atkins, the school reached their first final after beating Victoria College 1-0, with a goal by Rachel Hamill. Shauna Parkhill sent Ballymena through to a final they had won five times in seven years, but goalkeeper Cheryl Yorke, despite playing in her third decider, could not prevent RSD winning 3-1 on penalty strokes after a 0-0 draw. The champions later added the All Ireland Championship.

Dungannon's Kyra Forrest (centre) keeps her eye on the ball in the final.

Dungannon: Back, L-R: Jayne Nelson, Amanda Weir, Laura Burton, Rachel Hamill, Victoria Edwards, Lisa Hobson, Julie Nelson, Elaine Burnside, John Atkins (Coach). Front: Ruth Emerson, Joy Hadden, Kyra Forrest, Claire Redpath (c), Lesley-Ann Hall, Janice Williamson, Heather Greaves, Joanne Dugal.

Golf

Ralph Oakes, Northern Bank (Whitehead), presents the Froggatt Shield to **BRA** captain Kenny Smith, watched by team members (L-R) David Rush, Robert Hawthorne, Ian Barbour and Jonathan Hawthorne. BRA were later beaten in the final of the Irish Championship at Massareen by Tramore CBS.

Basketball

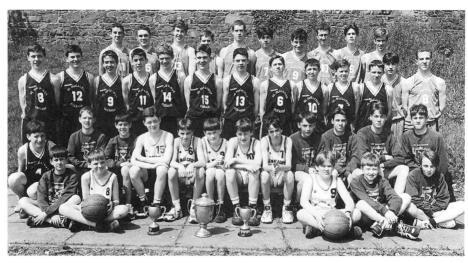

St Malachys, Belfast, won a hat-trick of titles in the Ulster Schools Series.
Back, L-R (Senior): Gary O'Neill, Neal McCotter, Matt McGuire, Gareth Fulton (c), Tom McCloskey, David McNeill, David Donnelly, John P.Walsh, Brian Lundy, David Wilson, Eamonn Lynch, James Boswell.
Middle (Under-14s): Ciaran Fox, Francis Joss, Peter Canavan, Eamon McElhinney, Damien Boylan, Andrew Brownlie, Simon Stewart, Paul Dunlop, Gareth Devlin, Chris Galloway, Brian McManus.
Seated: Michael McCann; (Under-13s) Mark Fulton, Deaglan Lundy, Declan Mellan, Gary McMullan, Paul McNally, Paddy O'Carroll, Michael Rogers, Paul Hill, Peter Greenwood, Diarmuid Phoenix, Ciaran Burns.
Front: Chris Whitson, Thomas Kane, Mark Taggart, Eamonn McManus, Adrian Hickey.

Athletics

Methody and Ballyclare High School shared the President's Shield as joint runners-up in the All Ireland Schools Athletics Championships at Tullamore. Pictured above is the Methody squad which struck gold in the high jump and triple jump, the latter thanks to Adam Smith (front), who was later selected for the Great Britain Junior team. Back Row, L-R: Mr.Davy Wells, James Magowan, Patrice Archer, Christopher Milligan, Ben Vrouhart, Neil Livingstone, Casey Blair, Neil Anderson, Richard Lloyd, Tony Shearer, Mr.Thomas Creighton. Front: Nathan Moore, Phil Murphy, David Browne, John Reynolds, David Irwin, Liam Nelson.

Cricket

Inst Make it a Treble! The cricketers of **RBAI** rounded off a superb year for their school by beating BRA by seven wickets to add the Ulster Bank Schools Cup to the successes of their rugby and hockey teams. Gareth McCullough and vice-captain Paul Arnold (pictured above with Dennis Aicken and the Stuart Grainger Trophy) also featured on the rugby fifteen, while Mark Frawley was also a member of the Burney Cup winning team. The rest of the cricket team was: Neal Notatowaski (c), Jonathan Burns, Ross Burns, Jonathan Corrie, Martin Dalzell, Connor McCully, Chris Murphy and Andrew Nixon.

Schools Football

NIE Youth Cup Final - St Malachys 1   La Salle 0

Solitude was the setting for a hard-fought North Belfast final of the NIE Youth Cup (Under-18, all Northern Ireland), which ended in a one-goal victory for St Malachys over rivals La Salle. The losers had Kevin Murray sent off and conceded a goal within the first 20 minutes, yet remained in contention to the end. St Malachys' goal came from Paul Kelly, after a corner from Damien Mooney, but Schoolboy internationals Liam McStravick and Gareth Fulton (also the St Malachys basketball captain) couldn't find another way past La Salle goalkeeper Barry McGreevy. The winners route to the final consisted of victories over Limavady High (2-1), Regent House (8-2), and Boys Model (2-0). La Salle needed replays to beat St Josephs and St Brigids.

Northern Bank Secondary Schools Cup Final
(Under-18, Belfast & District)   Castlereagh College 2 La Salle 1

Castlereagh College. Back, L-R: Martin Donaghy (Chairman, Belfast Schools FA), David Taylor Manager), Adrian Meredith, Ian Graham, Gary Bolton, Pat O'Hare, David Hopkins, Geoff Booth, Niall Hunter, Graham Montgomery (Northern Bank). Front: Raymond Carroll, Gareth Larmour, Peter Gillespie, Richard Cranston (behind), Colin Bell, Andrew McIntyre, Steven Jordan, Lee Feeney, Gary Wray (c), John McKendry, Colin Gill.

Termoncanice Retain NIE Primary Schools Cup

Goals from Gary Moore and Martin O'Doherty gave Termoncanice a 2-0 victory over Holy Family, Magherafelt in the final of the NIE Primary Schools Cup, played at Allen Park in Antrim. In the semi-finals, they defeated St Johns, Portadown, while Holy Family beat Slievemore 4-1. St John the Baptist won the Belfast Primary Schools Cup, for the 13th time in fourteen years, after beating Strandtown in the final. Their goals came from Damien Murray, Philip McFall and Jim Crossley, brother of Gerard, hero of La Salle's victory in the Connors Fuels Senior Schools Cup.

Dromore Boys Celebrate

Dromore Boys (under-11s) celebrate winning the Lisburn Credit Union Youth Cup final, after defeating Springfield Stars 4-3 in April.

Young Celt is La Salle Hero and Villain
Connors Fuels Senior Schools Cup

Glasgow Celtic signing Gerard Crossley scored in every round of the Senior Schools Cup (Under-15, Belfast & District) for La Salle, including four in the semi-final and both goals in the final, but he then marred his starring role by being sent off for retaliation fifteen minutes from time. La Salle beat Ashfield 2-0 at Ashley Park, Dunmurry, with Crossley scoring from the penalty spot after Sean Fox had been fouled, and from a corner. Stephen Matthews scored the fifth goal in the semi-final defeat of Corpus Christi while La Salle's other cup victims were Bearnagheeha (7-0), Orangefield (2-0), and Gransha (7-0), giving an impressive aggregate of 23-0. Ashfield beat Glengormley High (3-1) and Dunmurry (1-0) on their way to the final, with Colin Telford's winner in the latter game coming just five minutes from time.

La Salle: Back, L-R: Barry Mervyn, Philip Crossan, Rab Mervyn, Damien McAuley (c), Padraig Shortt, Johnathan Doherty, Sean Fox, Gerard Crossley, Gerard Boyle, Barry Lowe. Subs: Stephen Matthews, Brian Conlon, Martin Rodgers. Squad: Damien Stitt, Thomas Hall, Mark Muldoon.

Ashfield: Back, L-R: Mr.A.Jenning, Stephen McClung, Gary Armstrong, David McMullan, Philip Lewis, Michael Dougherty, Chris Holt, Stuart Greenaway, Anthony Reilly, Michael Downey. Front: Tyrone Bickerstaff, Martin Keyes, Jonathan Balloch, Colin Tedford, William Thompson, Vincent Harrison.

Tonagh Boys are the Real Thing!

Tonagh Primary School from Lisburn with the Coca Cola Small Schools Seven-a-side Cup.
Stephen Dougherty (captain), Simon Hull, Neil Campbell, Christopher Hull, Stuart Gore,
Christopher Kavanagh, and Richard Loughins.

All-Derry Battle in Bank of Ireland Senior Cup
St Columbs 1   St Peters 0

St Columbs, Derry, won the first all-Derry final in seventy years of Northern Ireland Schools Football, beating St Peters Secondary 1-0 in the Senior Cup (Under-15, all N.Ireland). A tense affair at the Brandywell required extra-time before St Columbs captain David Walker headed past the outstanding St Peters goalkeeper Paul McConway. In the semi-finals, St Columbs beat St Pats, Downpatrick 2-0, while Darren Murphy scored St Peters replay winner against Dunmurry, after a 2-2 draw.

Above: Brian Crossan (centre, St Peters) takes on the St Columbs defence. Others, from left: Paul Kearney, David Walker, Dermot Hegarty, Tony McLaughlin.   Below: Cup winners, St Columbs, Derry.

St Peters Secondary, Derry: Paddy Doherty, Mark Luukas, Mark McLaughlin, Brian Crossan, Paddy McLaughlin, Gerry Clifford, Philip Deehan, Gerard Reddan, John Lynch, Feargal O'Hagan (coach). Front: Darren Mooney, Declan Divir, Sean McSheffrey, Tony McLaughlin, Ray Green, Paul McConway, Darren Murphy, Liam Wilson, David Doherty.

Northern Ireland Under-15s

Back, L-R: Gareth Mackin (Glengormley HS), Brian Adair (Banbridge HS), Jonathan Topley (Clounagh JHS), Alan Parker (Crumlin HS), Philip McKeown (Carrick GS), Matthew Kerr (St Louis, B'mena), Aaron Hughes (Cookstown HS), Richard Graham (Kilkeel HS), Stephen Scullion (St Michaels, Lurgan), Paul Doherty (Limavady HS), George Doherty (Claudy). Front: Wayne Carlisle (Dunmurry HS), Paul Irwin (Coleraine Acad), Kevin Trueman (St Pats, Downpatrick), Gerard Crossley (La Salle), David Healy (Down Acad), Gary Hunter (Coleraine Sec).

Milk Cup has a Lotta Bottle!

The Northern Ireland Milk Cup 1983-95

"I'd heard about this competition but I never realised it was this good. It's the best I've seen in Europe, a real big jamboree, absolutely fantastic" - Everton manager Joe Royle speaking at the launch of the 13th Northern Ireland Milk Cup on July 24 at Coleraine Showgrounds.

58 teams, 1300 players, coaches and officials, 160 games, 14 venues, 40 referees, 300 volunteers and 40 flexibuses. This is a truly unique phenomenon and a tremendous tribute to the local organisers who had both the vision and the determination to establish an international youth soccer competition despite the backdrop of the troubles. "We obviously had an image problem, but people came here through the troubles and saw the normality of the people, and their warmth towards visiting teams, making them come back year after year", recalls Victor Leonard of the organising committee, which was originally formed by the Coleraine and District Youth League and the Northern Ireland Boys' Football Association.

In 1983, the first Milk Cup cost six thousand pounds to stage. A team from the Carnbane League had to be coerced into taking the numbers up to sixteen, and there was just one age group. Now, it's a three-tier competition with a new

Northern Ireland Under-19s receive their runners-up prize.

Everton and Norwich City contest the Under-14 Milk Cup final.

Under-19 section complimenting the Under-14s and Under-16s. The tournament really took off in the late 1980s, when Manchester United, Liverpool, Norwich and Rangers followed the lead shown by Jack Charlton's Newcastle United in coming to the North West. This year, the numbers were up from 44 teams to 58, with a top Premiership club among those unable to get in. The Milk Cup has paid dividends, not least for the local tourism industry, with 1300 beds required over four days in July.

Japanese team Shimizu S-Pulse were new this year, though they were on a double mission. First, they wanted to compete, and secondly, they wanted to win friends and promote their bid to stage the World Cup in 2002. Pens and badges were offered to anyone who asked, and they had their own television crew for the purpose of compiling a documentary. Australian team Perth United were also first-timers, having raised the cash in a novel way: the boys and their parents bought some ground, landscaped the site, built a house, painted it, and then auctioned it. Added to the money raised from other projects, they reached a total of $85,000 so that fifty parents could accompany the team on their trip of a lifetime. There's always a local connection of course, an exile who has an alterior motive for coming home, like Charlie Daze, one of "The Comedians", who brought the St Pauls club from Jersey. "I played a bit for Portadown but was injured at the age of 18 and had to quit. Now, I get tremendous pleasure out of seeing these kids play". Former Tottenham and Nottingham Forest star Johnny Metgod was in charge of the Feyenoord team which defeated the Japanese and Manchester United on their way to the Under-16 final against Russia. Unfortunately, the two continental finalists cancelled one another out in a drab nil-nil draw, leaving penalties to decide the winners. Spot-kicks were also required in the other finals, forcing the organisers to abandon extra-time in order to get through the programme on finals night at the Showgrounds.

However, the 8,000 crowd were compensated by the Under-14 and Under-19 finals, which produced plenty of goals and excitement. Martin O'Neill was present to see his Norwich City side throw away a 2-0 lead against Joe Royle's Everton, while Northern Ireland lost to Wales after leading 3-1 both in the game and in the shoot-out. Newry boys Chris Coffey (Arsenal) and Daniel Griffin (St Johnstone) had both headed goals from corner-kicks early in the game, while Philip Mulryne, the star of the tournament, scored Northern Ireland's third goal. Later in the summer, the 17-year-old broke into the Manchester United reserves.

International manager Brian Hamilton had initiated the involvement of what was really the Under-18 Northern Ireland team, as he recognised the value of such competition. Joe Royle echoed this view, "It gives lads experience of situations and it allows us to see how they learn, act and react in this type of situation".

Player of the Tournament

Past winners of the Golden Boot Award include John Spencer (1985) who has played in the first team at Rangers, and Nicky Barmby (1990) of Middlesborough and England. Barmby also won the Player of the Tournament Award, as did Lee Clark of Newcastle United in 1989, and Keith Gillespie in 1991. Other established senior players to have taken part in the Milk Cup include Steve Staunton, Steve McManaman, Nicky Butt and Ryan Giggs.

Wales "milk" their success in the Under-19 section!

12
Highlights of the Year
(Selected by personalities looking outside their own sport)

Peter Canavan (Gaelic Football) - "When you consider the size of Ireland in world terms, and the time and effort required for an athlete from here to be successful at the highest level, then Sonia O'Sullivan winnng gold at the World Championships in Gothenberg was just sensational."

Felix Healy (Soccer) - "For excitement, quality, drama, and sheer joy, look no further than the Ryder Cup victory by the European team. I watched it all, from Corey Pavin's chip-in on the Saturday night, when it looked all over, to Philip Walton's winning putt. Walton did extremely well, considering the fact that no-one was watching his match until the 16th and then the whole world tuned in!"

Raymond Burns (Golf) - "With being on the European tour, you can spend a lot of time watching television, and Miguel Indurain winning the Tour de France captured my attention for the duration of the event. His stamina is incredible and he is obviously a class above the rest."

Willie Anderson (Rugby) - "As a Tyrone man living in Derry, I particularly enjoyed seeing Tyrone's Ulster semi-final victory! On a spectrum of one to ten, the game had every emotion, and the passion of the contest reminded me of my own sport. I know some of the Tyrone lads and for them to win against the odds was unbelievable."

Garfield Harrison (Cricket) - "The Northern Ireland soccer team's performance in Portugal was outstanding. It showed how Brian Hamilton's enthusiasm and zest has transformed a young side into a very good one. Elsewhere, Nick Faldo's shot to the 18th at the end of the Ryder Cup, Dominic Cork's hat-trick for England against the West Indies, and Joey Dunlop's continued success, were all special, though I do wish Joey would call it a day."

Glynis Taylor (Hockey) - "Tennis is my second love, so I really enjoyed watching Wimbledon and Steffi Graf's success. Also, Sonia O'Sullivan has done superbly well to become a star in world terms."

Paul Hollway (Hockey) - "The Eric Cantona 'karate kick' incident was a negative highlight for me, as a Man.Utd fan. I can't condone what he did, but the abuse professional sports people at that level can be put under by large crowds is very intimidating. On more positive notes, Pegasus did well, Tyrone were unlucky, and the final moments of the Ryder Cup were superb. I was pleased for Bernard Gallacher at the end, and of course there had to be an Irish hero."

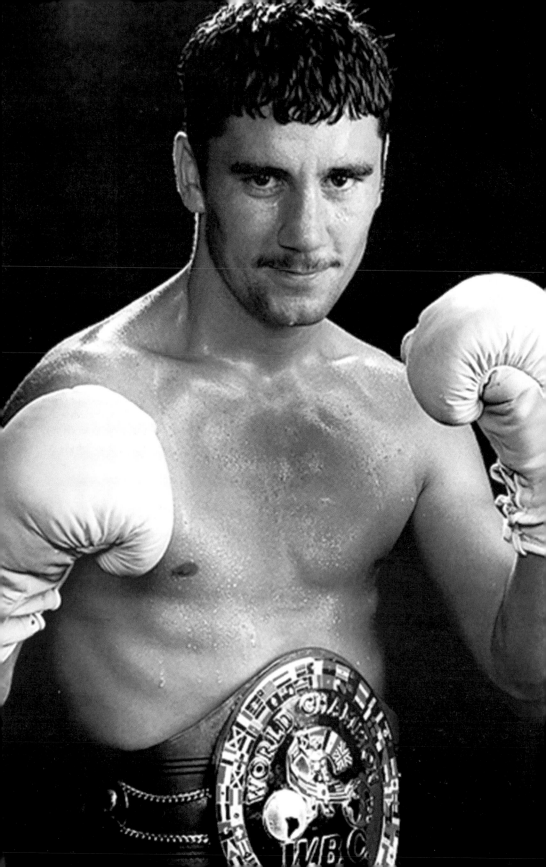

Joey Dunlop (Motorcycling) - "I've no time for other sport, what with racing bikes and running the Railway Tavern in Ballymoney, though I enjoy darts and pool. John Lowe is one of my heroes and I've been lucky to play with him."

Bertie Fisher (Motoring) - "It's always refreshing to see Irish men and women taking on the best in their chosen sport. Therefore, Sonia O'Sullivan beating world-class opposition, and Eddie Irvine signing for Ferrari, were my highlights. I'm also pleased for Eddie after the criticism he has had in his short Formula One career. Ferrari is the ultimate racing team and it is a very big opportunity."

Bryan Hamilton (Soccer) - "I felt terribly humble when presenting some of the medals at the Special Olympics at New Haven. The sense of achievement, and the expressions on the athletes' faces, left a lasting impression."

Sean McGuinness (Hurling) - "I really admired two young people who took on the world, and won. The first is Sonia O'Sullivan - for an Irish girl to be competing and winning at world level is unbelievable - and the second is Wayne McCullough. He's one of the most modest kids I've met, and he showed tremendous courage to leave Belfast for America in pursuit of his goal."

Trevor Anderson (Soccer) - "I'm afraid I have to stay within my sport because my clear highlight of the year was the FA Cup Final at Wembley. I had never been before - I always gave my tickets away - and it lived up to all expectations. The atmosphere was special, and Everton's victory made it a super day. Even though I played for United, I went as a neutral and was pleased for Everton, especially after the season they had had".

Mairin McAleenan (Camogie) - "Michelle Smith and Sonia O'Sullivan both caught my eye with their commitment and fantastic achievements, though for sheer emotion and excitement, the scenes at the end of the All Ireland hurling final were something to behold. It did your heart good to see the underdogs from Clare overcome Offaly and win their first title in 81 years."

Brian McLaughlin (Rugby) - "As a Newcastle Utd fan, I have delighted in their start to the season. Locally I was thrilled to see Neil Doak, a former pupil of mine at Wallace, take the prize wicket of Brian Lara when Ireland played the West Indies. Unfortunately, I can't take any credit as I only took Neil for rugby!"

Anthony Tohill (Gaelic football/Soccer) - "I admired Eric Cantona's courage for staying in England after all that had happened, and for a spectacular return in October. Miguel Indurain and Steve Collins also caught my eye, for their tenacity and determination to succeed."

Photographs Acknowledgements

Oliver McVeigh (Tyrone Times): GAA CS: Pages 1,2,4,5,6 bottom, 7 bottom ,8 top. FC: bottom right. BC: Top and third from top. BW: Pages 9,10,14, 17,18, 20,21,25,27,28, 29,31,33,34,36,37,38,39,41,42, 43,44,45,47,48, 51,52, 53, 54, 56, 59 bottom,63,66,68,69,70,71,72,76,77,78,79,81,99,105,112,115,117,120,127, 133,142,153,166,175, 176,189, 192, 194, 197,207.

Guinness Northern Ireland: FC: top right, bottom left. BW: 6 bottom,59 top, 125, 131,143,144, 147,149,155,159, 164,172,181, 182

Hugh Russell/Irish News: BW: 95,104,156,158.

Bank of Ireland: Gen.CS: 6 bottom. BW: 193,195,214, 215.

Ulster Bank: BW: 201,202, 204,209.

First Trust: BC: bottom. Gen.CS: 4 top. BW: 151.

Northern Bank: BW: 180, 205 bottom, 206, 208 top,210.

Donegal Democrat :BW: 74,75,90,196.

Derry Journal (Arthur Duffy): BW: 106 bottom,109,111.

L'Derry Sentinel (Michael O'Donnell): BW: 106 top.

John McElwaine (B'mena Observer): GAA CS: 6 top, 7 top. BW: 84, 97,100,101.

Tyrone Constitution (Gerry Knight) : BW: 203.

Dromore Leader: BW: 205 top, 211 bottom.

Ray McManus, Sportsfile, Dublin: GAA CS: 3 top + bottom. BW: 49.

AllSport Uk Ltd: Gen CS: pages 2, 6 top, 5 bottom. FC: top right.

Danny O'Kane, Dungiven : BW: 87,88, 192 bottom

John Smedley, Crusaders FC: Gen CS: page 7 top. BW: 119,121,123.

George Ruddell, Glenavon FC: BW: 124.

Smurfit International: BC: 2nd from top. BW: 161,162.

Joan McCloy: Gen CS: page 4 bottom. BW: 170.

N.Ireland Tourist Board: Gen CS: page 5 top. BW: 187.

Peter Watson: GAA CS: page 8 bottom.

St Malachys, Belfast: BW: 208.

Associated Press: Gen CS: page 1.

Irish Times: Gen CS: page 3.

NI Sports Council: BW: 6 top,8,183.

Bass Ireland: Gen CS: 7 bottom.

Gavin McCullough: BW: 170.

Paul Welch: BW: 184.

Methody: BW: 209.

Connors Fuels: BW: 212.

Owen McConnon: BW: 73.

Media Sports, Dublin: BW: 113, 114.

Lisburn Star: BW: 126,130.

RBAI: BW: 198.

Britannia Assurance: BW: 150.

Dairy Council: 217,218,219.

Seamus McAleenan: BW: 185.

NIE: BW: 211 top, 215.

Coca Cola: BW: 213.

Michael O'Rourke: BW: 86.

Guide
BW = Black & White
GAA CS = GAA Colour Section
Gen CS = General Colour Section
BC = Back Cover
FC = Front Cover